The Long Round

Dominic Calder-Smith writes regularly for *Boxing News*, *The Ring*, *Total Sport* and the *Glasgow Sunday Herald*. He lives in Oxford with his wife and two children.

Dominic Calder-Smith

The Long Round

The Triumphs and the Tragedies of
the Men who Fought Mike Tyson

YELLOW JERSEY PRESS
LONDON

Published by Yellow Jersey Press 2004

4 6 8 10 9 7 5 3

First published in Great Britain in 2004 by
Yellow Jersey Press

Yellow Jersey Press
Random House, 20 Vauxhall Bridge Road,
London SW1V 2SA

Random House Australia (Pty) Limited
20 Alfred Street, Milsons Point, Sydney,
New South Wales 2061, Australia

Random House New Zealand Limited
18 Poland Road, Glenfield,
Auckland 10, New Zealand

Random House South Africa (Pty) Limited
Endulini, 5A Jubilee Road, Parktown 2193,
South Africa

The Random House Group Limited Reg. No. 954009
www.randomhouse.co.uk

A CIP catalogue record for this book
is available from the British Library

ISBN 0-224-06381-2

Papers used by Random House are natural, recyclable products made from
wood grown in sustainable forests. The manufacturing processes conform to
the environmental regulations of the country of origin

Typeset by Palimpsest Book Production Limited, Polmont, Stirlingshire
Printed and bound in Great Britain by
Mackays of Chatham plc, Chatham, Kent

For Bim, Daisy & Max

Contents

Acknowledgements and Sources

This book would not have been possible without the cooperation, support, advice and assistance of many people. They are:

Claude Abrams, Leroy Berbick, Trevor Berbick, Tyrell Biggs, Tommy Brooks, Angelo Dundee, Steve Farhood, Bernard Fernandez, Mitch Green, Reggie Gross, Don King, Cedric Kushner, Patricia Love-Page, Donald McRae, Luke Matthews, Larry Merchant, Greg Page, Alex Ramos, Kevin Rooney, Ronnie Shields, James 'Bonecrusher' Smith, Emanuel Steward, Pinklon Thomas, Tony Tubbs, Tony Tucker and Carl 'The Truth' Williams.

In addition I would like to thank all those behind the scenes who supported this project and were involved in putting it together; everyone at Yellow Jersey, especially Rachel Cugnoni, Tristan Jones and Beth Coates, and my agent, Ali Gunn.

Many of the facts, figures and quotes used in the following pages were gleaned from a mountain of newspaper and magazine clippings, in particular from: *Boxing Digest,*

Boxing Monthly, Boxing News, Daily Express, Daily Mail, Daily Mirror, Daily Telegraph, Guardian, Independent, KO, Life, New York Daily News, New York Post, New York Times, The Ring, Sun, The Times, Today and Sports Illustrated. Several books also provided excellent reference sources, including Fire and Fear: The Inside Story of Mike Tyson by Jose Torres, Mike Tyson: For Whom the Bell Tolls by Reg Gutteridge and Norman Giller, and Gilbert Odd's Kings of the Ring: 100 Years of Heavyweight Boxing. Compiling the records featured at the back of this book would have been extremely difficult without access to the remarkably concise website, Boxrec.com.

The author and publisher would like to thank the following for permission to reproduce photographs: Action Images for the picture of the Tyson–Holyfield fight; and The Ring magazine for all other fight pictures, the Tyson–King 1989 press conference, Holmes and King playing golf, and Tyson in a Worldwide Wrestling Federation ring. All other photographs are reproduced courtesy of the author.

The author and publisher would also like to thank Reggie Gross for permission to reproduce extracts from his letters.

Prologue: Being Like Mike

Las Vegas, 22 November 1986

The taller man with the long black stockings and square-cut hair-style skitters on his feet as his younger, stronger, breezeblock of a challenger marches him down again, coal eyes peering above the rim of a high guard.

'Still Queer Avenue,' says Sugar Ray Leonard, as another combination stuns the champion. 'Tyson's punches even sound different from other fighters!'

The bell to end the first round chimes and Trevor Berbick holds his arms by his sides, juts out his chin and pokes a tongue at his tormentor. Mike Tyson isn't watching him. He is heading back to his corner, neck twitching and shoulders hunched. The crowd is on its feet. It knows the end is near. Everyone does. Tyson, the television audience, even Berbick knows.

'Where's the sponge?' shouts Berbick's cornerman, Angelo Dundee, as the fighter sits on his tiny, three-legged stool. 'Where's the fucking sponge?'

Trevor Berbick had been all smiles during the build-up to the first defence of his WBC heavyweight title, despite the screens placed strategically around the foyer of the Las Vegas Hilton, which depicted Tyson's bombardment of his previous victims. At press events and photo shoots Berbick wore crisp suits and crucifixes, but most prominently that constant beam on his face, as though he knew of some significant flaw in Mike Tyson that the rest of the world had missed.

On a twenty-seven-fight unbeaten streak, with only two opponents avoiding the ignominy of a scorching knockout, the twenty-year-old Tyson was the most vibrant figure in heavyweight boxing since Muhammad Ali had belatedly called it quits. He was an irresistible machine of war. And yet Berbick appeared unfazed.

Ironically it was Berbick who had ended Ali's career, defeating the self-proclaimed 'greatest' in the Bahamas five years earlier, where a cowbell had been used to ring in the start of each round. But just as Berbick had brought the curtain down on Ali's career, his own temporary paralysis would signal the dawn of the Tyson age.

'What we have to remember', urges Leonard's broadcast partner, Larry Merchant, 'is that Trevor Berbick has never been hit by punches as hard as the ones he's being hit with tonight.'

The second round starts, and no sooner does Berbick rise from his stool, arms held at full length before him, lower lip puckered as he makes two small, playful jumps in Tyson's direction, than he is sent crashing from a torrid combination of blows. He leaps to his feet, purses his mouth and fans a dismissive fist as the referee Mills Lane moves in to issue a mandatory eight-count. The action resumes, and Tyson continues to stalk.

'Tyson's throwing short, devastating punches,' explains

Leonard. *'My man's being patient against a guy who's got a great deal of experience.'*

That experience began in 1972, while Berbick was working on a US naval base in Guantanamo Bay, Cuba, where marines drained bottles of beer and grew belligerent as they counted down the days to tours of duty in Vietnam. Berbick likened the place to 'a war zone', and took up boxing to defend himself against intoxicated grunts. Four years later, he represented his birthplace of Jamaica at the Montreal Olympics, but failed to win a medal. Upon emigrating to Canada, he turned professional under the tutelage of Lee Black, the former light-heavyweight great Archie Moore, and the doyen of fight trainers Eddie Futch – who would later reveal that Berbick was the only student of his that he never liked.

Initially Berbick attempted to model himself on Ali, but his talent was too crude and cumbersome ever to be fine-tuned to such an improbable degree. On realising his limitations, he favoured the teachings of Moore, whom he described as an 'interior' trainer. Berbick was more comfortable as the aggressor, working his way in close to an opponent, rather than attempting the quicksilver, long-range boxing which Ali had perfected in his youth.

Tactically and mentally unpredictable, Berbick achieved a measure of success. In 1981 he retired Ali, and then in 1982 defeated the man Ali had tipped as his natural successor, the generously talented but generally lazy Greg Page. At the end of that year Berbick challenged Larry Holmes for the World Boxing Council (WBC) title and, though beaten comfortably, he became the first man to take Holmes the distance in a championship bout since Holmes had defeated Ken Norton for the vacant title four years earlier. Subsequently, the transplanted Canadian dropped fights he should have won, but emerged victorious from others he was expected to lose.

Titillated by his mercurial ways, the enigmatic, shock-haired promoter Don King took a liking to Berbick, calling him 'The Three Faces of Eve'. In the summer of 1985, while the FBI was pursuing King for tax evasion, Berbick decided to cheer the promoter's spirits. Late one evening, while King was in Las Vegas for a fight card, Berbick padded along to his hotel room. The fighter tapped on the door and thumbed his way through a bible as King emerged, blinking in the light of the hallway. 'The Lord is on your side,' said Berbick, leafing through the pages until he came to the 91st Psalm. 'Only with thine eyes shalt thou behold and see the reward of the wicked.' King chuckled, and there and then decided to give Berbick another shot at the title.

Eight months prior to facing Tyson, Berbick made the most of his second chance, upsetting the smooth rhythm of Pinklon Thomas to take the WBC crown. Success at the top level, however, failed to diminish his penchant for the peculiar. During the post-fight interview, live on HBO, Larry Merchant pointed out to the new title-holder that few people outside his inner circle had believed that he stood a chance against Thomas. Berbick replied: 'Well, Mr Merchant, I say this to you; that many people don't understand what mysteries I've been through. But I think right after this fight, and pretty soon . . . I won't say too much, but when I build my church and the gates of Heaven, Hell will not prevail against it. You don't understand that . . . people will understand it soon.'

They didn't, of course, but that made no difference to Berbick. Beating Thomas meant he had 'qualified' to meet Tyson, which in turn meant cashing in on a payday made substantial by Tyson's box-office appeal. First, Berbick was briefly attracted by an offer from a New York promoter, Denis Rappaport, to put his title on the line against Rappaport's big, Irish-American puncher, Gerry Cooney.

'I need money now,' Berbick told Rappaport during a period of negotiation on the telephone. 'A hundred-thousand-dollar deposit. I got a message from God. He said to ask you, and you'd give it to me.'

'When did you speak to God?' asked Rappaport.

'About twenty minutes ago.'

'Trevor?'

'Yes?'

'He spoke to me about five minutes ago. He changed his mind.'

Berbick hung up the phone, and instead signed to fight Michael Gerard Tyson.

Rushing to one's feet after being knocked down can be a grave error. It's an action taken by the unseasoned fighter who has yet to understand the value of a few seconds' respite, or the man whose ego has been burnt.

This is the latest of Berbick's mistakes. The first was to step haughtily into Tyson's threshing combinations. The second was to underestimate his opponent's quick power and employ a contemptuously loose defence. And now this, this scramble to his feet to show Tyson he remains unshaken and unconvinced. But Tyson can read the lie and already knows which machine-gun sequence of blows he will use to terminate his opponent's crumbling stand against the inevitable.

Berbick is sent fluttering again, short, hard hooks driving their way through the crooks in his arms, punching hard against his sides and chest and upper arms, every one of them forcing him to give ground. Tyson pauses momentarily, hands still held before his face, standing square on his disproportionately small feet. Berbick gathers himself, and the two come together near the centre of the ring.

In close, Berbick tries to cover and lean, but he is bending into the most potent heavyweight armoury since the days of Smokin' Joe Frazier and George Foreman. Tyson's facial expression does not change, but he sees the openings and pulls the trigger. A short uppercut bursts through Berbick's guard on the inside and jolts his head out of the fighters' huddled embrace. No sooner has the shot struck home than Tyson's right is drawn swiftly away from the cavern between the two men's interlocking bodies to land with equally swift delivery to the head. Then the left hook explodes against the champion's temple, barely seen by the crowds before it is buried on the inside once more. There is a delayed reaction, and then in virtual slow motion Berbick begins an unconscious, symmetrical collapse, which culminates in the back of his skull smacking the canvas.

Before the Tyson fight, Berbick had made a point of deactivating the air-conditioning system in his twenty-seventh-floor suite of the Hilton Hotel, for fear of being poisoned through the air ducts. At the time, he had permitted his wife and his wife alone to purchase his food and cook his meals. These precautions, he had maintained, were essential in light of his previous defeat – in 1983, to a relatively small heavyweight named S. T. Gordon – which Berbick attributed to foul play. A week before meeting Tyson, in response to questions about Gordon's victory, Berbick claimed to have met an individual who admitted to doping the fruit he habitually devoured before his pre-fight meal. This man, so the story went, even went so far as to produce the cheque which had been issued to him as payment for his services. It was an interesting account, prompting more questions than it sought to answer, but Berbick stuck to it. Nobody was going to inject his pineapple slices with anything suspicious before he got his hands on Mike Tyson.

When we speak about the fight in summer 2001, Berbick is living illegally in Miramar, Florida, breaking a long-issued deportation order. The intervening years have done little to dull his acute sense of paranoia. His Caribbean accent rises excitedly as he recalls a cold November night in Vegas, and pushes more outlandish claims my way.

'That was not a fight, and I've got all the proof in the world,' he wails. 'I was taken to the doctor for two weeks straight before that fight, but I made an agreement that I would go through with it. They made me sick. They made me sick! The real boys who controlled boxing knew there was no way Tyson could really beat me. They knew it, but the fight had to be made because they wanted Tyson to be the youngest heavyweight champion in history. I don't think they regretted it either, because it made them a lot of money. I had to go along with it. Watch the tape if you can . . . the original tape. The punch passed my forehead. It did not hit me in the head! What got me was the medication. Ten seconds after the punch missed my head I went down, because of the medication that

I took six hours before the fight. I wasn't dizzy, but my equilibrium just wasn't there. I don't know what they had put in that medication, but I just went down.'

The original tape shows the punch landing, but it's not the easiest shot in the world to catch, for the fighters are intertwined, obscuring the cameraman's angle when the *coup de grâce* is delivered. And the delayed reaction, though it falls short of the ten-second period Berbick refers to, adds a further degree of mystery to the spectacle for those witnessing it for the first time.

'The real mystery was how good I was,' Berbick persists. 'The mystery was that I was always just better than the rest, but people had to do what they did to make me lose. Somebody must have been spraying my room to make me sick, it's obvious! I was up against whatever it was, but I wanted to go through with it. I'm not blaming nobody. I did what I had to do, but they made me lose. I've got the proof. I'm not gonna call out no names, but certain people said I had to give up that title. I had to lose, OK? I had to lose!'

His eyes blurred and his limbs falling limp, Berbick fumbles desperately to regain his feet. Halfway there, he stumbles across the ring with his left glove scraping the ground, arms weakly hanging by his sides, and he staggers into the ropes. He piles into a row of photographers. Some race backwards, others hold out their palms to protect themselves from a human avalanche. Berbick reaches with a glove to propel himself forward, fails, tries again, and scrambles crab-like towards the referee.

'They injected me with whatever that was. I was taking that injection every day. The injections made me feel better, but they made me weak and my legs became very imbalanced. In the gym I was stumbling about all over the place.'

Berbick scutters across the ring on spaghetti legs and rolls on to his back. He has lost all control of his limbs. It is an awesome, brutal spectacle. He has been knocked down three times by one concussive punch. Tyson waits, devoid of emotion, eyes black and unblinking at the carnage he has caused. Eventually Berbick drags himself to his feet once more and he finds himself in a neutral corner. He steps forward as the referee comes towards him, his body shudders and his legs quake, and the referee holds him tightly, so that he cannot fall again.

'It's all over,' shrills Jim Lampley, the third man on the broadcast team. 'That's all. And we have a new era in heavyweight boxing.'

Trevor Berbick, 1986–2001

At about the same time as Berbick was being sent to sleep by Tyson in Las Vegas, I lay slumbering on a bench in Heathrow Airport's Terminal 3, a small pile of newspapers gathered together to form a makeshift pillow. This was the culmination of a friend's intricately planned and unauthorised expedition from our Oxfordshire school to the bright lights of London. But what I remember most about that evening – more than images of pretty Italian students in Covent Garden cafés and us bluffing our way into a Leicester Square cinema to see Demi Moore in various states of undress in *About Last Night* – are the hours I spent poring over the sports pages which had now become my headrest.

Within them were previews of that night's hostilities in Vegas, where the reportedly unstable Berbick would futilely attempt to repel the unstoppable young Tyson. Tyson, it was said, was a chilling force of destruction, and he had emerged to drag heavyweight boxing out of its doldrums and into an era of stark, no-frills brutality, the like of which it had not seen since the days of Rocky Marciano and Sonny Liston. Berbick, the newspapermen assured, would drown in a tidal wave of violence.

The pictures of Tyson in the papers resembled some of heavyweight boxing's past kings. He had the stoical glare of Joe Louis, and Liston's looming thunder; it would not be long before the rebellious shades of Jack Johnson emerged too. There was little mistaking the old-school aura Tyson generated. He was a throwback fighter, raw in his ambition and promising swift retribution upon the inadequates he would soon dare to challenge him with their 'primitive skills'. There were no fancy gimmicks or tinsel robes or glitzy footwear. Just a five-dollar haircut, black trunks, black shoes, sockless feet and cold steel beneath hooded brows.

By the time Tyson had finished wiping the floor with Berbick, he seemed as unconquerable as any heavyweight destroyer of old: as much as Louis had during the Brown Bomber's formative years; as much as Marciano had, in a career which remains to this day the only one unblemished in the record books of heavyweight champions; as much as the smouldering Liston had while twice stamping on the integrationist pieties of Floyd Patterson; and as much as Foreman in the wake of his predatory devastations of Smokin' Joe Frazier and Ken Norton.

But sooner than anyone could have guessed, Tyson's perceived indestructibility would be shattered by Buster Douglas in Tokyo. For this contest also, Berbick has a mysterious interpretation of events. Employed for the trip to Tokyo as a sparring partner, the old hand claims Tyson's team were so unconcerned about their charge's preparation that no official instruction was given to anyone in the training camp as to how they should help Tyson prepare for the underdog from Ohio. Berbick says the hired help would simply fix on their headgear and trade blows with the young champ for as long as they could stand it. As with the rest of his stories, there's not a shred of evidence, and he's getting more paranoid by the minute.

'I knew he was going to lose out there to Douglas,' Berbick says, his claims getting wilder and wilder. 'I tried to help him, to advise him that he was being set up, but I could never get the opportunity. I don't think he could ever have won that fight. I think there were people with him who wanted him to lose. He got what I got, but he got it worse because he almost got killed. That's the reason he's how he is today, you see, because he is still badly hurt. He still hasn't recovered. That fight damaged him. He took so much punishment, I don't think he'll ever recover from it.'

By the end of 1990, the year Tyson fell to Douglas, Berbick was serving a six-month probation for attacking a former financial adviser. Not long after being released the following year, Berbick was accused of raping his family babysitter. He stood trial in Miami in 1992, before a virtually empty courthouse. Eleven days earlier, legions of press had descended upon Indianapolis to watch Tyson sentenced for raping a beauty-queen contestant named Desiree Washington. Tyson was at times oafish and monosyllabic during his trial. Berbick's behaviour in Miami was so irrational he was ordered by the judge to undergo a psychiatric examination.

'He kept telling me that he hadn't had sex in a long time, that God would understand, and that I should too,' Berbick's victim testified. 'When it was over, he turned to me and said, "Go ahead and report it. No one will believe you."' When it was his turn to take the stand, Berbick rambled, 'She's on the payroll. She is being used,' before inexplicably adding, 'I am still the best fighter in the world. No more mister nice guy.'

Handed a four-year jail sentence, Berbick was released in 1994 but quickly broke his parole conditions and skipped to Canada. Resuming his career, he won the Canadian heavy-weight title. He even pocketed an $82,500 payday for engaging in less than three minutes of a boxer vs. wrestler match-up at Tokyo's Sumo Hall – a contest which saw him flee from the ring after taking one kick up the backside too many from a Japanese opponent named Nobuhiko Takada.

It was not long before his flagging fortunes took several bad, consecutive hits. On discovering that Berbick did not legally hold citizenship status, the Canadian Boxing Commission withdrew his title. After the whole affair had raked up Berbick's past criminal activity, the authorities voided his immigration documents. He informed the press in Montreal that God had recently visited him in his apartment, and his state of mind was once more called into serious question. When a subsequent MRI scan revealed a small blood clot on the brain, his boxing licence was revoked completely.

Penniless and by now pursued by the IRS, Berbick some-how managed to return to Florida to be with various exten-sions of his family, which is where I located him. Ever delusional and highly volatile, Berbick insisted that dark forces continued to prevent him from reclaiming his old crown, but that he was on the verge of securing a new, multi-million-dollar deal with Don King which would soon see him retake control of sport's richest prize.

His intended storming of the heavyweight ranks, however, never gathered so much as a breeze. Weeks later, he was arrested at Syracuse's Hancock International Airport while on his way to attend the annual International Boxing Hall of Fame induction weekend in Canastota, upstate New York. Extradited to Broward County, Florida, to answer charges of failing to make court-ordered payments for previous offences, he was then deported to Jamaica.

Both Tyson and Berbick had become outcasts. The only difference was money. While Berbick was banished to the Caribbean, Tyson's exile was less tangible – a removal from society's acceptance, yet one which permitted him to remain within pay-per-view distance because there were still so many who wished to gloat at his destruction.

Tyson's menace sparked mainstream fascination with heavy-weight boxing in the 1980s, but the men who, like Berbick, made their doomed bids to thwart him piqued my interest just as profoundly. While legitimately great fighters such as Larry Holmes and Michael Spinks, as well as Frank Bruno – whose public profile in Britain was at one time almost as high as Margaret Thatcher's – enjoyed a level of widespread recognition, the majority of Tyson's early rivals rose from obscurity for mere nanoseconds, before submerging themselves in a wasteland of unfulfilled promise.

Years after their physical prime, Tyson still treads the pugilist's boardwalk of broken dreams, desperate to resurrect his career and profit from handsome paydays against fresher champions who lack the wear and tear and deep-rooted damage which so handicap his search for redemption.

'It's mind-boggling, what became of him,' remembers Steve Farhood, a former editor of *KO* magazine. 'The Tyson of 1985 is almost unrecognisable in that respect to the one of today. Back then he was just another fighter in the crowd. He was extremely shy, and didn't talk much. He would just sit around the locker room with all the other fighters, and that was it. Everything was so much less complicated for him back then.'

Those whose job it is to commentate on his career wonder what will become of Tyson. Will he fight on until every last cent of potential revenue from his one-man industry has been drained? Will he wind up like Joe Louis, haunted and bankrupt? Will he die young like Sonny Liston, desolate and superfluous? Or will he drift away from public spectacle and slip quietly into a life of undisturbed comfort, when so few before him have managed to do so?

In delving further into the lives of the men Tyson fought between 1985 and 1989, I discovered mirror images not only of Tyson's past, but also his subsequent fortunes. The first to bring this to my attention was Berbick, the very man who had vainly attempted to block Tyson's initial rise to the world championship. Like Tyson, Berbick's hot-headedness was legendary. Like Tyson, Berbick displayed an increasingly disturbing trend for illogical behaviour. And like Tyson, Berbick found himself convicted of rape and locked up. But there were others, aside from Berbick, who had tripped and stumbled as they tried to move on.

For each of them, life after Tyson had become the longest round of all.

One: Blood

Atlantic City, 29 May 2002

IT WAS A WEEK BEFORE *THE* FIGHT, BUT ON THE NEW JERSEY COAST Don King was promoting another contest: between former champions Evander Holyfield and Hasim Rahman. In the camp of the King, any suggestion that Lennox Lewis vs. Mike Tyson was a genuine 'superfight' was unceremoniously shot down. In the formidable shapes of Holyfield and Rahman, he had the ammunition too, and the video clips had he wished to use them: here comes Holyfield again, shaking off Tyson's early fusillades and grinding the rusting Iron Man against the ropes with one rat-a-tat volley after another; and here's Rahman, with a jab, then another, stepping in towards his retreating prey and then lowering the boom, striking Lewis's jaw with the most ferocious right hand he's ever thrown. But within the dark, addictive confines of professional boxing, fortunes change as drastically as they do at the blackjack tables, and while the cycle had dipped for Holyfield and Rahman, it had risen once again for Lewis and Tyson.

King, always a master of regeneration, had been caught

on the hop for once. His frustrations at being continually thwarted in attempts to realign himself with Tyson were becoming harder to assuage.

Unusually he would not be in town until two days before this latest promotion of his. There were rumours that he was desperately trying to coax Tyson away from Lewis with a lucrative offer that would steer his former charge into a series of fights against far less formidable opponents than the dreadlocked Englishman. Stung, however, by the realisation that all was not as it should have been after an investigation into his financial records four years earlier, Tyson could no longer be persuaded.

Despite King's absence, business continued on the shore-line. In a hotel reception room, Rahman was singing 'bling, bling' at passers-by, hands in tracksuit pockets, a grin fixed on his partially scarred face. He had come close to an appointment of his own with Tyson after beating Lewis in Africa. They had met at an all-stars basketball game, where a mutual friend had asked Tyson if he would meet Rahman's mother, who was a big fan. 'Fuck his mother,' Tyson had whispered.

After he had dethroned Lewis with his thunderous right hand, one of the offers put Rahman's way had been a contract with the cable TV giant, Showtime, which guaranteed $10m for a first defence against Tyson and a deal for further fights on the station even if he were to lose. He turned it down, though. And he turned down a rival HBO bid too, and all its similarly favourable terms. Instead he met King in a hotel room, watched the Benjamin Franklins tumble from a duffle bag and on to a smoothed-out eiderdown, and his mind was made up. And even though he was forced to grant Lewis an immediate rematch anyway by a New York court, and even though he lost that rematch, and even though he now had no title and no contract with any TV outlet, or any guarantee of future millions or any prospect of a match-up with Tyson, he insisted that his gamble had paid off. Once upon a time Tyson himself would have said the same thing about his dealings with King.

Holyfield looked old when he came out from behind the microphones and name cards and stood among the well-wishers. Looking away from the smooth cut of his face and moustache, one could sense his age by the stiffness in his legs and a weariness in the way his arms moved as he put mineral water to his mouth and grabbed at chairs before seating himself down. Like Tyson, he was coming to the end of the road. Unlike Tyson, however, he had repeatedly bounced back from defeat with triumphs over men who were supposed to have been too much for him. And unlike Tyson, Holyfield's future beyond boxing was reasonably assured. He had his fair share of outgoings, but his life was settled. Tyson had purchased and then deserted mansions and estates in Las Vegas, Ohio, Massachusetts, New York, Cleveland, Connecticut and Maryland. He had decorated them with bronze statues of Genghis Khan and Alexander the Great, built cages in his gardens for Bengal tiger cubs and filled vast wardrobes with Roman minks and brand-name tracksuits and footwear. He partied in his mansions and grew bored of them, and then he sold them and moved on. Holyfield stayed put in a marble palace in Georgia, complete with the obligatory multiple bedrooms, giant swimming pools, acres of lush greenery and asphalt plains to exercise his thoroughbreds; a real home all the same, and well equipped to assist with his uncontested responsibility for almost as many children as the local orphanage. In addition, he had already launched his plans for the future: his own clothing label, Warrior Wear – with its strange winged shield emblem emblazoned upon backgrounds of ecclesiastical mauve – a recording company, urban scholarship schemes and a foundation for underprivileged children.

Where was Tyson's future? Lost amidst the emotional outbursts, press-conference brawls, bouts of road rage, prison sentences, counselling sessions, spiralling debt, and daily revelations of wrongdoing. Tyson was a manic depressive, whimsically fatalistic at the best of times, borderline psychopathic at others. His latest team of advisers may well have had his best interests at heart, but they were all owed money too and none was about to erase his debt in a fit of goodwill. Tyson had a deadweight of troubles on his shoulders; Holyfield enjoyed an array of options at his fingertips.

'I don't worry about what Tyson's gonna do, because if I do that, then shoot, I won't be concentrating on where I'm going,' said Holyfield with a shrug, that morning in Atlantic City.

In fact, despite the sub-human finish to their second fight – in which Tyson had elected to munch the living daylights out of Holyfield's ears – a bizarre kinship had grown between the pair. They had not become friends. Tyson still insisted that Holyfield was a serial headbutter, one of the dirtiest fighters in the game, yet simultaneously he would describe Holyfield as 'beautiful, awesome . . . just one of the most hardcore fighters there's ever been'. And Holyfield, for his part, spoke of Tyson almost as though he were a younger brother who had misbehaved too often for most people's liking, but still needed love and affection.

In every sense, Tyson was miles away from Holyfield. But as his showdown with Rahman neared, Holyfield was not the only man in Atlantic City whose experiences with Tyson had been as dramatic as they were now resonant. The gathering had begun.

Atlantic City, 31 May 2002

A lone voice wailed, drunken and slurring, but still distinguishable from the low hum of expectation which awaited the arrival of Don King.

'What about Mike Tyson?'

By Friday the heat had intensified and a sheet of cloudless blue filled the sky; sunshine pierced the eyes and baked the wooden floorboards and amusement piers. The pale and the portly wobbled around the boardwalk in garish T-shirts covered in decals of kittens and unicorns, buying chintz from the market stalls and great pink towers of candyfloss at the salt-water taffies, while eighties music spilled from fluorescent jukeboxes. The blocks nearest to the shoreline and the boardwalk offered visitors a choice of brunch, jewellery and porn – all of it cheap. In the city's residential areas, car wrecks lay abandoned in unattended back gardens behind clapboard houses with carpets of plastic grass rolled out on porches, white picket fences, broken windows and dried shrubbery.

Beneath the expanse of virgin blue, bathed in the heat and occasionally rocked by gusts of wind, a band of school children in black and grey uniforms and ribbons twirled batons, struck drums, shook pompons and clashed cymbals as they marched slowly into the city's central complex of court-houses, libraries, police stations and governmental build-ings. In the midst of their party King's face was fixed in wrinkled elation, his huge presence rising from the crowd of young musicians who trumpeted his arrival at City Hall, the glittery buttons and silver braids on his 'Only in America' denim jacket glinting in the fierce light as the cavalcade brought him towards a podium opposite the library.

A loose crowd had gathered in the square: council workers on their lunch breaks, biker cops in black shorts and protec-tive helmets, representatives of the National Association for the Advancement of Colored People (NAACP), local politicians and one Lorenzo T. Langford, the mayor of Atlantic City, whose task for the day would be to present the promoter with a key to the city and the intriguing accolade of 'Promoter of the Millennium'.

Throughout the many speeches and zealous welcomes offered by Langford and several others, King's huge smile remained plastered on his face, a small American flag in his left hand. He didn't falter once, not even as the noisy onlooker with the grey dreadlocks and brown paper bag called out once more, *'What about Mike Tyson?'*

Most of the crowd ignored the old man and applauded King as he mounted the two steps up to the podium, flag waving, lips upturned, soaking in both the attention and the sunshine. This was the man, so one of the councillors hinted in a previous address, who that morning had donated $10,000 to the Martin Luther King High School from where the young band members had trooped. This was the man, another orator had stated, whose mere presence in the city ensured that 'everyone who lives and works here profits in some way, from schoolchildren to police officers . . .'

And as King began his speech by quoting Roosevelt, the drunk's cries on behalf of Mike Tyson were made one last time before the biker cops moved him away from the festivities, leaving the spiritual descendant of P. T. Barnum to assure all whose lives had been changed since George W. Bush's declaration of war against terror, that 'we have nothing to fear but fear itself'.

Later in the afternoon, with my nose pressed up against King's star-spangled jacket, we took an elevator up to one of the offices made available in City Hall for the promoter to speak to a small gathering of writers. Away from crowds he was not nearly so rambunctious, instead preferring to speak in hushed tones, and listening sporadically to a close-knit team of aides and publicity reps updating him on the latest developments affecting his promotional empire. The showman's act had many faces; that of humble humanitarian, playful rogue, master of hyperbole. They were all in essence a mish-mashed variation of one another, but genuine emotions had been known to seep through the one-man carnival, and anger was sometimes one of them.

King wore a tie dotted with American flags, which came to a halt two-thirds of the way down a white-collared shirt which bulged at the stomach. His face, as he spoke, appeared less tired and worn behind his spectacles. Occasionally when he felt it necessary to appear indignant, he would gaze wide-eyed in feigned stupor, dipping contours around puffed-out cheeks lending him the fleeting appearance of a hamster storing away provisions.

'I'm not closing the door on Mike Tyson,' he muttered, drawing his chair closer to the conference table, and failing once more to focus attention on the principals involved in his own show that weekend. 'I never close the door. But let me borrow an old Southern line and say, "Quite frankly my dear, I don't give a damn." I just don't care about Lewis fighting Tyson.'

He did though. He cared deeply; cared and hoped and prayed that if the fight had to happen at all, it would be a financial and theatrical disaster. Certainly he cared more about it than anything else right then, including the fight between Holyfield and Rahman.

'This Lewis–Tyson fight has been fraught with all types of dangers,' he blathered. 'The spirit of the fight isn't there. You've gotta take heavyweight fights and make them into a big extravaganza, and to do that you've gotta have spirit. You've gotta always respect the public. You can never disrespect the public. I think somebody said, "You can do anything with a climate of public opinion and support, but you can do nothing without it." Uncertainty is the most lethal thing to any promotion, and every day – even though we're just a week away from the fight – people are still asking, "Is it gonna come off?" Dubiousness and doubt kills a promotion, you know what I mean? We should just be human beings and say that this man, Mike Tyson, is sick and needs help. I mean, this whole promotion is fraught with trickery. It is sheer charlatanism. It is amateur time in Dixie! The wannabes and the greedy people is there. I couldn't get a scriptwriter to make a script better to show how to destroy a promotion. But let's examine this in detail, because Tyson did something just the other day which I didn't like. And what he did was this: I've seen him and his behaviour insult the nation and disgrace our class of people. African-Americans. He talks with this lady from the television and tells her that she's gotta fornicate with him to get an interview. Even after she goes away and then comes back to try again, he tells her to perform fellatio on him. "I still want a blowjob," he says. I mean, this is depraved activity, it is behaviour that is unacceptable, it is . . .' And he was away again, on his endless rant, knowing that he had failed to stop Tyson and Lewis reaching their destination.

Atlantic City, 1 June 2002

Saturday night. The Boardwalk Hall was packed with officials in bright suits, players in Armani, fans swathed in fight-night memorabilia, undercard boxers freshly showered, curious forty-somethings in tropical-print shirts, journalists with plastic credentials hanging on their chests, TV reporters with earpieces, technicians carrying rolls of masking tape, freshly brushed commentators, round-card girls in sequined brassieres, fighters' wives and girlfriends, paramedics sitting beside stretchers and boxed resuscitation units, cutmen with cotton buds behind their ears: all the particles of boxing's kaleidoscope.

An R&B tune welcomed Rahman into the arena. He stepped towards the ring, head occasionally bowed, gloved fist on the shoulder of a young son, a blue and silver robe wrapped around his back, the name of a clothes store he had recently opened in his hometown of Baltimore embroidered on matching shorts. Then it was Holyfield's turn, his shining pate and solemn face rising from his entourage as he walked in uncharacteristically stilted fashion towards the canvas battleground, gospel music filling the air, rose-coloured gown and satin shorts shimmering under the lights.

There was a low, rippling surge of excitement, handclapping, whistling and shrieks of anticipation while the enduringly tanned Michael Buffer made his customary, rumbling introductions.

Several feet back from my press seat, a line had formed behind a cordon of metal barriers separating the media from the rest of the hall. Amongst them, a giant stood between a small, moustachioed figure in a jacket and tie and a young woman with hair dyed the colour of straw who had squeezed herself into a tight, pale pink dress. Towering above his companions, glistening locks of hair tumbling over his ears and down the sides of his neck, he kept tottering on his feet, as though dizzily recovering from being spun around in little circles. He wore a baggy, cream suit and white tennis shoes, and from his lips dangled a splintered toothpick. He smiled oddly one minute, pulled a face at no one in particular the next, and then slap-jabbed in the direction of the young woman by his side, smacking his shoulder with a right hand and shooting a mock blow in her direction with his left. This little routine amused him greatly, even more so when the object of his playfulness tried swatting him away, a pen and a notepad held firmly in her spare hand and an increasingly irritated scowl on her heavily made-up face.

'Gotta be quick,' Mitch Green kept mumbling gleefully, as he smacked his shoulder again and let rip with another wild jab at thin air. 'Gotta be quick!'

Mitch 'Blood' Green, 1986–2002

A young, impressionable Mike Tyson was attracted to those who had carved themselves ominous reputations. He didn't have far to look. In the New York ghetto, Mitch 'Blood' Green had established sizeable notoriety by the late 1970s. As a teenager, he had marshalled The Spades, a gang of Harlem toughs which would provide the inspiration for a violent B-movie entitled *The Warriors*.

A while after taking up boxing, Green flew to the Soviet Union as part of a touring squad of top American amateur fighters. In the late seventies American amateurs were boys using their unpaid work as a springboard for professional contracts. Their Soviet counterparts, meanwhile, were grown men banned from making money out of sport – artillery officers and paratroopers hardened by Communism's vigorous physical training regimens.

On the occasion of Green's visit to Russia, he was the only tourist to win his contest, outfoxing his opponent with a blend of slickness and peculiarity. By means of celebration, he combed his Afro into a high crown, popped a baseball hat upside down on a street corner and proceeded to tap dance for loose change while bemused Muscovite housewives queued for loaves of bread.

Though boxing was an outlet for Green's quirky forms of self-expression, it could not stall his more chaotic out-of-the-ring behaviour indefinitely. The wizened old gym rats in Brooklyn and the Bronx would nod their heads and mutter how Blood knew his way around a ring, but his boxing instinct was not supplemented by any consistency in training, nor an eagerness for clean-living. Heavyweight contenders went jogging at dawn and were in bed well before the midnight hour. Green had a vampire's antipathy to daylight and executed his roadwork evading cops under the glare of early-morning illuminations. Heavyweight champions showed abstinence and discipline. Mitch Blood Green snorted angel dust.

When a pre-adolescent Tyson was thundering along the sidewalks of Brownsville, stealing handbags from old ladies and knocking senseless anyone who maltreated his pigeons, Green ruled swathes of gang territory and reeled in four New York Golden Gloves titles. When Tyson became just another unruly juvenile offender, Green was a king of the ghetto. Within years, however, Green's professional boxing career had spluttered, while Tyson closed in on a challenge for the world title and the prospect of a lifetime's legally earned affluence.

Brought together by King, the two New York boxers signed to fight each other at Madison Square Garden in May 1986. Tyson, for all his awe of the ghetto and fondness for gangsta types, appeared to relish the opportunity to make an impression on Green's sneering, almost comical features with his lethal fists.

A day before the fight, Green learned that he was being paid $30,000 to Tyson's $200,000. He went berserk. He threatened to pull out of the contest, launched himself at King and had to be held back by bodyguards as his huge hands reached out to snatch at the promoter's throat. With the fight put in sudden doubt by Green's threats, a compromise was sought: Blood settled for being released from his managerial contract with King's stepson Carl in return for his acutely short end of the purse. While Green roared how badly he was going to knock his opponent out, the man-child Tyson smirked sheepishly in the background.

Tyson's entrances to the theatre of war were stark. He disdained the tasselled boots and psychedelic robes, quick-stepping it into the ring dressed only in black shorts and matching shoes. That didn't necessarily mean he turned his nose up at flamboyance, but in his early days of iron, he preferred an approach that was reverential to the great fighters of the past.

Green knew his way around a ring, it was true, but that wasn't enough. Although he was able to ride Tyson's storm he had little hope of blanketing it. Instead he fiddled, slapped and smothered his way out of serious trouble without ever coming up with an effective response to his opponent's relentlessness. Tyson dominated him in almost every round and won a unanimous decision. 'If I'd been paid right, I'd have knocked the faggot out,' Green claimed afterwards, though there was little justification for his bombast.

Life was seldom dull for Green after losing to Tyson. He faded from the boxing scene immediately afterwards, more interested in robbing liquor stores than fighting men his own size at the Garden. One night, a dose of PCP sent him on a rage through Harlem. It needed half a dozen cops to take him into custody. On another occasion he was arrested while driving with a portable television set switched on in his front passenger seat.

Superficially, Blood had become a carnival act, a lumber-ing street hoodlum with a deafening bark and a dwindling bite. He led a life so wacky it would have been funny, if it hadn't been so damned frightening for all those he bumped into. He held up a Mobil station beside the Grand Central Parkway in New York, but the money he snatched from the cash register would not suffice, so he made waiting vehicles form an orderly queue before filling up the engine of his Lincoln Continental and then those of his fellow motorists, pocketing their payments and sending them off on their way, one after the other.

Then one September day in 1988, Tyson decided to go shopping at a Harlem boutique named Dapper Dan's at four in the morning, and he and Green were to become fatefully reacquainted. By now, Tyson had defended the heavyweight championship of the world seven times. But the men who had taken him to the top were no longer there: his mentor Cus D'Amato had died of pneumonia in 1985, and his beloved co-manager Jim Jacobs had fallen to leukaemia earlier in 1988. Around Tyson, three separate parties tore at the strings which orchestrated his career: the waspish, egocentric Bill Cayton, Jacobs' former business partner; Robyn Givens, his wife; and finally King, the promoter who kept telling him that Cayton and Givens (in conjunction with her mother, Ruth Roper) were all devils set on wringing his financial resources dry.

When Tyson, close friend Rory Holloway, a bodyguard named Anthony Pitts and a handful of flunkies hit Harlem, Harlem quickly knew about it. Tyson loved the atmosphere there, especially the lurking danger – not of walking through the neighbourhood in the twilight hours, but of stepping out of the suffocating control with which his warring custodians kept trying to envelop him. These were similar streets to the ones he had roamed wild on with Holloway, thieving, mugging and running, back in the days when they were a pair of overweight thirteen-year-olds. And now, here he was again; the self-styled baddest man on the planet, the undefeated, undisputed, heavyweight champion of the world.

Revelling in the commotion around him, Tyson purchased bags of designer clothing, body-popped to the music blaring from shop stereos, and signed his autograph with a marker pen upon the cleavage of adoring female fans. Word spread that the champ was in the hood, stirring Green out of another of his funks. Still simmering at the disparity between their purses for the fight at the Garden two years earlier, Green decided to confront Tyson in the environment he knew best. From across the block, Blood marched up to the Tyson entourage, whose leader was now haggling over a $500 leather jacket with the slogan 'Never Mind The Hype' across the back. Green's hair trickled down his back, chunky swathes of jewellery swung like pendulums across his open neck and chest; his ill-fitting suit was baggy at the ankles, draping over scruffy, patent-leather pimp shoes.

Blood howled at Tyson like a banshee, screaming gibberish and profanity. And then Tyson struck him with a fist made doubly persuasive by the square rings on his fingers. Green was sent hurtling back, left eye closing and a deep gash which would need five stitches spouting blood from the bridge of a broken nose, all caused by the impact of a solitary blow. Tyson was enraged by Green's temerity and wanted to punish his old rival further, but Pitts and Holloway wrestled him into his idling limo as Green snatched off one of the vehicle's side mirrors, then cupped his hands around bloodied lips and screamed in fury as Tyson was whisked away. Green would later announce with a degree of juvenile pride, 'He still didn't knock me down.'

It soon emerged that Tyson had broken his right hand filling Green's face, and a scheduled title defence against Britain's Frank Bruno had to be postponed. In the meantime, Green succeeded in putting his split mouth and broken face into all the papers. He wore dark glasses several sizes too big for him, chewed on his toothpick and swore he would make millions suing 'Michelle the Homo' Tyson. He ridiculed Tyson's high-pitched tones, even carrying a grotesque rubber doll which he dressed in nappies and named Michelle.

Very soon, Cayton stepped in and proposed an ingenious deal. If Green agreed to drop all assault charges against Tyson, then Cayton would deliver him a rematch with Tyson for the world championship and the huge payday which would come with it. There was a proviso, however: Green first had to defeat a top-ten contender. Green, as Cayton had suspected, paid heed only to the prospect of making a quick million against Tyson, agreed to the deal, and Cayton was laughing. Green was far from in love with boxing. He didn't object to a street fight, but having been institutionalised for most of his adult life he couldn't stand rules and regulations, and he was never going to enter into a legitimate title eliminator with another contender. His hopes of cashing in on the bust-up in Harlem were set back, and though Tyson would go on to further bedlam, things for Green would get even worse.

Rage and the Streets

It is said that the successful fighter is the one who knows how to control his violence and his passion and his anger and his fear. Certainly, this was what D'Amato had tried to instil into Tyson. There is seldom any use in a fighter hating an opponent or losing his temper and allowing his heart rather than his mind to dictate his actions in the ring. But staying in control is more easily said than done when a man who weighs more than fifteen stone is hitting you in the face. The nature of boxing is such that an innate volatility exists within each and every man who takes up the sport for a living. It is largely a question of how well a fighter can suppress his primal instincts. This is not to say that such emotions have no place in the ring; faced with the task of bringing the cool-tempered, analytical Lennox Lewis to another level, the esteemed fight trainer, Emanuel Steward, would often speak of his quest to tap into the street thug inside his charge, to draw out the nastiness that needed to be a constant rather than sporadic companion for Lewis's polished talent.

It was a difficult line to tread. Another opponent of Tyson's, Carl 'The Truth' Williams, would maintain a level of contact with friends from his past which, although helpful in maintaining his street edge, was dangerous nonetheless. Those of his contemporaries who had not been killed were embroiled in drug wars, and one had even taken out a contract on the life of a New York police officer.

At the age of nine, when popular legend has it he exacted revenge upon a local bully who had torn the head off one of his beloved pigeons, the genie of Tyson's anger escaped.

Suppressed at first by his mother, and to some degree by Jacobs and Cayton, Tyson's keen temper would never again be fully contained. 'My mother didn't believe in violence,' he recounted several weeks after destroying Berbick. 'She detested it. With her being that way, I was very shy, almost effeminate shy. My brother was five years older, so I only had my sister to play with. I guess I picked up some habits talking with her, because when I was younger they used to call me "fairy boy". I was always gentle, really gentle.' He was also an object of ridicule, taunted for wearing ragged, second-hand clothes while his peers purchased flash tracksuits with the proceeds from a night's muggings. On the streets of Brownsville he was forever seen wandering about aimlessly, with an ill-fitting hat upon his thick head and a polythene bag full of stale cookies in his hand.

Fed up with the mockery, Tyson took to purse-snatching, but he was less than adroit at plotting his escape routes. Tyson had been arrested thirty-eight times before he was sent to the Spofford Youth Detention Center in 1978. A year later he was moved to the stricter Tryon School for Young Offenders in upstate New York. This was where he met a social worker and former boxer named Bobby Stewart, who subsequently took him to the Catskills to work out before D'Amato. D'Amato, a cynical, inscrutable eighty-year-old who had defied the sport's mob rulers in the 1950s and guided the careers of former heavyweight champion Floyd Patterson and former light-heavyweight champion Jose Torres, remarked there and then that Tyson would one day become world champion 'if he wants it'.

Up until the defeat of Berbick, Tyson seemed to play the

game well. Even so, there had been times when the street thug within him would not be denied. A number of sexual-harassment claims were silenced with hush money, and a $105,000 payment was made to a car-park attendant and his female colleague after Tyson attacked and molested them outside a Run DMC concert in Los Angeles in 1987. By the time of his street fight with Green, there was no stopping the champion's downward spiral into anarchy. Allegations of what one judge would later describe as 'serial buttock-fondling' were hitting the headlines, as were reports that Tyson had become addicted to anti-depressants, that he was growing disenchanted with his career and was becoming suicidal. He had smashed the camera lenses of photographers who interrupted his early-morning runs through Central Park, and admitted to landing 'the best punch I ever threw in my life' on Givens.

Living a life so reckless that pundits predicted an early grave, Tyson was frequently seen rampaging through nightspots in Manhattan and Los Angeles, wasted on Long Island Iced Tea – for which he had no tolerance whatsoever – and itching for confrontation. 'Combat, the ring, is my great tranquilliser,' he would admit. 'When I go into the ring, everything is simple. Outside is where I've had my problems, my worst fears.'

New York, September 1998

Newspaper vendors huddled inside the entrances of High Street Brooklyn Bridge station, tabloids held down by pebbles and spread out on the covered ground beside their feet as the spatter of rain persisted outside. Beyond the station, the Manhattan skyline struggled to make its presence visible through the thick shawl of mist which had settled upon the East River, and the chatter of the A train faded as it rolled towards the Rockaways.

At a block nearer to the borough's connection point with the bridge, a line of cardboard letters spelling the words 'Gleason's Gym' leaned against a set of window panes on the second floor of a corner building on Front Street. Outside and below, lorries were parked up against the loading bays of a warehouse, and steam filtered out of a series of ventilation shafts.

Blood was making a comeback. Blood wanted to be king of New York once more. Blood still wanted a piece of Mike Tyson.

I climbed the granite steps up to the steel door and plastic drapes which separated the second floor landing from the gym, and as I did so the continual thrum of the speed ball and crackle of the skipping rope grew progressively louder, merging with the other sounds of the gym to produce their own little symphony – the drumbeat thud of the heavy bag, the hushed gasps of exertion and the gunshot combinations fired at hand pads.

Blood was back on the scene, still trying to persuade everyone he had what it took to whup the man he persisted in calling Michelle, still drifting in and out of his own little dream world like a patient slipping in and out of an anaesthetic, still deluding himself that the public craved a fight between him and Tyson as much as he did. He was back training at Gleason's because he had been lined up to fight for something described as the New York State heavyweight title. He had been inactive for almost seven years, but some excitable soul had agreed to take over his managerial contract and in the process started pushing the occasional pay cheque his way. The semi-retired boxer had been whisked off to Lake Worth, Florida, to notch up a quick warm-up victory prior to the New York title fight, and a Mexican with a poor 5–11–2 record had taken advantage of his half-hearted approach and hustled him out of victory. But he was Blood – a name everyone in boxing had heard of – and so he remained faintly marketable, even if the prospect of a quick buck every now and then was, as he claimed, the only motivation left in his life.

In the late afternoon, when the shadows darkened the interior of Gleason's and the heavy, wet greyness outside was enough to make the heart sink, Green appeared in the gym, chewing his toothpick and waving a handful of pamphlets advertising his fight the following weekend. A broad white bandana covered lank hair that ran down to his shoulders.

Throughout his workout he released exaggerated growls as he stabbed at the heavy bag and unleashed cuffing shots on a sparring partner who looked almost embarrassed to get the better of their exchanges. Green grunted as he thrust out his left arm. He tried vainly to ward the younger man off with an open-palmed burst of shots, punctuated by snarling war cries which made the younger, flashier fighters giggle as dour trainers wrapped their hands with yellow gauze. The sparring partner dipped and swayed his head from one side to the other, forewarned of incoming fire by Blood's excitable efforts, the crude missiles easily evaded.

'He's timing you, Mitch!' an old man croaked from beside the ring.

Green turned away from a stray elbow, but intentionally kept himself entangled in his sparring partner's limbs. Droplets of sweat fell from his brow and hair, into the cracks of his bleeding lips and on to the stained blue canvas beneath his feet.

'Yeah?' he growled.

'Yeah!'

'Shuddup!'

'But . . .'

'Shuddup!'

'But he's making you miss every third shot,' the old man stuttered, his eyes rolling crazily in their sockets, arms shaking at his sides, feet marching him nervously around the perimeter of the ring.

'Yeah?'

'Yeah!'

'Shuddup, bum!'

'But . . .'

'Shuddup!'

A hook crashed into the side of Green's head guard, and his critic was splashed with the boxer's grimy perspiration. 'Said you should shuddup, you bum,' he spat.

Green smiled when he stepped down from the ring. His ageing face looked tired and the flesh around his eyes was creased and baggy, lending him an almost Oriental appearance. His cheeks were swollen, and although his body appeared to be in reasonable shape for a man who had walked a wilder side than most, at that moment I felt that his name was surely all that Mitch Blood Green had left to trade on. He had offered little more in his sparring session than an ability to get hit without resigning, and he would offer little more than this the following weekend when the action was for real.

'You wanna talk, then you gotta pay,' he said after emerging from the locker room a short while later. I shook my head. 'You gotta quarter, then?' I handed him a coin and he made a call from one of the payphones at the side of the gym. He launched into an animated diatribe at the unfortunate on the other end of the line and then suddenly broke into a conversation with a small girl who wandered past, a brightly coloured toy pony held in her hands as she waited for her father to complete his workout. Green, the ex-con and former gang leader who had thumped police officers, snorted coke, and collected sixty-three driving offences (and counting), stroked the glittering lilac mane of a plastic pony as he chatted amiably with its five-year-old owner. And then, after abruptly terminating his telephone conversation, he gave a small boy a gentle hug and handed him one of the cheap posters for his upcoming fight with Brian Nix.

Since the incident with Tyson in Harlem, Green had fought on only four occasions, though he had bailed out of another contest minutes before the start by wounding himself above the knee with a penknife. Nearly ten years on from his violently abbreviated tirade at Tyson, with Cayton's deal long forgotten, Blood had also had his day in court. With Tyson in attendance, Green's time to humiliate his old nemesis had arrived, and he did so by mocking the former world champion with pouts and blown kisses. But Tyson had not reacted, instead remaining impassive throughout the hearing and eating ice creams at the bottom of the courthouse steps in the afternoon.

The jury had ruled in his favour, but Green's reward was scant: he had been looking for a minimum of $1m in damages for the assault; the judge presiding over the sorry affair awarded him $45,000. Any modest celebrations on Green's part were dampened further still when it was pointed out that the sum would not even cover his legal fees.

'I still beat him in court,' Green said when I brought up the subject. 'And all he did was sit there and say in his sissy voice, "He hit me first! He hit me first!" What kind of man is he? I called him a homo on national TV, and he did nothing. So I say, "Well come on then, sissy-boy, if you don't wanna talk, then let's make the fight." He's scared, but I ain't never been afraid of no man in my life. I'd bust him up good if I had the chance now.' He mimicked Tyson's lisping accent as he stood up, ripped the shirt off his back and jabbed and slapped at the air. 'Money,' he sneered as he sat down finally, his shirt slung over a sweaty shoulder. 'Nothing else means a thing. Money's my motivation. It's the only thing that can make me fight my best, and I had no motivation the night I fought Mike Tyson. Pay me right and I'd have knocked the bum out. That's what he is. Just a fuckin' bum. But now I feel good. I've got my homeboys supporting me. I'm in good shape, even though I jus' got out of jail again the other day. I do nothing now but work out and watch TV. I've still never been hurt and never been knocked out, and it's not about to happen either – never. After this fight on

Saturday, the sky's the limit. A title shot will be mine and then I'll kill everybody. I'll kill 'em all.'

'Can you tell me about Dapper Dan's?' I asked.

'No, you gotta pay me for that,' he said.

'I can't do that.'

'Gimme a quarter then,' he demanded, and for the second time that afternoon I relented. 'I was just in the neighbourhood at the time, and someone told me he was around,' he said dismissively. 'All I wanted to do was talk to him about King and the money we'd made for our fight. You see, King blackballed me through my career. He never gave me any chances . . .'

'Well, you did try to strangle him, Mitch,' I said.

'He pulled me out of a fight on short notice,' Green mumbled. 'I was gonna break his fucking neck. He never gave me any chances because he knew I was a dangerous fighter who would beat all his homos. He made them all duck me. Never paid me what he said he was gonna pay me. I call him Don *Queen* now.'

'So . . . Dapper Dan's?'

'We were talkin' trash for a bit,' he continued. 'Then he sucker-punched me. I really had nothing against him personally, but since then I do. Please give me Mike Tyson now, someone. Please give him to me.'

'So you're still not exactly friends then?'

'He ain't my friend, he's my girlfriend!'

'Your girlfriend?'

'That's right, my girlfriend. Somebody tell me where I can get hold of my girlfriend, because I wanna knock the homo's ass right out! He hit me with his best shot, with no gloves on, and he still couldn't knock me out. He won our fight, but that really wasn't me. Like I said before, you gotta pay me right.'

'And then?'

'And then you get to see the real Mitch Blood Green.'

Even as he approached his forty-fifth birthday and a life destined to be spent whiling away his time in Harlem projects for as long as he could keep out of the slammer, it was troubling to think of Green still chasing that elusive, legalised rematch with Tyson. But I found something sneakily admirable about the way he continued to buck the system. In the end, boxers often wound up submissive and beaten and living on welfare, and Green was halfway there. But no other fighter had tried literally to wring Don King's neck, and few had ever responded to the news that they had once again been ripped off by turfing the entire contents of their manager's office out of a tenth-storey window.

Those now guiding Tyson's career were practising exactly what Green had for years – trying to perpetuate a myth of invincibility. While Tyson's excuses for defeat usually had much to do with his mental state, Green had always tried to qualify his own setbacks by claiming a lack of money meant he could not be motivated, and that a lack of motivation equated to poor performance. If he were paid a million dollars he would fight like a million dollars, he said, and even though everyone knew this was a charade, there were those who remained entertained by the notion of Blood trying to boil once again.

That Saturday night, inside an inflated tent on a Staten Island

Park, Green kept Brian Nix waiting for a full five minutes before making his appearance. 'Let's hope he's not sticking a knife in the other knee,' the promoter sighed as he sipped from a Styrofoam cup of vending-machine coffee.

When Green eventually came bounding into the makeshift arena, he wore a big grin on his wet face. He bit down hard on his toothpick, his legs kicking out wildly at various angles, his black silk robe etched in lime piping and the word 'Blood' sketched on to his shorts in thin, stencilled crimson.

It was a perversely watchable fight – not for any display of talent by either boxer, but due to Green's insistence on playing the clown. He showed off his toughness by taking more of Nix's shots than necessary, rubbed his dank hair into the faces of his trainers between rounds, wiggled his hips and jived with the round-card girls and leaned over the top ropes to tell the meagre crowd of onlookers a few bad jokes. He huffed and puffed at the advancing Nix for ten rounds, but Nix was no timid little pig and kept tossing wide hooks into the sides of Green's head. Whenever Green landed a punch of his own his legs jolted spasmodically in celebration as though he were auditioning for a part in *Riverdance*, and his right hands were launched in Nix's general direction as though they were serving for the match at Flushing Meadow. When the fight was over and the judges told Green he had lost again, his goofy smile refused to fade. 'I seen guys out there . . . never done nothing and they get paid ten million dollars and look like garbage,' he would complain to me later on. 'Give me that kind of money, man. I'd fight a lion, a baboon, a bear if I was paid right.'

As Green was given a helping hand back to the dressing

room, a muscle-bound freak in a sleeveless vest came hurrying over. He had a close-cropped hairstyle and the smell of lager on his rancid breath. He was the kind of guy Greg Haugen, a former lightweight champ from Alaska with an acid tongue, would have labelled a 'steroid monkey'.

'I was there when you fought Mike Tyson, and I thought you kicked his ass!' yelled the man.

Green's legs quivered slightly, and he sagged while his cornermen held him upright. 'I did, didn't I?' he mumbled, looking back at the man who now stopped and stared and drank from a can of Budweiser. 'I kicked his butt good and I'm gonna do it again!' And then, despite the shaking in his limbs and the throbbing pain inside his head, Mitch Blood Green let out one last bellow before disappearing into his dressing room to recover. 'Where's Michelle Tyson? I want Michelle Tyson! Someone get me Michelle Tyson!'

Atlantic City, June 2002

The post-fight press conference was in full flow. King stood in the middle of a stage, putting his own spin on things and trying to find the bright side to the evening's unsatisfactory ending. To his left sat Rahman, glum and hurting, his wife holding an ice pack to the haematoma of John Merrick proportions which was still swelling on the left side of his head. To his right glowed Holyfield, triumphant and unapologetic about the clash of heads which had exacted Rahman's demise. The win had ensured that Holyfield's malfunctioning bandwagon would sputter on, its captain hoping to be next up for the winner of Lewis against Tyson.

In front of the fighters sat row upon row of reporters, behind them hovered relatives, trainers and friends, and to the sides of the room gathered hangers-on, hard men and posers, gangsta types and women in expensive suits. Behind them all, Green leaned against a back wall, chewing and listening, and occasionally finding himself rebuked by his companion – the lady in pink – for not paying her enough attention. If King had spotted the presence of a man who had once had to be restrained from clamping fingers around his neck, he failed to let on, and for once it seemed as though Green was comfortable keeping a low profile.

Wherever he went that evening, it seemed as though Green's new-found companions – the lady with the dyed hair and the little guy with the moustache and shades and no discernible sense of humour – remained by his side. A few reporters made attempts to approach the giant, but all were blocked off by one or the other, and instead interrogated about the nature of their business and fobbed off with business cards hastily run off a newsagent copier. These two were Green's newly hired agents, positions which needed to be filled because the legendary trouble-maker had just won something called the WBS heavyweight belt (a more accurate title might have dropped the 'W'), having only to defeat a veteran journeyman named Danny Lee Wofford for the organisation's inaugural title.

'Now that Mr Green is world champion,' spluttered the male agent, who introduced himself to me as Alonzo, 'it is only fair that a stipend is charged for his agreement to any further interviews.' Green was no closer to being world champion than Ralph Nader was to being sworn in as President.

And a stipend was no more a prerequisite in securing an interview with a real champion like Lennox Lewis than it was for a reporter to provide evidence of a degree in English literature. At some point in the evening, Green's companions left his side, perhaps in search of an exclusive contract with HBO, and Blood whiled away his time performing magic tricks for a young kid called Malik.

'Well, Malik, you gotta be quick man, you gotta be quick,' Green rasped, flipping a quarter from one hand to the other, catching it in his fingers, and then making it disappear before plucking it from behind the boy's ear.

'Wow, he made a quarter come out of nowhere,' said the boy excitedly.

'Can you do that with hundred-dollar bills?' I asked. Green lurched from one foot to the other, swayed towards me and whispered conspiratorially a barely decipherable 'I wish', before continuing his routine. 'Gotta be quick, Malik. Gotta be quick.' This time he took two quarters out from behind the boy's ear and then started jabbing at the air above Malik's head.

'Are you a fighter?' asked the boy.

'Sure I am,' Green replied. 'And you're gonna be hearing a lot more about me too from now on.'

'Because you've won a title now,' I said to him.

'That's right,' he said, jabbing in my direction now. 'I'm putting this new organisation on the map.'

Behind us Rahman and his wife were departing, while Holyfield continued to hold court with the press. 'Are you looking for a fight with anyone in there?' I asked, jabbing a thumb back towards the throngs in the conference room.

'No. I wanna fight Tyson still, that's who I want.'

'You fought Mike Tyson?' asked the boy incredulously.

'Ask him,' replied Blood, pointing at me and spinning one of the quarters on the tip of his forefinger. 'He knows . . . he'll tell you. Yeah, I fought Mike Tyson. And I've never been knocked down or knocked out, and all these other bums have – all of them; Tyson, Rahman, Lewis, Holyfield. But nobody's ever knocked out Mitch Green.'

I watched Green shadowbox for the boy's entertainment, then lay on some more old magic tricks, and before long the lady in pink was back, asking me for my name and affiliation, and the humourless short guy was asking how much I was going to pay to talk to Mad Mitch some more. 'Yeah man,' muttered Green in the background. 'Give me some chuddar, man. That's what I want, man. Chuddar! Chuddar!'

As our conversations came to a close and the agents finally accepted there would be no money changing hands, I broke away from the three of them and started heading towards the exit to the Boardwalk. 'Hey man, hey, whoa there,' said a voice at my shoulder. It was Alonzo and his moustache. 'Listen, if you're not able to come up with a stipend of any kind, then perhaps you can see what you can do about getting tickets for Mr Green and ourselves for the Mike Tyson fight next weekend. See, it's our job to make sure that fight happens; Tyson–Green II. And we want to go to Memphis to drum up some interest. Can you help us?'

'Sure. I'll see what I can do,' I lied, and left them all behind me.

Two: Night Shifts

Ground Zero, May 2002

IT WAS FLEET WEEK, ALMOST MIDNIGHT, AND 42ND STREET WAS black, hot and teeming with drunken sailors chasing elegant women in cocktail dresses, straight out of a scene from one of those old Sinatra movies. I met Carl Williams outside Grand Central station and we took the train to Ground Zero, walking the last few blocks to his workplace, past an unmanned police checkpoint into a building overlooking the devastation of 9/11.

Inside a front yard, cordoned off with thick sheets of plastic marked 'Danger – Keep Out: Asbestosis', we signed in at a desk and Carl handed me a respirator, goggles and two protective uniforms. Behind the desk, a marine in a navy boiler suit and baseball hat read *Catch-22*. We stepped through into the marines' rest area, where lockers were decorated with cartoons of Osama bin Laden snipped from the papers, and pornography lay scattered on the trestle tables amongst discarded coffee cups and dirty plastic plates.

'Lookee here, we come to work and the first thing we see is a guy getting his dick sucked,' sighed Carl, whistling

47

through his teeth and turning one of the magazines around for a better view. 'Now don't you think the marines should have somethin' better to do than read this shit?'

We pulled the outfits on over our clothes, then the goggles, and disinfected the respirators with alcohol. Carl checked his walkie-talkie and penlight were working, then we passed through the drapes and the claustrophobia kicked in. More than a decade ago, Carl had jabbed at Mike Tyson for $1.3m. Today, he padded through broken debris for two hundred bucks a night, while a bunch of marines read Heller and porn in the ghoulish silence of a dusty basement. A lone guard took us up to the twentieth floor in the lift. On the way he re-secured my respirator, and then I was alone with Carl, following him as he picked his way across rubble and loose wiring, and eventually on to office floors where marker boards still bore the minutes from meetings held in the early hours of 11 September 2001. We trod through each open-plan area; half-eaten Hershey bars on desktops alongside wallets and nine-month-old cups of coffee and cartons of milk with 09/01 expiry dates on their sides. The calendars had stayed on September. The plants had died. They were deathly grey and withered, and they were everywhere. On each floor, in fluorescent orange spray, the emergency services had drawn crosses on the exteriors of all the doors.

We stared down at what remained of the graveyard for thousands.

Spotlights peered into the blackness of the pit, and where once had stood the financial centre of the world, the clearing of the ruin continued. The men and women working below us in the depths were no longer rescue workers but discarders of glass spears and broken masonry, deformed steel girders and melted iron. The end to an awful task was approaching, and the city waited for the last day of May, when salutes, bells and taps would signal the departure of a symbolic, empty stretcher and the final column of steel. There was just a smattering of activity beneath us. A pair of bulldozers crept across the ground on lightweight tracks; a man paced along one of the perimeter walls with a pickaxe over his shoulder; a woman in a hard hat spoke into a cellphone. An orange ramp slid down from ground level to Ground Zero, and in a week's time it would be lined with uniformed members of New York's Fire and Police Departments.

'This is the heart of the devastation,' Carl muttered. 'You're standing in it right now. Can't get closer to it unless you're one of the rescue workers yourself.'

As a fire-safety officer for a Manhattan-based security company, he would continue to be stationed at Ground Zero until the client who had enlisted security details to patrol its gashed premises eventually decided whether or not to move its operations uptown.

'The heart of the devastation,' Carl repeated, leaning over a makeshift barrier. 'But in here it's like a silent world. A lost world. You don't hear nothing unless the guys downstairs are trying to get through to you on the radio. And in the darkness, moving from one room to another, you get lost. It can be frightening sometimes. You never know if someone's gonna jump you when your back's turned, because they've had problems with this building already – whether it's been homeless people, opportunists or people from another company trying to break in to steal confidential information. The silence is frightening, but then any noise which breaks the silence can be frightening too, you know?'

With that admission of fear, he stepped away from the gaping divide and shuffled through the debris with his torch, pointing it into far corners and at the cobwebs knitted around scaffolding hinges, a hint of unsteadiness about his gait which may have been caused by the broken surface beneath his booted feet.

I lost him for a short while as I continued to stare into the depth of the city's wound, but intermittently I would hear him as he moved from one nearby pocket to another. Then I caught the thin beam of his light searching into the distance. He was like a ghost in the half-wrecked edifice, whispering words of dismay and resolution every few minutes, his tall, athletic, slightly stumbling body swathed in white.

The city had been told to prepare itself for another terrorist attack. The newsreaders on NBC and CNN were telling everyone another strike was imminent, and police commissioners, mayors and White House spokespersons weren't arguing. It was becoming a lot easier to get paranoid if you journeyed to work on the subway and looked at every abandoned paper bag as a potential smallpox container; or if you commuted across one of the many bridges dividing Manhattan from its outer boroughs and viewed each passing boat as the fanatics' next improvised missile; or if you took the Greyhound to Atlantic City for a day's gambling and wondered how difficult it could really be to drive a truck packed with Semtex into the Lincoln Tunnel and let the whole thing blow in the thick of rush hour.

An emergency vehicle skittered up the ramp, paused as it approached one of the men in dungarees and boots, and then moved on and away. A single drill could be heard on the far side of the crater, near to the Federal Post Office building, and a few tiny figures in yellow helmets stopped and drank from beakers. 'I think they'll strike again,' said Carl, as he rejoined me. 'I hate to say it, but I do. I hope they won't, but they will. They'll attack America again because this is the Land of the Free. And it'll be New York that they target again too, because this is the financial centre of the world, man. This is where it is. This is the heart of America. It'll always be New York they go for first.' The air was still. 'I stood here and stared for a long time too, when I first came here to work,' he said, switching his torch off. 'It's unbelievable.'

Five days a week, from Sunday to Thursday, Carl Williams left his home in Sleepy Hollow, arrived at Grand Central station just after 11 p.m., and took the 6 Train to City Hall. And from midnight until 8 a.m. he scoured this building, from the top floor down to the basement, for fire and vagrants and gas leaks and anything else which might signal further danger either to the stability of the building itself or else the client's resources. He'd travel home in the morning, eat some breakfast, spend a little time with his wife, and then sleep before the alarm clock roused him to prepare for his next shift. 'Come on,' he said, stepping back towards the fire exit and on to the main hallway beside the disused elevators.

'We're finished here. Let me check in with the others and tell them we're going down to the twelfth.'

In less than an hour he would be leaning against an empty reception desk, his respirator off in clear violation of the rules, telling me things about his life, his past, his loves and his future that I would never have asked him about, spilling them and asking me to keep half of it to myself, which I promised, though it troubled me at the time to hear it all.

As we emerged into the emergency-lit elevator hall, I thought of our first meeting the previous summer, when Carl had sat opposite me in the penthouse suite of a major banking organisation and talked to me about war in the Middle East and his fear of flying.

Carl 'The Truth' Williams 1959–1989

Carl was born in South Carolina in 1959, the year Floyd Patterson lost the world heavyweight championship to Ingemar Johansson and a brash young light-heavyweight named Cassius Clay was only dreaming of fighting at the Olympic games in Rome. For the first few years of his life he was raised by his grandmother and picked cotton for pocket money once the school day had ended. Aged seven he moved to New York, where he lived with his mother and stepfather in Jamaica, a rough neighbourhood in the borough of Queens. The golden rule was to keep off the streets if you wished to keep out of trouble, but when it came to making a choice between the volatility of his home life and sidewalk skirmishes with fellow bored teenagers, the streets won.

By the time Carl reached fifteen, Patterson was washed

up, Olympic champion Clay had long since established himself as the incomparable Muhammad Ali and, several subway stops away, a nine-year-old Mike Tyson was learning how to thieve from department stores.

Carl idolised Ali. When it became clear that he could fend for himself better than most in street tussles with his peers, he chose to fight all-comers with one hand. Holding his right fist behind his back, he jabbed circles around a dwindling number of antagonists. When the impromptu bouts on the sidewalk were won, his mouth would kick into overdrive. 'I laugh about it now,' he would later reflect. 'But down on the street I was known as a guy who had his game, and they always said that my game was very good. My game was speech. They used to say that I was "game-tight and bullshit proof", because if I thought something was bullshit I would say so. I was never afraid to speak my mind or tell people how I felt about something. That was my game.'

By his sixteenth birthday he had readily accepted membership into the Seven Crowns, a pistol-packing, thousand-strong local gang which had its regular haunts and coded greetings and hand gestures. But the more friends and rivals who wound up with their toes tagged, the more Carl was lured towards the brighter prospect of a career as a prize-fighter. At nineteen, he joined a couple of gyms – one in Jamaica, the other in Manhattan's Times Square, both now long closed – and became 'The Truth'. He won the Spanish Gloves tournament at Madison Square Garden and prestigious National Golden Gloves titles in 1980 and 1981 as a heavyweight. In 1981 he was crowned world amateur champion after defeating both a Cuban and a Russian in Belgrade.

All along, the most effective item in his arsenal was the left hand – a pump-action shotgun of a weapon, a thing of beauty, marvelled at by the purists within boxing's close-knit fraternity. Williams also gained a reputation for his movement, natural rhythm and sheer athleticism.

Growing up in the same city, Carl had been familiar with the emerging Tyson, even if Tyson had moved from the grim projects of Bedford-Stuyvesant to the verdant Catskill mountains after his introduction to Cus D'Amato. The year he turned pro, The Truth shared a training camp with the sixteen-year-old prodigy, and from the first day the two came together in the ring, he could not help but be impressed by the shy, lisping hulk who sought to mow him down. 'He bloodied my nose,' Carl confessed. 'I vowed that the next day I would punish him. I was a young pro, and this kid hadn't even fought as an amateur yet. I went home that night and contemplated what had happened so much. I had been the number-one amateur in the world, I was an up-and-coming pro, and here comes this young kid who busts my nose, busts me up and embarrasses me. I said, "Now I have to punish him!" And I did just that. Come the next day, I used my movement and hand speed to give him a boxing lesson like I don't think he'll ever forget.'

Carl racked up fifteen straight victories before challenging the world's waning heavyweight champion, Larry Holmes, on 20 May 1985. The two possessed similar styles, but while Holmes had vastly more experience, youth was on Williams's side. They boxed for fifteen solid rounds in the heat of Reno, Nevada, and The Truth's left hand severely hindered the elder man's vision. But Holmes was the recipient of judicial generosity and Carl went home without the title. In the years which followed, the defeated challenger would describe this moment as the bitterest setback in his career; worse than being knocked senseless, worse than being stopped controversially in contests he felt he had a chance to save, worse than anything else he ever experienced in the prize ring. In some eyes Carl was the people's champion – many thought he had deserved the judges' verdict – but sentimentality in boxing never lasts long. Unlucky losers may be slapped with sympathy on the way back to the dressing room and consoled by the morning's press reports, but then the world starts looking for the new kid on the block. By the time Carl was preparing for another run at the title, the next big thing had arrived.

In 1986 the veteran Mike Weaver knocked Carl out in two rounds. Before the year was out, Tyson had become one of the sport's three reigning heavyweight champions and its hottest commodity since the retirement of Ali. Pulling himself together long enough to train appropriately for a match with Bert Cooper, a fireplug from Philadelphia who had Tyson firmly in his own sights, Carl earned redemption of a kind the following summer when he drummed Cooper to defeat in eight rounds. 'All I was thinking about when I was fighting Bert was Mike Tyson,' he said afterwards. 'Now I've got Tyson clocked to a tee, man.'

All of a sudden The Truth was a viable contender again, and on 21 July 1989 he challenged Tyson for the undisputed world title at Donald Trump's Taj Mahal casino in Atlantic City. On paper Carl had the style to compete with Tyson. Tyson had lost a few of his dimensions since sacking long-time trainer Kevin Rooney a year earlier, and Carl was a smart operator. But Carl had a glaring Achilles' heel: he had been knocked into the ground more times than a tent peg. The match-up of Tyson's power and the challenger's chin was only ever going to produce one result. For about a minute the young champion had to move his head in and out and around Carl's darting left hand, but once he had his challenger in position, Tyson ducked another jab and came up with an impeccably timed hook. The shot launched Carl into a sprawling heap, his arms draped along the ropes, backside slapping the canvas, his knees bent up before him. Moments after referee Randy Neumann had asked him twice to answer a basic question and been met with blinks as his only response, the fight was waved off. By the time Carl was back on his feet, he had decided that 'politics' were involved and that he had been set up as a stooge so that Tyson could advance towards more lucrative showdowns. In his very next fight, Tyson would lose the championship in one of boxing's greatest ever upsets. Carl would never challenge for the title again.

Midtown, New York, June 2001

When I first met Carl, he had been retired from boxing for four years. Tyson, meanwhile, was tormented by a wish to terminate his career, strangely at odds with his urgent need to clear himself of debt and set up sufficient retirement funds.

It was a suffocating New York summer, but the air conditioning on the top floor of the Fleet Bank International building in midtown Manhattan provided relief from the dripping humidity. I was taken by Carl's youthful appearance as he came striding towards me, ushering me away from a reception desk surrounded by plants and pieces of modern art, and into a small office where we could talk in peace. Forty-one-year-old ex-fighters usually had a fatigued look about them, but Carl could have passed for five or six years younger, and his face was unmarked save for a horizontal scar across his nose caused by his slipping on ice several winters before. His speech did not betray any impairment either, which was a welcome sign, though one which encouraged unscrupulous souls to woo him still, as they sought to lure him back to the ring. Becoming a name was a poisoned chalice towards the end of a fighter's career. One of the first things a manager looks for when he feels the time has arrived for his young protégé to move up a level is an opponent who, despite having been put out to pasture for some time, has a familiar public profile. In the short term it suits most of those involved. The manager gets to sell a marketable fight, the name gets a bit of extra cash to boost his diminishing finances, and the protégé gets to boost his unbeaten record by effortlessly beating someone he can then brag about to the ignorant.

In October 1997 Carl had accepted just such a fight, and he had been beaten in so brutal a fashion that observers suggested his life would be on the line were he ever to box again. In the time since, he had told a lot of determined persuaders where to put their offers. 'It's very hard for your mind to accept what your body's been telling you for a long time,' he said, lucid and clean and smart in his pale grey suit and spotted tie. 'People come up to me when they see me at the fights and say, "You look so great, man, why don't you get back in the ring? Let me tell you what I can do for you . . ." And I say to them, "No, let me tell you what I can do for you – get the fuck out of my face! Are you crazy?" I mean, I'm not that old, but I'm not looking to get beaten up in the ring. Next thing you know, you'll be talking to me and you'll say to yourself, "Damn, I was talking to Carl a year ago and he sounded great, and now he can barely get his own name out of his mouth." When you get older and you're still in the game, that's when you take your real beatings, because your skills will have definitely declined. I most certainly miss those days when I was younger, and I have been tempted on a few occasions to make comebacks because the fighter inside of me still says I can do this. Then reality sinks in and says, "Hey Carl, you did it once when you were at the top of your game and you were one of the best, but you can't do it any more." Even though there's no killers around today, at forty-one years old I'm just not gonna have the same jab, speed or anything that I once had. I don't wanna end up getting beat up by a kid young enough to be my son.'

After retiring from the ring, Carl had taken a job in security at the same Taj Mahal building in which he had been flattened by Tyson, but he was far from happy with his circumstances. On a trip to the International Boxing Hall of Fame's annual induction weekend in Canastota, a meeting with another former heavyweight contender, Gerry Cooney, resulted in a change of scenery and a new outlook on life. Cooney had plunged into alcoholism after being crushed by

Holmes in a bid for the world title in 1982. After his recovery he had set up an organisation entitled FIST (Fighters Initiating Support and Training) with the help of a businessman named Norman Weiss. With their wives assisting them, Cooney and Weiss aimed to help out former fighters as well as active boxers who needed to retire for their own safety, offering support and guidance for them all as they sought housing, help with their rent, healthcare funding and employment which kept them away from the temptation of agreeing to sacrifice themselves in exchange for ready cash.

'Gerry and Norman reached out to a lot of people,' said Carl, 'and one of those people was me. You see, once you're out of boxing nobody gives a shit about you any more, at least not until they came along. It was like, *Carl who? Truth what?* Believe me, just as happy as some of the guys are today, running around getting their picture took here, there and everywhere with all those rich folk at ringside, in a few years' time when most of them are finished, the rich ladies will hold on to their handbags real tightly when they next see them coming. "Hey, remember me? It's me – we met two years ago when I was world heavyweight champion, remember?" And they'll say, "Get the fuck away from me – who the fuck do you think you're talking to?" But I'm one of the lucky ones. I may not seem like it because I've been through some wars in my time, but I still have my faculties. I don't mean wars in the respect of getting beat up, because I never took a lot of unnecessary punishment or had my head jerked around too much. But I fought everyone in the division, and their uncles! I was always very aware of the risks involved in this sport. You have to accept them, or else you've got no business doing it, and if I had to do it all over again, I would. You see, boxing helped cultivate me in so many ways. I was a kid from Jamaica, Queens, where people joined gangs as soon as they could. I didn't escape that lifestyle but I was able to go through it and I'm still alive today, thank goodness. And I try not to complain. Boxing was good to me. Certain people in boxing weren't good to me, and they know their names, but the bottom line is that the responsibility to do things right is ultimately yours. There were a lot of people during my career taking a bit here and a bit there, but where was I when this was all going on? Spending money like I was a billionaire, that's where. So here I am, working as a security guard, and the transition from being the employer – which is how I saw myself as a professional fighter – to becoming the employee, is very difficult. It's a big adjustment. You have to put yourself in situations where you have to kiss a lot of ass. You've gotta be like, *How are you sir? Oh, hi there, how are you sir?* You know? Give me a fucking break! I've gotta be like this with this fucking person? But there you go – you do what you gotta do, until you can do what you wanna do, and I do thank God that I was able to push a lot of things aside and move forward with my life when boxing was over.'

'At least you can accept where it all went wrong,' I said.

'Oh, the responsibility is mine,' said Carl. 'When you look in the mirror and you wonder where all the money went, why you ended up where you are today, you have to say to yourself, *Yo man, you fucked up. This is your life now. Along the way, a lot of people screwed you over, and you know all their names, but you're the real culprit because you allowed it all to happen*. It's especially bad for me, since I felt I was a little smarter than most of the other guys in the game. But guess what? I was chasing girls and partying and spending like the best of them. Before I knew it, there was nothing left to eat. I was broke. If I had looked after my money better back then, I wouldn't be working for Fleet Bank today, I'd own Fleet Bank!'

Larry Holmes had attempted to warn Carl about the need to invest his money wisely while he had it. Instead, of his $1.3m purse for challenging Holmes, The Truth chose to blow $125,000 on the latest Mercedes, and the rest gallivanting in Miami and Hollywood, 'while the wolves raided the hen-house back home'.

'There he is, about to become world champion once again,' sighed Carl when I mentioned Tyson's name. 'But I always liked Mike, you know? Aside from that time when we sparred those two days and it became a bit of an incident, we got on well and we used to talk a lot, even though in those days he was pretty robotic . . . the way he spoke. He couldn't really talk to too many people . . . he really couldn't socialise at all. Out of the ring, I'm not so sure his people did the right thing by him because they always had him locked down, but they built him up the right way professionally.' He paused for a moment and shook his head in disbelief before saying, 'Tyson used to be my sparring partner, can you believe that? And now the fucking guy's making ten million dollars per fight, whilst I'm sitting here saying, "Hello sir, how may I help you?" Talk about the dynamics of life. I hate my work. I can cry, but that's the price you pay if you fuck up. Who knows though, maybe I'll hit the lottery one day.'

42nd Street, New York, May 2002

The peak on Carl's Kangol hat deflected the early-afternoon brightness as he sat against a concrete barrier, waiting for me on 42nd Street. He looked bigger in his boots, tracksuit trousers and Spiderman sweatshirt than he had in his suit and tie, and I could see now that he would have been some-what intimidating himself once upon a time – not Mike Tyson intimidating, but pretty daunting nonetheless, with big shoulders and a wide chest, and an intermittently sour expression in his eyes.

It was a year on from our last meeting, and Carl hadn't hit the lottery. All the same, things could have been a lot worse. He was taking home the kind of money the average man on the street would not have sneezed at, and living in a decent neighbourhood with his Dominican wife. He didn't have a drug problem to tackle, he wasn't collecting welfare cheques, and he remained in apparent good health after all his years in boxing.

Shifting himself off the concrete and turning us into the crowds heading downtown, he began a sprightly stroll towards 34th Street until he stopped beside a street vendor flogging black-market CDs on the sidewalk. He scanned the rows of merchandise on the ground for a few moments, asked to be shown the latest Ashanti album and examined its list of tracks. 'Yeah, this is the right one,' he sighed. 'Gotta get this for my daughter, Nija, or she'll kill me when I next see her. She's in hospital with leukaemia, and I always like to take her something when I visit.'

'I'm sorry she's ill.'

'Yeah, you know . . . and she's only eleven years old too. It breaks my heart, man.' He toyed with the CD for a moment, then handed the vendor a five-dollar bill and asked for it to be put into a small carrier bag. 'But this'll cheer her up. She loves Ashanti, man. She's wanted this one ever since it was released.' He took the bag and we resumed our journey, me pacing faster to keep up with him, Carl still making his way through the crowds, easing other pedestrians out of his path with the slightest of hand movements. 'She's responding well to treatment,' he said. 'They'll have a better idea how she's doing in a couple of weeks' time. But it's just terrible, man, seeing my little girl get struck down with something like that. I love her, and I think the world of her. Even though her mother and I don't get along, if she's there when I visit I just put a smile on my face for my daughter's benefit, you know . . .'

We met a friend of Carl's appropriately named Big Larry and ended up in an Italian diner across the road from the Madison Square Garden forecourt. As I sat down with a soda, Carl and his pal queued at the hot-plate counter and gawped at a woman dressed in a pair of silver-effect trousers which weren't so much skin-tight as fused to her legs. Carl and Big Larry had grown up together in Queens, and attended the same gyms. Big Larry had known Carl when he was a nobody who wanted to be a somebody, when he was a somebody fighting for big cheques in Las Vegas, and now as the might-have-been who worked shifts as a security guard and commuted to and from his job on the train just like the average Joe. Throughout it all, Big Larry had remained Carl's friend, which had to mean something.

Big Larry sipped at his Coke through a straw, and Carl played with his food. 'I really don't think I've been that fortunate, because I've been in a lot of trouble myself,' Carl said gloomily, when I suggested he had wound up better off than many of his peers. 'I went through years of abuse and being abused by people. I brought a lot of those problems on myself, I guess. But I realised that if I kept on the way I was going, I would end up dead. And I didn't want any child of mine visiting me at the morgue. I don't know why it is I've been able to get on with my life better than some of the others. I suppose I just knew that I had to move on when I realised I've got my children – especially my eldest daughter, who needs looking after. Her mom and I having a very volatile relationship, which all started when I was coming up as a pro. Right from the start we were going through a very volatile, very physical relationship. It landed me in a lot of trouble, and as a result they took my daughter away from me. I was taken to court, and I had five hundred dollars taken out of my pay every two weeks . . . and that's a lot, man.'

'And now that situation's resolved?'

'It's resolved,' he replied, unconvincingly. 'I still harbour a lot of hostility towards her, but I just don't show it. Our daughter is more important than anything. Even so, it's not easy.'

One moment he was proud of what he was doing with his life, keener than a kid on the way to the fairground for me to meet his superiors at the security company. The next, he was downcast, embarrassed by the notion that his new job might cast an air of servility about him. Still, he wasn't dead, like John Tate, who had suffered a brain haemorrhage back home in Knoxville. He hadn't ended up beating his long-term girlfriend to a pulp, as Michael Dokes had done in Vegas. And he wasn't still looking for fights in the mistaken belief he remained the best heavyweight in the world, as did the ever-delusional Trevor Berbick.

'Some of those other guys haven't been able to make that transition into a normal working environment because they've never had the social skills,' Carl ventured. 'See, I've always been the kind of guy who knew how to get along with people. And I'm game-tight, remember?! That's very important. It's all about how you apply yourself, you know? *We* all have it. *I* have it, *you* have it, *he* –' Carl glanced at Big Larry and then back at me – '*he* has it. We're lucky. We know how to apply it. It helps to be articulate. Some of those other guys just haven't learned how to be articulate. That's why they're having problems now.

'You're not in the game of boxing any more, this is the game of life. You're not being catered to any more, you're doing the catering for other people. I'm dealing with executives and VIPs every day, people with big heads; that's what I have to deal with. Fifteen years ago it was me whose ass was being kissed, can you believe that? If somebody had told me then that I'd be doing this today, I'd have said, "Get the fuck out of my face," because I was in a cloud.'

The phrase reminded me of Trevor Berbick, who had almost completely lost the plot in recent years. For Carl, one of many who had defeated the West Indian after Tyson had become champion, the reality checks had been hard hitting. Unlike Berbick, however, Carl had dealt with them.

'Last time I spoke to him, Trevor Berbick told me his fight with Tyson was fixed, and that he's going to be champion again,' I told Carl.

'Trevor *Ber-bick*?! That's sad enough. He said his fight was fixed?'

'That's what he told me.'

'His fight was far from fixed, man! He went down three times from one punch. How fixed can that be?'

'He said the knockout punch missed him.'

'Missed him? Yeah, it missed him all right. He got hit so hard, he didn't see or feel it coming! He thinks he can be champion again? He shouldn't even be allowed to fight again. Goes back to my friend, Iran Barkley. He's my buddy, but he's talking about fighting again also, and that's very sad.'

'Oh dear.'

'Oh dear. Exactly. Nobody's gonna allow him to fight. But take his case as a prime example. Barkley is now living with his mom, in the projects. That's gotta be hard medicine to swallow – going back to live with your mom, in the projects of all places. *Man, you fought your way outta the projects, and now you're back there.* It's a sad case, man. It's a sad case. Those guys; they just can not move on, because they look back at when they could do this, and for most of them they were the best years of their lives. They want to recapture the past.'

Two more girls in denim hotpants and T-shirts, sauntering around the café, looking at menus and deciding to head elsewhere, and Carl and Big Larry lingering at them with their eyes, smirking and chewing on their soda straws. 'Caught me again,' said Carl, with a grin. 'But you know it's true!' He settled back in his seat, cheering up a bit and warming to the topic as Big Larry disappeared into the bathroom. 'Guys like Berbick – they don't have the money any more. They don't have the fame. Nobody stops them in the street any more. They want to recapture that. They watch their old fights repeated on TV, and they hear some announcer say they're better than the guys around today, and they just wanna get back into action, man . . .'

'Do you get recognised much yourself?'

'Sometimes I do, man. Yes, sometimes I do. People can't believe how young and well I look. You know, sometimes I don't like to be recognised. They say, "You're The Truth, right?" But sometimes I just don't feel like letting them know what's going on in my life right now.'

'But you don't want to fight again like all the others?'

'I'd fight Larry Holmes again for five hundred thousand dollars,' he replied half jokingly. 'But no, the reality is I know better. When it's over, it's over. You've gotta realise that. You've gotta know that in your heart and just move on with the rest of your life. You just can't say to yourself, "Well, maybe I got another fight within me." No man, it's over. It's over. You know, I'm forty-two years of age now, and people still say to me, "No man, you look so young. You look so great." I don't give a shit how great I may look on the outside. Those forty-two years of age are inside me, not on the outside. If I look all right on the outside, well that's good . . . that's great . . . thank God. But it's not happening any more.' He lowered his voice and looked around. 'It's over,' he whispered. 'I look at tapes of myself every now and then, but I always say to myself that I'm not gonna live in an illusion of grandeur. I take reality as it is. I know my reality. I don't believe I can fly. Those guys sitting out there, thinking they can get back in the ring and do it again, they think they can fly. Hey listen, it's over. Be grateful that you've got some friends, you've made some contacts, you've still got your health. That's the most important thing. You've got your health, you can spend time watching your kids grow up. Be grateful. Unfortunately, a lot of people just can't do that or say that to themselves.'

In a fortnight's time Tyson would challenge Lewis for the world heavyweight championship at the Pyramid Arena in Memphis, Tennessee. Half the world anticipated a show-down for the ages, convinced Tyson had been preserved since those faraway days when he had fought like a demon. The other half saw a mismatch: a beating in waiting for the man whose recent years had been spent for the most part duck-ing lawsuits, fondling strippers and threatening to consume Lewis's non-existent children.

But whether Tyson was seen as the destroyer or the doomed, the fascination was mounting. People who didn't usually give the sport a blind bit of notice – even those who dismissed the whole business as a dated, laughable exercise on the far fringes of entertainment – wanted to know about the fight. It didn't really matter that Lewis–Tyson was being flogged to the public for in excess of $59.95. Lewis–Tyson was front-page news. It was an event. It was *the* event of the year. Over 20,000 requests for press accreditation had been made from around the world. The fighters were to be paid $17.5m each for their services, with additional revenue sure to follow once the pay-per-view figures were totalled. And join-ing the bulging interest in the fight, Tyson's former opponents were all reading and watching and waiting for this latest act in his macabre play, phantoms from his past all gathering together in mind at least, to see what was to become of the man who had extinguished them on his march towards what at the time had been described as assured greatness.

Tyson was looking up at Carl, Big Larry and me from the cover of *Sports Illustrated*, joyfully exposing the teeth which had ripped a segment clean off Evander Holyfield's right ear, beside the heading, 'Monster's Ball'. 'As he storms toward his showdown with Lennox Lewis', the piece said inside, 'is Mike Tyson the ultimate psycho celebrity in the midst of a public breakdown – or the shrewdest self-promoter in boxing history?' Carl didn't give the magazine more than a fleeting glance as I asked how he thought it would all turn out for Tyson.

'I don't think he'll ever be brought down to the level of Berbick, but you never know.'

'But if he was brought down to that level, and he had to find a job to survive . . .?'

'You mean, like me?'

'Something like that.'

Carl shook his head. 'He wouldn't be able to do it. He just wouldn't be able to. That would be too hard for him. He's always been on a pedestal. For him to adjust like that . . . well, I just don't believe he'll ever have to cope with that anyway.'

'But he's effectively fighting for nothing against Lewis,' I ventured.

'Oh, I know he owes the IRS all that money, but if he wins or loses admirably, that means he'll have put up a good fight and deserves a rematch. Of course if he loses because of one of his fucking escapades and does all that shit he normally goes through, nobody will ever wanna see him again. As a matter of fact, those same people will help to bury him even deeper than he already is. When the people turn against you, it's unbelievable.'

'But a lot of guys in your position have got through large amounts of money. How much is enough, Carl? What's going to be enough to satisfy Tyson that he can just retire and get on with the rest of his life in peace?'

'He's made over two hundred and fifty million during his career, that's the figure that I hear . . .'

'More,' muttered Big Larry.

'Well, whatever . . . somewhere along the line, someone somewhere has got to have got through to Tyson that he had to invest his money more wisely. I can still sympathise with Mike though. Trouble comes to him all the time. People say, "Oh, there's Mike Tyson, we'll give him some problems." And they're on to him like a fucking ghost. But the problem is Mike Tyson isn't the kind of guy you can approach in that kind of way and expect him to just get a little upset. These people who approach him; they don't have the same status as Mike. They can't understand the way his mind works, or relate to him as a human being. But I can. Look, Holyfield and Lewis aren't gonna have any problems if this ever happens to them, because they don't react the same way as Tyson. If someone comes up to Holyfield and does something crazy, he's gonna walk away, shake his head and laugh. Tyson's gonna snap the guy's neck! Believe me. That's the way he is. It would be impossible for him to work a normal job, because of that reason.'

'Tyson needs to surround himself with good guys,' said Big Larry, chewing his food and waving a hand at Carl. 'This guy . . . this guy does just that. You don't wanna be hanging around with no hoodlums and drug dealers and things, you wanna be hanging around good people. I can never remember Carl associating himself with bad people, and we go back to seventy-nine. And you've never heard anything bad about him aside from his personal life . . . his marriage break-up . . . and that was solved. But Tyson, he's always running into trouble. As a matter of fact he just ran into trouble with a personal friend of mine at that press conference he did with Lennox the other day, Mitch Rose. Mitch started calling him out. Yeah, personal friend of mine Mitch, but I'll be honest with you – who gives a fuck?'

Carl saw me flicking through *Sports Illustrated*, and glanced down at the timeline of photos chronicling Tyson's days as a delinquent, his marriage to the actress Robyn Givens, those heady championship years when no one thought he could be beaten, the shocker against Buster Douglas, the rape conviction, the release from jail, the savaging of Holyfield's ears and the recent press-conference brawl with Lewis.

'If he can't get Lennox out of there early, he may well self-destruct,' he sighed. 'You know why? Because this is do or die for him. This is the fight which will take him away from all of his problems. Everything's riding on this fight for him. It's much more important for him to win this fight than it is for Lewis. This is for respect and pride for Lewis. But this is for his life as far as Tyson's concerned.'

Carl stretched his arms above his head. 'Tyson's really a

great guy, you know? I'm not being funny, it's true. But he doesn't have a lot of skills as far as human-being skills are concerned. Tyson's not the kind of guy you can walk up to and say, "Hey buddy, how're you doin'?" I can, but the average person couldn't walk up to him and do that. I could go up to him and say, "Yo man, wassup?" But he would kill the average fellow. He would kill them. He's from the street, and if he sees another person from the street coming up to him, he won't think the guy's coming to say hello – he'll think he has a confrontation on his hands. He'll say, "You can't come up to me like this, you can't do this with me!" Man, that's the kind of guy Mike Tyson will always be.'

Ground Zero, May 2002

We went from floor to floor, moving slowly and cautiously, checking computer rooms, private offices, water coolers and filing cabinets and around the crude balconies created by the plummeting devastation. Intermittently Carl's walkie-talkie would crackle, he would respond, and then we would move on after he had registered our whereabouts with the marines. He talked about his daughter. She had liked her CD. He spoke again of the sorrow he felt for those who had perished when the towers came crumbling down. And then we stopped. Carl snatched his respirator off, leaned back against a reception counter, elbows up on the ledge, and threw his head back a little. 'I've been through some shit in my life, man.'

'You mean your wife?'

'That's not all, but that's a large part of it. You see, I was abused long before I ever met her.'

'How do you mean?'

'When I lived in South Carolina, I was so happy,' he sighed. 'I looked upon my grandmother as my mother. To me, *she* was my mother. You know what I'm saying? I loved her like my mother. She was the most beautiful person in the world, and I loved her more than anybody or anything in the world.' His eyes clouded a fraction and he tipped his head back some more. I stopped worrying about him endangering himself by breathing in the undiluted air, and felt somewhat ridiculous standing there before him, my face masked, arms crossed, listening to him speak like this. 'When I went to live with my mother in New York, she abused me.'

'I'm sorry.'

'Yeah, she abused me. She hated me and my sister, because she hated our father. See, our father was darker skinned than her, and we were always a constant reminder of that. She didn't like that she had dark-skinned kids.' He shook his head slightly and said, 'She was my mother, so I loved her. But I hated her too. She had a little drinking problem there. At night she would wake me up and beat me with a belt. And sometimes she would lock us in our rooms for days without food.'

'No one noticed?'

'She was clever. She didn't beat us so bad when we were at school. And when she had parties and we went out she was always so nice to us. She was the kind of person everyone warmed to. I loved her. And I hated her more than anybody. She died the year my daughter was born. How about that? My sister has gotten over it. She went and got a degree, and she's a computer analyst now, making a good living for herself. I can never forget though.' He pretended to examine his hands for a moment. 'You know, I feel so sorry for my wife. All the things I could have offered her fifteen years ago, yet she has nothing and my ex-wife got it all.'

Love, Sex and Violence: The Heavyweight Marriage

On the eve of Williams's fight with Tyson, he was awoken repeatedly throughout the night by his first wife, Diane Donaldson, who kept calling from her separate quarters to complain about the hotel's room service. Later committed to eleven days inside a jail cell for slapping her in a fit of anger, Carl was just one in a long line of heavyweight boxers whose careers were drastically affected by tempestuous personal relationships.

Jack Johnson infuriated the bigots of early twentieth-century America by cavorting with a string of white women, and even being so bold as to marry one. Jack Dempsey's image as an icon of the 1920s would take a bruising from the biographical disclosure that he had once been employed as what was sinisterly described as 'a professional rapist of women'. Max Baer's reign may have stretched beyond 1935 had he not been so enamoured by the Hollywood lifestyle and the pretty young starlets who caught his eye. And Muhammad Ali, though married four times, was for long tormented both by an inability to quench his own riotous libido and the refusal of his stunning first wife, Sonji, to conform to the strict teachings of Islam.

The Lost Generation of the 1980s – the very crowd Tyson

swooped on with a vengeance – was riddled with broken marriages and scores of tales of domestic disturbance. More than half of the men Tyson fought during his first reign as champion were either estranged from their wives at the time, or else on the road to divorce, but even William's problems were diminutive when measured against Tyson's encyclopedic catalogue of run-ins with and offences committed against women.

The first sign of Tyson's battle with his sexual demons appeared in 1982, when as a burly teenager indulged by the besotted D'Amato in the Catskill mountains, he was rumoured to have made lewd sexual advances towards an eleven-year-old girl. The girl was the niece of Teddy Atlas, one of the young trainers employed by D'Amato to oversee the development of his aspiring fighters. Atlas, who had once gently cradled Tyson's head in his hands as the youngster sobbed at his own insecurities, confronted Tyson about the rumours and, on being convinced of Tyson's guilt, was reported to have pressed the barrel of a pistol against the teenager's head, vowing to pull the trigger the next time he heard of such behaviour. Ironically, it was Atlas who wound up packing his bags shortly after the incident, as D'Amato continued to shield Tyson from his own fallibilities.

The cosseting of Tyson extended beyond D'Amato's death in 1985. After Tyson was accused of sexually harassing first a shop assistant and then a cinema usher in an Albany shopping mall, Jim Jacobs and Bill Cayton managed to gloss over the incidents. But they tried to drive home to Tyson the importance of resisting such behaviour if his good image was to be maintained.

'I go for sweet girls, honest girls,' Tyson coyly revealed to a female reporter just over a year later. 'I like them to be independent, confident, but not too confident. I'd like to settle down eventually and marry, but not for a long time yet.' It was all too squeaky clean and rehearsed, echoing Joe Louis's care not to be photographed either standing beside a white woman or gloating at a fallen opponent. Still, Tyson couldn't resist describing the Albany apartment he had just finished decorating as '. . . kind of Playboy style. It's all maroon, beige and brown. The girls, they walk in and are stunned.'

Already, Tyson – accompanied by childhood friend Rory Holloway and a failed stand-up comedian named John Horne – was addicted to 'tramping', endless romps with conveyor belts of women eager to throw themselves at celebrities. Shortly before training commenced for his fight with James 'Bonecrusher' Smith in March 1987, the champion remained in a Pennsylvania hotel room for forty-eight hours uninterrupted, as he and Holloway engaged in an orgy with two dozen women.

Two months later, perhaps to his management's relief, Tyson appeared to have settled down with a steady girlfriend. He had been smitten by Robyn Givens after watching her in a TV series called *Head of the Class*, and Horne, who had contacts in the entertainment industry, arranged for the pair to meet on a date. Introducing her to the media before his title defence against Pinklon Thomas, Tyson declared that Givens was '. . . very good for me. She has shown me there is another life outside the ring,' before adding quickly, 'Don't think I'm losing my concentration. I know how much there is still to do. I don't plan to be one of those champions who comes and goes before you really know him. I'm going to be around for some time.'

It all appeared to be great news for anyone who had a vested interest in Tyson's career, and lent some much needed grounding to his personal life. His ambivalent attitude towards the treatment of women, however, coupled with the revelation from basketball star Michael Jordan – one of Givens' former beaux – that 'she's the kind of girl who, when she throws her arms around you, makes you check for your wallet', did not bode well for a cosy future together. Indeed, two months into their romance, there were reports that Givens had already called the police from a New York apartment belonging to one of Tyson's inner circle, Steve Lott, for fear of being attacked by the boxer.

By the end of 1987, Tyson was growing incensed about unfounded rumours that the property mogul Donald Trump was conducting an illicit affair with Givens. Tyson's own infidelity was undisputed, and when he returned to Atlantic City in January 1988 to ruin any pretensions that a thirty-eight-year-old Larry Holmes had to remaining glory, a trio of women in pursuit of the champion's affection – Givens, the British supermodel Naomi Campbell and a former Miss USA named Suzette Charles – were carefully positioned in separate ringside seating areas.

It was Givens who succeeded in getting her man, marrying Tyson in February 1988 and a month later flying out to Tokyo to watch her husband wipe out Tony Tubbs. In Japan, the couple was all smiles, a picture of bliss as Tyson donned a bandana after the fight and gently nuzzled his wife. But the honeymoon period was cut short when Givens unearthed a condom in Tyson's jacket pocket. They had an explosive row as they drove home, which culminated in Tyson crashing his $183,000 Bentley near the entrance of New York's Holland Tunnel.

Tyson and Givens lived in an enormous New Jersey mansion, but it wasn't large enough to protect Tyson from his mother-in-law, Ruth Roper, who was living with the happy couple. Such a household was hardly conducive to a life of marital tranquillity, and within four months of Tyson pledging his wedding vows, Roper was informing the press that he was repeatedly abusive towards her and her daughter. In September, Givens and Tyson sat beside each other on a sofa for an interview with Barbara Walters on the ABC TV series, *20/20*. An inanimate and mumbling presence beside his wife, Tyson listened in silence as he was described by Givens as 'manically depressive', and their life together as 'a living hell'. Two nights later, the police were again called to their home to investigate an incident of alleged domestic violence, triggered by Tyson's humiliation. By the end of the week, Givens was suing Tyson for divorce, and Tyson was countersuing.

By now, the lid had burst off Tyson's private life, and there was little anyone could do to contain the champion's wayward indulgences. That December, Tyson was slapped with two lawsuits for molesting Sandra Miller and Lori Davis in a Manhattan nightclub. In 1989, his inappropriate impulses resurfaced during a court hearing against Cayton. Spotting an attractive lady across the chamber, Tyson decided to win her favour with some none-too-discreet hand gestures.

Unfortunately for Tyson, the lady in question was singularly unimpressed, and also happened to be an attorney.

In June 1989, a year to the day since Tyson had obliterated the previously unbeaten Michael Spinks, the Tyson–Givens divorce was finalised. The following month, the champion defeated Carl Williams in Atlantic City, and at a post-fight press conference waved bundles of dollar bills at the press while a flock of beautiful women crammed around him.

In the wake of his loss to Buster Douglas seven months later, however, Tyson was to become more melancholy, openly chastened by his disastrous marriage. 'The last two years have seemed like a hundred,' he explained. 'I believed in a woman with my heart, and she tore my heart out. Now I have to think with my brain and not my heart. I gave this woman so much of myself and now it burns me up knowing that she is out there knowing so much about me, so much of what a man wants to keep secret.'

There were those tempted to believe a more abstemious Tyson had emerged; one who would temper his cravings and regain his old focus, if for no other reason than a desire to harness his prodigious talent once more and reclaim the world championship. It was not long, though, before Tyson had slipped away from the serenity of the pigeon lofts in which he had sought sanctuary after the Douglas debacle, and regressed into further, alcohol-fuelled promiscuity. A former employee of Givens sued him for sexual assault and for making death threats against her; while beaten opponent Razor Ruddock was having his shattered jaw rewired in a Las Vegas hospital, Tyson surveyed a line-up of six girls in mini-skirts after polishing off a late-night meal, made several choices and disappeared to his hotel room; and a month later, deprived of sleep and stinking of beer, he slobbered all over a group of swimsuited beauty-queen contestants at the Black Expo in Indianapolis, and wound up being arrested for the rape of Desiree Washington in Room 606 of the Canterbury Hotel.

Tyson always maintained his innocence of the charge of rape, conceding only to crude and ungentlemanly conduct. But he was indicted on counts of forcible rape and oral sex by a Marion County grand jury in September 1991, and sentenced to six years' imprisonment the following March. Already slapped with a paternity suit by a former girlfriend named Natalie Fears, Tyson soon received correspondence from Givens while languishing in his jail cell, asking – according to reports in the *New York Post* – for an unlikely reconciliation. Tyson passed on the offer, and seemed close to marrying another ex-fling, Geraldine Ecclestone, upon his release from the misleadingly named Indiana Youth Center. As things turned out, when Tyson was released into the soft, white sunlight of a March morning in 1995, it was Monica Turner – a doctor whose first husband was a convicted drug dealer – who secured his hand in marriage. There was a quiet dignity about Turner, who displayed an understated determination to help Tyson bring some order to his chaotic financial affairs. When in March 1996 Tyson regained the WBC title, held on loan by former victim Frank Bruno, there appeared to be a semblance of order in the fighter's life. Tyson's disposal of Bruno was majestic in its choreography, and he had gone many months without a whisper of discontent about his home life.

Although Turner refrained from looping a noose around her husband's ankles and keeping him tethered to their picket fence, she appeared to have calmed Tyson's habitual agitation.

It didn't last. In April 1996, after spending an evening in the company of his old sparring partner, Oliver McCall, at the Clique nightclub on Chicago's South Side, Tyson was accused of sexual assault by a twenty-five-year-old beautician named LaDonna August. Five years earlier, the veteran *New York Times* boxing writer, Phil Berger, had found proof of Tyson's occasional innocence in this department. 'I've known Mike for two years, and he's the best man I've ever been with,' a Washington beautician named Sherri Brown told Berger. 'He's been a caring, compassionate friend to me.' And a twenty-one-year-old student from the Bronx, Jeanine Mayers, recalled an occasion when she went to a disco with Tyson and saw a woman touch the champion boxer in a suggestive fashion. 'Mike told her, "If I touched you, you'd sue me,"' Mayers recounted. 'She looked over her shoulder and said, "Yes," and kept walking.'

The Chicago police department elected not to press charges against Tyson after nightclub staff and August's friends raised doubts about the beautician's version of events. Yet this did little to remove the mud which had been flung at the boxer once more. A year later, after a motorbike accident on a Connecticut highway left him with broken ribs and a bruised lung, Tyson admitted that his marriage was 'pretty much working, but only because [Monica] is putting more work into it than I am. I [would] really hate to lose her. Anything's a possibility in life, but if I do, it will be my fault. It wouldn't be her fault.'

By now, there was enough strain for Tyson at work even without the ones he was admitting to at home. He had lost twice to Evander Holyfield – systematically pounded the first time, disgraced by his disqualification defeat in the rematch. He was commencing a year-long expulsion from the sport as a penalty for biting part of Holyfield's ear off, and was a few weeks away from being sent to jail again for assaulting two elderly motorists in a much publicised road-rage episode. From then on, the allegations of misconduct against women, whether fabricated, exaggerated or genuine, came in torrents. Two women in a Georgetown DC bistro filed suits after Tyson verbally abused and threw coffee over them. His provocation? They had scolded Tyson for blanking a pair of autograph seekers, then ordered clams and bacon off the restaurant menu. There were fresh paternity suits, allegations he had raped a fifty-year-old supermarket cashier in California, and even that he had abducted and imprisoned women and forced them to become sex slaves at a residence in Phoenix – which resulted in his home being encircled by a SWAT team. All these allegations were made only months before he was due to challenge Lennox Lewis for the world title; all were quashed. Tyson was leading a borderline nefarious lifestyle that was driving a succession of trainers to distraction, whiling away the night-time hours carousing in lapdance clubs; but there was no evidence to prove he had raped, abducted or enslaved anyone.

But ultimately, another heavyweight marriage – like Trevor Berbick's and Pinklon Thomas's and Carl Williams's and Tony Tucker's – was doomed to a grinding end. By the time

Tyson arrived in Memphis for his showdown with Lewis, Monica Turner was on her way out of his life.

Ground Zero, May 2002

We took the elevator down to the ground floor, binned our uniforms in the disposal devices, shed our respirators and moved outside, past the police booth where a cop now gazed at us suspiciously. It was 4.15 a.m., and the chattering of drills and hammering of pickaxes still went on around us. I shook Carl's hand a couple of blocks away from his workplace. 'I hope we meet again soon, and that things work out well for you and your family – especially your daughter.'

'I hope so too man,' said Carl, checking the sidewalk from left to right.

'You'll make it eventually,' I said. 'You never know what's around the corner.'

'I'll never get all of what I had back,' he replied. 'I know that, but I'm not satisfied with the way things are, you know? I need to get some of it back. Not all, I know, but I've just gotta get some of it back.'

We made our farewells. I started walking home, turned to wave and saw a bearded Korean man emerge from his all-night grocery store. He and Carl greeted each other warmly, and I heard the man say, 'Someone told me you fighter.' Carl just said, 'No, man, they got me mixed up with somebody else,' before turning on his heels and heading back to work.

Three: Undisputed

Searching for Tony, 1998–2002

IN MARCH 1998, DON KING'S MATCHMAKER PAYTON SHER TOLD
the press that he never wanted to see Tony Tucker in a boxing
ring. 'I've retired him,' Sher announced. 'Wherever he is, I
wish Tony well, but I won't be booking him for fights ever
again.'

It had been more than a decade since Tucker's commend-
able stand against a prime Mike Tyson, and almost five years
since he had lasted the distance with and rattled a young
Lennox Lewis, but nothing had dampened Tucker's dreams
of glory. Nothing, that was, until March 1998, when a medical
report announced that he had suffered grave visual impairment in his right eye, and advised that he no longer be
permitted to box in the state of Nevada. This, then, had
signalled the end of the road after a line of improbable comeback bouts which had resulted in concussion, fractured
orbital bones and any number of physical traumas which lay
dormant and disguised. The Nevada State Athletic
Commission (NSAC) vetoed a proposed bout of his in Las
Vegas, and there was not a state in the land which was going

to defy their ruling. Tony Tucker's professional boxing career had been terminated.

Carl Williams had referred to 'the dynamics of life', and here they were in their bluntest form: Lennox Lewis and Mike Tyson were jostling for extra fiscal guarantees to boost already massive purses for their impending clash in Memphis; Tony Tucker had been reduced to scratching a living as a doorman or a greeter in Las Vegas, a city he would once have jetted into to earn small fortunes of his own. Each morning, after dropping his daughter off at elementary school, Tucker would return to his residence on East Indian River Drive and prepare for the grinding monotony of another day. His life had grown empty and depressing. Eventually all fighters had to lay down their gloves and start gluing clippings into scrapbooks for their grandchildren, he knew that. It was just that that moment had arrived so soon. One minute he was one of the sturdiest heavyweights in the world, the next people were imploring him to get the hell away from the sport and find himself a proper job.

Living in Vegas hadn't helped much. Every weekend it seemed there were shows at the Aladdin or the Sahara or the Thomas & Mack Center or the MGM Grand or the Stratosphere or the Mandalay Bay casino and resort. The monotony had let up only briefly when Tucker was asked to play a cameo role in a movie, *Play It to the Bone*. That had been a lot of fun, rubbing shoulders with Antonio Banderas and Woody Harrelson. Whenever Tucker thought about that time, he would laugh out loud and pray for a similar opportunity to come along. But it never did.

Instead, he buzzed residents in through security doors,

while his income dropped, his second marriage capsized and Tyson and Lewis – men he had not backed down from during his wonder years – talked telephone numbers. How was it that he could give Tyson all he could handle and make Lewis look ordinary, yet today he had wound up as just another of the sweet science's forgotten players?

Far away amidst the Hollywood hills, an old friend of Tucker's, Alex Ramos, was on a mission to help former prize-fighters struggling with their day-to-day existences. Ramos, for one, had not forgotten about Tucker. His company, the Retired Boxers' Organization (RBO) was an outfit which specialised in conjuring up resources from wells which others had written off as dry. Ramos had plans, and just as Gerry Cooney's organisation had sought to help out Carl Williams, Ramos had every intention of lending his outfit's support to Tucker. Ramos had once enjoyed a reputation as an exciting young middleweight from the Bronx, which had helped secure him a spot on a mid-eighties TV series, *Tomorrow's Champions*, alongside Tucker. This show featured a generation of young talent, including future champions Davey Moore and Johnny 'Bump City' Bumphus, as well as the rugged Tony Ayala Jr. They were going to be the sport's new wave of stars, youngsters poised to succeed the likes of Thomas Hearns, Sugar Ray Leonard, Roberto Duran and Marvin Hagler. Instead, many of its members became boxing's most damned. Moore became a champion too soon. Not long after he was brutalised by Duran, he was killed in a freak accident, run over by his own truck after forgetting to put on the brakes. Bumphus became a drug addict. Ayala raped and sodomised a young school teacher and was sent down for years. Ramos's career progress was not without setbacks, and by the time a title shot came his way he was tired and over the hill.

Ramos kept in touch with Tucker as often as he could, but shortly before Christmas 2001, they lost contact after Tucker's second marriage dissolved and he moved away from Sin City without a forwarding address. For several months Ramos heard nothing. His secretary sent every subscriber to the RBO's newsletter an email asking for anyone with any knowledge of Tucker's whereabouts to get in touch and let them know he was safe and well.

When he was a young amateur standout, Tucker was known as a quiet guy with a ready smile, pleasant to be around, never boorish or obnoxious; fun, without having to be the life and soul of a party. But since he had stepped into a Las Vegas physician's office to hear the results of a routine eye exam, he too had become that little bit sullen and embittered, just as all prizefighters seem to somewhere along the line. As the weeks went by, Ramos's anxieties rose.

Eventually, however, Ramos got the news he had been waiting for: Tucker had resurfaced in Tampa, Florida. 'Vegas was upbeat all the time,' Tucker told Ramos on the telephone. 'But it's always there, surrounding you. Everyone knows you. Here in Tampa, I can kinda settle down. I've met some good people and made some good friends. I like Tampa a lot, man. This is a beautiful place. I heard they had some promising kids down here, so maybe I can train a champion.'

This was good news; Ramos thought Tucker had the potential to become an excellent trainer. He had been a world champion. He had a wealth of knowledge to offer some young buck with the tools to do something in the game. Just so long as he didn't try to take to the ring himself.

Still, as things stood, Tucker was doing no fighting, no training, no nothing at all – just soaking up the rays in Tampa and taking life easy. Knowing that for former prizefighters so much free time tended to lead to an unhealthy indolence, Ramos was keen for his friend to take up the vacant position as Florida spokesperson for the RBO. Tucker didn't need any arm-twisting.

'I'd definitely like to be involved,' he said. 'Who's more deserving to be in this kind of position, but we fighters ourselves?'

'You've got it, Tony,' said Ramos.

'I mean, we lived it Alex, you know? We lived it.'

'Yes, Tony,' said Ramos. 'We did.'

Grand Rapids, Michigan, 1966–1980

It was a vivid memory from Tucker's childhood: one of the first times little Tony had been allowed to attend one of his dad's fights, and he remembered the crowd on their feet, cheering and screaming, and the blows which landed on his dad's body and face. He could remember it all. As Bob Tucker retreated on to the ropes, his opponent advanced and smashed him to the canvas. Above Tony's daddy, the referee hovered into view and counted. Bob Tucker knew that his opponent's supporters were on their feet and stamping now, but he didn't hear their jubilation or the numbers tripping from the referee's lips. The only thing he could hear as he raised himself groggily and shook his head was a high-pitched wail from behind. '*Daddy, get up! Daddy, get up!*'

Little Tony was hollering and screaming, his fists curled into balls as he watched his father prepare to be ushered back into battle. His daddy was his hero. Back at school in third grade, everyone knew who Tony was. If he was ever bullied by kids in the fourth grade or manhandled by a teacher, he would go back home in the afternoon and tell his daddy, and the very next day his daddy would handle it. Now, as always, Tony wanted his daddy to beat the other guy to death. Before the round was over, Bob Tucker hammered his opponent into submission, and little Tony stopped screaming.

Growing up surrounded by boxing had seemed as natural to Tony as waking up in the morning. In Michigan at the time, there were really only three ways out of poverty: crime, working the car-plants in Detroit, or boxing. And in Tucker's hometown of Grand Rapids, boxing was booming. In 1963 and '64, Bob Tucker represented Michigan in the US National Team Championships, and saw his side win on both occasions. After school, Tony would spend his afternoon in the gym, watching his daddy and the rest of the team prepare for competitions. When his daddy turned pro, Tony carried on watching and learning some more. When Bob Tucker finally retired, he began tutoring men himself. Little Tony would sit and digest everything while his daddy instructed fighters like Floyd Mayweather, who would go on to test the great Sugar Ray Leonard, and a hulking behemoth named Buster Mathis, who had bested Smokin' Joe Frazier twice in the amateurs and would take Muhammad Ali the distance as a pro.

That Tony would one day become a fighter himself was never really in dispute. But if anyone thought the father was prepared to put his son at risk in a bid for the fame, success and wealth which had evaded his own professional career, they were mistaken. Two years after Michigan had captured its second successive national championship, Bob Tucker was involved in an horrific automobile accident which left him badly hurt. Some who were aware of his near miss with death noticed subtle changes in him from that moment on. While his family and loved ones were simply relieved to watch Bob recover from his ordeal and return to a normal life, a few of the faces in the gym picked up on the extra caution with which he went about his everyday affairs. A handful of them even felt their friend had developed a sense of paranoia about his well being, and even more about that of his son.

One of those who clocked this change was Emanuel Steward, one of Bob Tucker's teammates on the all-conquering Michigan amateur squad. Like Tucker, Steward had also decided to focus his energy on training fighters. During their time together, he became acutely aware of Tucker senior's fears. By the time Tony reached his late teens, it was obvious to someone with Steward's eye for talent that he was developing into a classy boxer. On top of that, Tony was a good kid: he'd steered clear of the gang culture and drug scene which was starting to run rampant across Michigan, and unlike so many of his contemporaries, he had managed to graduate from high school.

As a slim light-heavyweight Tony represented his country at amateur tournaments in Europe and the Americas. Simply getting the opportunity to travel was an education in itself. None was quite as memorable as a 1978 trip to Cuba, where he won his bout in front of Fidel Castro at the Coliseum in Havana. After Tucker collected his medal that night, he walked past Castro's balcony and flashed a smile in El Presidente's direction. He was disappointed that his host seemed unwilling to move away from a cortege of body-guards to mix with the American visitors.

A year later, the twenty-one-year-old established himself as one of America's finest amateur fighters, defeating Cuba's finest at the Pan-Am Games in San Juan, and then winning the World Cup in New York. The only prize which had thus far eluded him was the Olympic gold medal, and the Games were just around the corner. But while politics had not disrupted the regular US–Cuba tourneys, events way beyond the world of amateur boxing were going to rob Tucker of the chance to follow in the footsteps of Cassius Clay, Joe Frazier, George Foreman, and Michael and Leon Spinks. Tucker had been filling out, and was preparing for a move up to heavy-weight. The American coaches had failed repeatedly to discover a heavyweight capable of overcoming the legendary Teofilo Stevenson; Tucker was their chance of toppling the giant Cuban and interrupting his march towards three consecutive gold medals. In Tucker's eyes, victory over Stevenson would have been the ultimate stepping stone towards turning professional, and he had fully intended to kick off his pro career with more noise than anyone had generated since Clay returned from Rome with his bag of jaunty magic tricks and imperfect poetry. It wasn't to be: the USSR invaded Afghanistan and President Carter ordered the

US team to stay away. Tony Tucker was distraught, and Stevenson powered his way to another victory. The 1980 Moscow Olympiad was the first in a succession of three Games blighted by boycotts. As a result, American, Cuban and Soviet Bloc fighters wouldn't compete together in the same Olympic championships for a span of sixteen years.

The dejected US squad was asked to participate in a tournament in Poland. Tucker won his light-heavyweight contest, and the next day the team flew back to New York to board various internal flights home. Tired and disgruntled, Tucker was waiting for his daddy to arrive by car from Michigan when a message came through from one of the team's hierarchy. Would Tucker be willing to fly back to Poland and take part in a different competition, this time as a heavyweight? At first he thought the request was crazy. He had just flown all the way from Warsaw, why would he want to put himself through that journey all over again, in such a short space of time? But the more he thought about it, the more the idea appealed to him. He was never going to have the opportunity to humble the awesome Stevenson. But he could fly back to Poland and whip every heavyweight in the tournament to show the world what might have been. He would fly to Poland, but only on one condition; his daddy was also to get a seat on the flight. The officials agreed.

Tucker sat in the airport and waited. He passed most of the time with his best friend, Lemuel Steeples, a welterweight from St Louis who was also taking part in the second competition. Steeples had earned his place on the team by knocking out an opponent from Texas named Donald Curry and another from Detroit named Milton McCrory. When

Tucker and Steeples went to camp, they always shared a bunk. And when each of them fought, the other would be his most vociferous supporter. Tucker thought Steeples was certain to become a dominant world champion. Curry and McCrory would themselves win world titles.

As the hours ticked by, Tucker became more anxious. There was no sign of his daddy. Soon, Steeples had to check in his luggage. The team officials asked Tucker to board the flight without his father, but the boxer refused. His daddy had driven miles to collect him from the airport; he wasn't just going to fly back to Europe and leave him to it. They tried getting messages to Bob Tucker by calling the rest of the family in Grand Rapids, but all anyone knew was that Bob Tucker had set off for New York the previous day and should have been there with Tony by now.

As the rest of the team boarded, Tucker waited. An increasingly irate group of officials eventually shrugged and headed for the boarding gates. Tucker waited some more, and it was announced that the gate for his departure to Warsaw had closed. He hoped the guys would all do well. He knew Lemuel would.

After the flight took off, Bob Tucker arrived, and Tony forgot all about Poland. The pair embraced, and prepared for their long trip home. In the car, they talked about boxing and family, stopping only to use the bathroom or to eat at one of the roadside grills. Occasionally they would tune in to one of the R&B stations. When they returned to Grand Rapids and parked the car outside their home, Tucker's mother and sisters flooded out of the front door, crying and clenching him to their necks and shoulders, their tears

wetting his face and shirt. Bob Tucker looked on incredulously as his wife and daughters grabbed and kissed his son.
Hadn't they heard the news once during their trip back home?
Hadn't they stopped for breakfast and seen the pictures on
the TV screen behind some coffee bar? Didn't they buy the
newspapers that morning?

'I had no idea. Didn't hear nothing about no plane crash
until I got home. I was like, "Wow, they're so happy to see
me," and then they told me about the plane. Man, I lost
some of my best friends ever on that flight. Especially
Lemuel. He was a bad man, and he was my best friend. He
would have been a sure champion.'

Romancing Tony, 1980–1987

Later that year, Tucker turned pro under the management
of Steward. Another Michigan fight face, Luther Burgess,
was appointed his head trainer. But neither Steward nor
Burgess had Tucker's ear the way his daddy did.

From the outset, Bob Tucker had two criteria in mind: his
son would fight no one even moderately competitive until
his father agreed to it; and, wherever money could be made,
that was the direction to be taken. Few could have blamed
Bob Tucker for taking the tried and tested road of maximum-
reward minimum-risk, but he took this method to the
extreme. His son was pitted repeatedly against opponents
who were incapable of providing him with the necessary
seasoning for the big time.

Even more damaging than this line-up of soft touches was
Bob Tucker's irresponsibility with Tony's business affairs. As

well as being managed by Steward, Tucker was also signed to a managerial contract with Mike Tyson's future adviser, Shelly Finkel. In turn, Finkel had a firm relationship with Main Events, a relatively new promotional entity based in New Jersey which was overseen by a former truck driver and union official named Lou Duva. Main Events were to promote Tucker in conjunction with Top Rank, a rival organisation headed by a former Attorney General named Bob Arum. The situation was unhelpfully elaborate; it was to become even more so in time.

In April 1984 Tucker caught the attention of Cedric Kushner, a Chicago-based immigrant from South Africa, who had worked as a Ferris-wheel operator and lion-cage cleaner before dabbling with boxing. Kushner was managing a popular but limited middleweight named 'Irish' Teddy Mann when Tucker caught his eye. At the time Tucker had compiled an unbeaten pro record of 12–0, but Kushner had heard there were problems between the numerous parties promoting and managing him. 'Before I knew what was really going on, I discovered that Tony had actually become a free agent,' Kushner would recall. 'And it was at this stage that I decided to start seriously romancing him.'

But getting to Tucker meant getting to the father first. That summer Kushner arranged for the Tuckers to be flown to New York, and on a warm Saturday evening he drove them upstate to Syracuse, where he was promoting a rock concert. Kushner had previously worked with Van Halen and Fleetwood Mac, and on this occasion he drew a crowd of 60,000 to watch Foreigner perform at the Carrier Dome. The Tuckers attended the concert as Kushner's guests of honour, and while Kushner suspected that the music was not quite to their taste, his belief that the sell-out crowd would impress Bob Tucker proved well founded.

'We'll sign with you for a hundred-thousand-dollar signing bonus,' was Bob Tucker's decision at the end of the evening.

'That's twice as much as Bob and Lou have offered you,' replied Kushner. 'In fact, that's twice as much as Don King has offered you as well.'

'That's right,' said Bob Tucker. 'But they're more famous and experienced, and we're taking a big risk with you.'

Kushner smiled wryly, the two shook hands, and before long the contracts were signed. It was a deal which Kushner would remember fondly for years to come. Tucker had won numerous Michigan State amateur titles, the Pan-Am Games and the world championships, and had compiled a 12–0 record as a pro: such a pedigree would have easily demanded a $1.5m signing bonus in the twenty-first-century marketplace.

In meetings with both men, Kushner effectively spoke to Bob Tucker and Bob Tucker alone. It wasn't that Tony was unable to speak for himself: he simply found business matters tedious, and besides, as far as he was concerned, his daddy knew the ins and outs of boxing's machinations far better than anyone else. While Kushner was happy to deal directly with Bob, he found Tony's inability to be his own man strange, especially his continuing to live with his dad at the age of twenty-six. To someone like Kushner, who had taken gambles in life from the moment he had stowed away on a German steamship bound from Pretoria to New York, this level of dependence seemed unusual in a grown man. It amused him that the two hung out together so often that they were taken for brothers. And though he would groan inwardly whenever the simplest of matters was brushed aside with an 'Oh well, Pop will take care of it', he genuinely liked his new fighter. Not only had Kushner signed a top-flight heavyweight, but he'd taken on an extremely personable young man in the bargain. The presence of a somewhat domineering father on the scene seemed a small price to pay.

But Kushner discovered that Bob Tucker's input would be more problematic than he had at first calculated. Twelve fights into his contractual deal with Kushner, Tucker had fought a collection of stiffs. He had won all twelve bouts with ease, but that was hardly the point: eight of his opponents had lost their previous match; only three had won more often than they had lost; one had never previously boxed as a professional. And still Tucker senior was not a step closer towards letting Tony exhibit the full extent of his repertoire against a fighter worthy of the description.

Kushner knew that this was the era of unbeaten boxers. Without an undefeated record to brag about, a fighter found it tough to acquire regular work on television – the lifeblood of a promoter's success, especially a relative neophyte like Kushner. But just as the TV people loved to hear a ring announcer bellow '. . . *with a record of 24–0 and 24 big knockouts*', the majority of prizefighters with such glossy résumés had never fought anyone plausible. Kushner did not want to see Tucker beaten, but Bob's super-cautious approach was beginning to chip away at his patience. As the big paydays and meaningful matches seemed to recede into the distance, Kushner began to suspect that the father was stalling for fear he would be without a job if anything goofed up in his son's career.

Bob may have wanted Tony to fight nobodies, but he had no qualms about him fighting lots of them. Kushner was contractually bound to pay Tucker a minimum $10,000 per fight, which in addition to the opponent's purse and training expenses usually amounted to a cost of $22,500 for each match. With Tucker fighting almost once a month, the whole operation was costing Kushner far more than he had planned. The sheer economic consequences of the situation eventually drove Kushner into the arms of other investors.

Attracting further investors was fine by Bob Tucker, for it initially meant a further cash injection. If he realised the long-term implications he didn't say so, and purportedly no one ever made it clear to Tony himself. By the time the Tony Tucker pie had been carved up among investors old and new, as many as ten people had a financial stake in the fighter's career, including Finkel and Steward, Arum, Main Events, Kushner, Josephine Abercrombie and Bob Spagnola in Houston, Denis Rappaport in New York, Jeff Levine and Bob Tucker himself. Tony Tucker had yet to lose a professional boxing match, yet already the rot had begun to set in.

Eventually, the quality of Tucker's opponents began to improve – marginally – and he won decisions over a pair of crusty old veterans in Jimmy Young and James Broad. Still, it was too late to escape the suspicions of a national press which ridiculed Tucker's record as manufactured, and yawned its way through his soporific wins. Despite tremendous atheletic ability, a wide-ranging and effective arsenal and what one reporter described as 'film-star good looks', Tucker just could not capture anyone's imagination. Young was washed up and feeble, and Broad was gross and predictable, yet Tucker had boxed each with all the zest of someone preparing for the Monday-morning commute. Tucker had fast hands and good movement, but he was so laid back he often seemed to lounge around the ring, posing. He had an explosive uppercut, but he seldom used it, and at times he preferred to carry opponents rather than find a creative way to dismiss them.

Even so, he climbed the ratings, and in May 1987 was matched with James 'Buster' Douglas for the vacant IBF portion of the world heavyweight championship. Originally Tucker had been expected to challenge Michael Spinks, but Spinks's promoter, Butch Lewis, persuaded his fighter to drop out. Simply put, Tucker posed Spinks too much risk for too little reward. Instead, Spinks relinquished his IBF title and cashed in on a showdown with the more marketable Gerry Cooney.

Typically, even though this was his chance to become a champion, Tucker fought Douglas with even less alacrity than usual. Douglas was not quite as naturally gifted as Tucker, but the two were similar in many ways. The biggest personality in the Douglas corner was his own father, Billy 'Dynamite' Douglas, who had once been a pretty formidable middleweight. Like Tucker, Douglas fought tall, possessed good skills and could hit with respectable, though not over-whelming, authority. And like Tucker, he often needed a firecracker placed under him to bring out his best. Douglas, however, had lost a few during his career, and there were question marks surrounding his commitment and ambition.

For nine rounds, Douglas took charge of the fight, maintaining a game plan of steady pressure and combination punching to stop Tucker from settling into a rhythm. Maddeningly for his own corner, Tucker allowed Douglas to command the flow of their contest. Maybe he knew what he was doing, was perhaps certain that Douglas's focus would crumble, but to everyone else it seemed like sheer laziness. Eventually, in the tenth round, Tucker raked Douglas with hooks and uppercuts, and the outsider from Columbus, Ohio, gave ground and wilted. The fight was stopped, and Tucker was pronounced IBF world heavyweight champion.

'Even then, I really didn't get a chance to enjoy being champion. I was welcomed back to Grand Rapids when I came back from the fight. They gave me a parade and the keys to the city, but then I went back into camp straight away. I had started to see the mismanagement going on in my career. Man, that's when I started to turn sour on boxing, and just wanted to get away from it all.'

Tucker and Tyson, July 1987

When he wasn't in the gym, sweating inside a T-shirt and leggings and lacing the pads with sharp combinations, Tucker was always immaculately attired. His father talked to him constantly about the image he now had to uphold, emphasising how he had to spend in order to look the part. Tony inherited his father's habit of not sparing a dime, purchasing whatever he wanted no matter what the cost, even wearing three-piece suits to the cinema, on the basis that a champion's image meant everything.

Despite his victory over Douglas, Tucker wasn't the real champion – at least not in the public's eyes. That recognition was accorded to Mike Tyson the night Tyson scrambled Trevor Berbick's senses in Las Vegas, and if Tucker really wanted the status of a true champion, he'd have to go through Tyson first. Yet it seemed that all Tucker ever wanted to talk about were his new threads. Kushner would sigh, humour his fighter, and then get on with the business of making a Tyson fight while Tucker went shopping. Bob kept repeating that this was the way it should be, and Tony kept listening. Even when the match with Tyson had been arranged, Tucker's priorities were in doubt: he flew his favourite hairdresser from Detroit all the way to Vegas so that his curls would look right on television.

In 1986, Don King had sold the idea of a heavyweight unification tournament to HBO. A championship series, predominately featuring King's fighters, would give boxing its first undisputed champion since Leon Spinks had shocked Muhammad Ali eight years earlier. Within a year, King's more established fighters – Tony Tubbs, Pinklon Thomas, Tim Witherspoon, Larry Holmes, Trevor Berbick and Bonecrusher Smith – were eliminated from the tournament. Tucker's victory over Douglas propelled him into the grand finale against the twenty-one-year-old Tyson. But to suggest this final pairing was anticlimactic would be like describing the tournament's promoter as a touch flamboyant. The fight nearly everyone wanted to see was the darkly vengeful Tyson against the unfathomable, quirky Spinks. But, by forfeiting his IBF crown, Spinks had given up his place in the final. Tucker, coming off a string of lackadaisical victories over journeymen opponents, was thought to have next to no hope of being competitive, let alone victorious, in a fight of such magnitude. It wasn't that people were dismissing him as a fraud. Some sections of the media knew he had the size, mobility and power to trouble Tyson. But there was no buzz about Tucker, no magic ingredient to make his showdown with Tyson special.

Tucker set up camp in Texas, and trained in a big old barn with his daddy, Luther Burgess and Emanuel Steward watching his progress. Sporadically, Kushner would visit the camp, his almost sorrowful gaze fixed on Tucker as the fighter pounded away on a sparring partner with the inappropriate *nom de guerre* of 'Young Joe Louis'. On the surface, they were preparing to shock the world, but deep down, the men in that barn had mixed feelings – not only about each other, but about the outcome of the fight.

Steward, like everyone else who came into contact with the young athlete, was immensely fond of Tucker. He even felt Tucker was fundamentally and technically sound enough to beat Tyson, to expose him and stop him in the middle rounds, so long as there were no hiccups along the way. Steward could see that Tucker was confident of victory, but he also sensed something which he didn't like: he thought that Bob Tucker was scared to death of Tyson, and he suspected Tony had detected this fear and was dwelling on it. This, more than anything Tyson brought to the table, concerned Steward enormously.

Tucker's self-assurance was genuine. There were no fits of bravado or outrageous claims, just an inner confidence and resolution. But he had started to cotton on to the disastrous state of his managerial affairs; he knew there was an ever-increasing number of investors poised to take their cuts from his $1.75m pay cheque. He was no mathematician, but he guessed that whatever he would eventually clear from his purse would be mere scraps. Every now and then, as he hit the speedball and thumped the heavy bag, Tucker would think about the prospect of challenging the world's most dangerous fighter for what had effectively become chump change, and his buoyancy would sag.

Kushner knew that his promotional relationship with Tucker was nearing an end, but so far he had little to show for his $750,000 investment. The Tyson match would be a pay-off of sorts. It had been an interesting ride, but a trying one too, and it was coming to an end. Kushner still liked Tony, but he wasn't certain his man could handle Tyson. And even if he could, Don King was promoting the fight, and had already begun to manoeuvre himself into a position of favour with the Tuckers.

Eleven days before the fight, Tucker's fate was sealed. Like Tyson, Young Joe Louis was a short, compact heavyweight. He was not in the same stratosphere as Tyson when it came to punching power, but Louis was Tucker's Tyson clone, and on this day Tucker decided to show everyone in his camp exactly what he intended to do to Tyson the following Saturday night. *Bop! Bop! Bang!* Tucker bounced on his feet, and shot out jabs and long right hands as he outmanoeuvred his plodding sparring partner. *Bop! Bop! Bang!* His legs felt fantastic, his arms loose and ready, and the shots crackled into Louis's face with impressive accuracy. *Bop! Bop! Bang!*

And then as the pain shot through Tucker's right hand, he dropped his fist and turned towards his father. 'It's really hurting, man,' he said softly, as the gym hands looked on in concern. 'Well, use your left,' whispered his daddy. The sparring resumed for a few moments and then Tucker winced again, his right arm falling to its side and his left signalling to Louis that their workout was over.

Tucker knew what the damaged hand meant; the fight was at risk of being postponed. Both Tucker and his dad worried that they would be blackballed if it fell through so close to the date. They were advised that Tony should rest the hand for ten days. But ten days was all the time that remained before the fight. Tucker considered backing out and giving the hand proper time to repair and heal, but then convinced himself he could handle Tyson with just the one good hand. For the remaining ten days, Tony Tucker shadowboxed.

Las Vegas, Nevada, 1 August 1987

When he walked to the ring, Tucker looked the part at last. Alongside the squat form of Tyson, who now sported an unattractive bald patch on the top of his head, Tucker cut a dashing figure in his crimson and gold lamé robe, carefully coiffed jheri curls bobbing around his shoulders as he danced around his opponent's cornermen.

In thirty previous fights, Tyson had never been hurt. He had lost a couple of rounds, been frustrated and jabbed at, and taken a couple of solid blows to the chin. But not once had anyone jarred him, made him take a step back, compelled him to reassess his reputation as invincible. In the first round of his fight with Tucker, this changed. Performing his habitual opening bell skip – which usually preceded an immediate charge into a terrified opponent – Tyson had an early night in mind. He saw Tucker make a fast retreat to the ropes, and moved in accordingly. But instead of covering up and waiting for the onslaught, Tucker rebounded and sprung a perfectly executed left uppercut which nailed Tyson square on the point of his chin. It was a shocking blow, and as Tyson moved back under the impact, his legs juddered and his ankles wobbled – only fractionally, but they wobbled.

A minute into the fight, Tyson had taken the biggest punch of his professional career. For Tucker, however, that upper-cut would prove to be the end of his fight. Moments later, he fired his damaged right hand. It was the first time it had been used with purpose, and the effect was shattering. He'd broken his hand and he was in agony.

'The pain shot all the way over to the back of my head. I remember wishing Tyson would hit me in the face rather than me having to hit him with my own hand again. All the way throughout the rest of the rounds, all you can see me doing is winding up my arms, all that kind of stuff, showing everybody watching that I just couldn't use my right hand again. I just clowned around for the rest of the fight. I was losing the fight because of it, but I did it really just to show everybody that Tyson really ain't doin' nothing. He really ain't all that, you know? Man, if I hadn't went in there with a bad hand, the whole outcome would have been different.'

Tyson controlled the contest from the fourth round on, but he remained wary of his opponent throughout, unaware that Tucker had broken his hand. For eight rounds, Tucker backpedalled and clinched, occasionally sending a few soft flurries in Tyson's direction. At one point he stepped accidentally on Tyson's 'big-assed' feet, ripping off one of Tyson's nails. As the final bell sounded, their exchanges ended and they hugged, Tyson pressing the side of his face against Tucker's chest, the palm of his left hand on Tucker's shoulder, congratulating his opponent on a good fight.

The Demise of Tony Tucker

A day never passed by without Tucker second-guessing all that had taken place during the build-up to his showdown with Tyson. Losing to Tyson had been a life-changing experience. Although Tucker had guessed his purse was going to be shaken down – he knew too many people had a piece of him by now – he was not prepared for the extent of its depletion. 'Well damn, I've lost, but I've still got *some* money,' he had sighed to Luther Burgess in his locker room afterwards. He was right: but only just. After deductions and taxes, he had come away with $28,500. He swore he would turn his back on boxing for good. He felt betrayed and used, that he should have been granted more time to prepare for the fight and more time for his hand to heal. Of course the fight should have been postponed. He should have overruled his team and pulled out. And he should never have let his father handle his business affairs. There were a thousand could-haves and shouldn't-haves. Kushner never promoted Tucker again, and Steward stepped down as his manager. Luther Burgess soon passed away, and Bob Tucker's relationship with his son began to suffer.

After being extended the full twelve rounds by Tucker, Tyson embarked on a streak of performances which filled the rest of the division with dread. His outings became increasingly violent and abbreviated as he tore through Tyrell Biggs, Larry Holmes, Tony Tubbs and Michael Spinks. With each paralysing knockout scored, the more impressive Tucker's stand seemed.

For a while Tucker was determined to remain true to his rejection of boxing. Tormented by his experiences, he broke contact with his father and embarked on a wild spree of fast living and cocaine nights, until the well ran dry. Eventually he cleaned up his act, announced his inevitable return and signed a promotional contract with Don King. But in the ring his performances were hardly extraordinary: he destroyed the no-hopers but laboured against the journeymen. Soon into this comeback campaign, he cut his father loose and sent him back home to Grand Rapids with a cheque for $35,000. 'I still love my dad dearly,' said Tony. 'But I won't ever allow him within a million miles of my career again.'

It wasn't until 1992 that anyone began to think of Tucker as a viable contender again. He tackled Oliver McCall for the instantly forgettable North American Boxing Federation title and won a drably contested twelve-round decision on a Don King-promoted show in Cleveland, Ohio. 'Give me two more rounds for the title,' McCall's cornerman, Richie Giachetti, had implored his fighter before the bell rang to begin the eleventh round. 'What title?' McCall had responded incredulously. Afterwards, the director of boxing at Don King Productions, Al Braverman – whose job it was to help promote Tucker – told reporters that Tucker 'looked like a piece of shit'. Tucker's stumbling resurgence was hardly setting the world alight.

In May 1993, largely through his connections with King, Tucker was granted a shot at the new WBC champion, Lennox Lewis. As much as King wanted to see Lewis deposed, it wasn't necessarily because he wanted Tucker crowned champion. If Tucker won, King would have himself the carrot he needed to ensure Tyson re-signed with him on his release from jail. It wasn't to be. Tucker was drilled to the floor in the third and ninth rounds, and though for the final nine minutes he had Lewis on the back foot and looking concerned, it wasn't enough to save himself from a lopsided decision defeat. After that, Tucker's more dependable qualities – his athleticism, skills and durability – crumbled. Two years later, and still with King, he was paired with Bruce Seldon for the vacant WBA portion of the championship. Seldon had a notoriously weak chin and Tucker was favoured to take advantage of it, but in a vicious encounter Tony's nose and right orbital bone were broken and the fight was stopped. Later that year, Tucker met Henry Akinwande on the under- card of Tyson's fight with Buster Mathis Jr in Philadelphia, and lost by a wide decision. In the summer of 1997, on the same night Tyson bit Evander Holyfield in Las Vegas, Tucker fought Herbie Hide in Norwich, England, for the WBO title. He was blown away in two rounds. Tucker's demise was horrible. Hide and Akinwande and Seldon would have struggled to resist the untarnished model which had rocked Tyson to the core. A decade on they were embarrassing him.

Tucker didn't give up. King agreed to loan his services as a name fighter to Oliver McCall's manager, Jimmy Adams, who was promoting on a small scale in Nashville. Adams soon put Tucker on his regular shows in the city's clubs and hotels, against some of the worst opposition he could muster. After a couple of wins, Tucker signed for a fight on Showtime against a resolute Puerto Rican named John Ruiz, and was halted in the eleventh round. Adamant that the fight had been waved over too soon by the referee, Tucker boxed again, this time making mincemeat out of a burly white brawler in Mississippi.

'Bing! I was back. Then I went to Vegas, and that was when they found out this thing about my eye. I said, "Doctor, please – let me just do this next fight." "Nope," he said. "I can't let you do it." Broke my heart, man. I went and had the operation in Atlanta. Got the retina reattached, and while I was getting my sight back, I was told I couldn't fight no more. It was just a scratched retina man, nothing worse than what Sugar Ray Leonard came back from. But no, that was it. And it broke my heart, man.'

Lewis vs. Tyson Is On

Just as King had unashamedly kept Tyson away from Lennox Lewis and Riddick Bowe in the mid-nineties, Shelly Finkel

assumed a similarly cautious approach on taking over as
Tyson's manager in 1998. In the lead-up up to his eventual
collision with Lewis, Tyson did not tackle a single top-ten
contender, instead disposing of a motley assortment of opponents who were either pasty, overweight, soft-hitting, weak-
chinned, unstable, or any combination thereof. Yet the
illusion still worked. Tyson had an almost inexplicable hold
on people. So what if he had spent more time groping pole-
dancers in smoky nightclubs than getting his hands on sparring partners at the gym? So he was getting flabby, smoking
pot, slamming tequila, fornicating for America, proposi-
tioning reporters and repeatedly being accused of sexual
assault? Big deal. He was Mike Tyson. Given the opportunity, and the right preparation, he would annihilate any man.
Nothing else mattered. Douglas and Holyfield were simply
bad days at the office. Against Lewis, the world would see.
Tyson, when he was right, was unbeatable.

Lewis was a chess master with gloves on, premeditated
tactics and analytical calm, efficiency personified. Tyson was
raw, uninhibited, prehistoric danger. Lewis's craftsmanship
was admired by the connoisseurs. Tyson was naked excitement for the masses. Tyson put bums on seats and heads
into orbit. He broke wills and hearts and noses. The public
paid good money to see Tyson punish men no one had ever
heard of before. Lewis had to fight stars in order for anyone
to care less. Lewis inspired apathy. Tyson inspired terror.

Yet it was debatable whether Tyson had ever wanted to
fight Lewis at all. After all, he had paid $4m to avoid facing
him in a WBC-mandated title fight back in 1996. Shortly
after that missed opportunity, Tony Tucker had run into his

old adversary in Las Vegas. 'Man, if you really gonna fight Lewis, I can help you,' Tucker had offered. But Tyson had just flashed his golden teeth and admitted, 'Oh man, I ain't even *thinking* about fighting Lewis. I ain't thinking about fighting at all no more!'

The press conference to announce the April match-up had hardly got underway before a bloated figure, his face semi-disguised by a black mask, leaned over the balcony, waved a bag of fake grass in his hand and screamed at Tyson, 'You're a homo, man! You touched up my ass in that club! Your wife needs a real man like me!' By an uncanny coincidence, Tyson's latest tormentor was another dormant but hyperactive heavyweight named Mitch.

Shortly before Christmas 2001, Mitch Rose had introduced himself to Tyson at the Sugar Hill nightclub in Brooklyn. A part-time fighter whose greatest exploit in the ring had been the deflation of a three-hundred-pound carnival act named Butterbean, Rose had a bigger reputation on the street than he had as a prizefighter. At the Sugar Hill, the pair of them talked, joked and mingled with the ladies until 6.30 a.m., when Rose claimed he left to sober up in the front seat of his truck. When Tyson himself exited the club moments later, heading for his limo with several women in tow, Rose leaned out of his window and advised Tyson to 'be careful with those chickenheads' – a reference to oral sex. It was enough to ignite one of Tyson's infamous tantrums. In an echo of his assault on Mitch Green fourteen years earlier, Tyson missed Rose with a punch, then grabbed and wrestled his man to the ground, ripping apart Rose's five-thousand-dollar mink coat.

Now, on stage, Tyson managed to keep his cool while another mad Mitch was removed from his vicinity by security guards. The calm didn't last. As Tyson and Lewis were announced by an invisible MC, they appeared on opposite sides of the stage: Lewis in a pale, checked suit; Tyson in dark slacks and T-shirt, with a black leather hat on his head. Then Tyson strolled towards Lewis's side of the podium for an up-close stare-down that Lewis would later swear had not been prearranged. One of Lewis's bodyguards pushed forward to protect his boss and Tyson took a swing at him, triggering a mass brawl. Tyson missed his target, but as the various minions turned the stage into a sea of thrashing limbs, Lewis rapped Tyson on the side of the head. He later claimed that Tyson had bitten his leg as he dropped to the ground.

A few days later, the Nevada State Athletic Commission convened in a Las Vegas sports centre to discuss Tyson's request for a new licence to box in their state. The NSAC and Tyson were old friends. The commissioners had banned Tyson from the sport for a year after he had ripped at Holyfield's ears. Soon after his subsequent return, when he had knocked out Orlin Norris with a blow launched after the bell to end the first round, they had told him to 'take this show on the road'. 'You don't know my horror stories,' Tyson told the commission. 'I found last week's events humiliating and embarrassing. I was embarrassed. It was just a horrible situation. I wish certain people who I cherish had never seen that situation. I am going to have to explain it to my kids and nephew, why I conducted myself like a fifteen-year-old.' It wasn't enough: despite the huge amounts of money riding on the fight, the NSAC's commissioners rejected Tyson's application, 4–1.

In an instant there was a stampede of interest from cities across the globe to secure the rights to the richest prizefight in history. Under the recommendations of the Muhammad Ali Act – a piece of legislation which sought to standardise various ethical and safety practices within the sport – Nevada's veto was supposed to be respected by all other state commissions in America. (Before the Ali Act it had been difficult to get rival commissions to cooperate, especially where states not considered major players in boxing were concerned, which was why a former champion declared completely blind in one eye was once permitted to launch a comeback in Wisconsin.) But when Nevada refused to stage the Lewis–Tyson fight, American cities from Washington, DC, to Los Angeles broke ranks. It wasn't just American cities displaying interest either: venues in Panama City, Montreal, Amsterdam, Milan, Madrid, Paris, Copenhagen, Glasgow, London, Kuala Lumpur, Berlin, Beijing, Seoul, Jakarta, Singapore City, South Africa, Tokyo, Lagos and even Beirut were rumoured to have offered unimaginable sums to pay for the rights to host the event.

One by one, however, the overseas sites dropped out, and whether from political pressure or lack of funds, so too did the majority of the American cities, until only Detroit, Washington, DC, and Memphis remained. Lewis's people, especially his trainer Emanuel Steward, had influence in Detroit. Tyson, formerly a resident of neighbouring

Maryland, preferred DC. Memphis won the race, a date of 8 June was set, and the final countdown commenced.

Lewis vs. Tyson was back on.

While Tyson trained for the fight on the Hawaiian island of Maui, sporadically taking a break to keep reporters up to date on the many lurid details of what whetted his sexual appetite, he appeared to have found himself an unlikely defence counsel for his latest indiscretions. In Atlantic City, Evander Holyfield was telling the press that there were major differences between his history with Tyson and the recent rumpus with Lewis in New York. According to Holyfield, New York was a confection of media bias against the monster they had all helped to create. 'All my antagonists,' Tyson had sighed mockingly, as a group of writers trooped into his beachfront cabana in Maui for a meeting with their favourite whipping boy. 'I ought to close the gate and beat your fucking asses, you all crying like women. Just close the gate, kick your fucking asses . . .'

'I've been in press conferences, and I'm a heavyweight, so I know how heavyweights think,' Holyfield had said, twirling his Clark Gable moustache across his upper lip as he gave a satisfied smirk. 'Lennox Lewis is a big heavyweight and Mike Tyson is a kinda small heavyweight, and anytime you have a big heavyweight gotta have a bodyguard to keep the little guy from jumpin' on him, then something's wrong! When the bodyguard jumps in and pushes the guy, what do you expect Tyson to do? Then, while the little guy is down and the big heavyweight hits him, what then? Shoot, you're not boxing now, you're in a fight,' he whistled. 'So what do you do in a fight? Anything. When you box, you box, and you box within the rules. A fight is a fight and you do what you can to survive.

'And the fact is Lewis violated Tyson anyway by hitting him when he wasn't watching. Tyson weren't gonna hit him, he was just going up there to scare him. You know, when this thing broke out, everyone said, "Tyson." But he didn't do nothing. He just wanted to show Lewis he was tough. What – everybody else do it, but when he do it, it's wrong? Everybody took sides, and most of them took sides against him. And you know how it feels when everybody's accusing you of doing something when you didn't do it. Shoot, it don't feel good at all.'

'I think Lennox thinks I'm afraid of him,' said Tyson in Maui, after throwing up on the semi-comatose form of sparring partner Leroy Seals lying at his feet. 'I'm going to show him differently. He lacks respect for me, the way he talks about me. The previous time he talked about me, he said, "He's not a fighter. He's an actor." If you're a true fighter, you don't accept nobody calling you nothing else but a fighter. That's a big disrespect for me.'

Memphis, Tennessee, 8 June 2002

In Memphis, both fighters switched on the charm. Lewis met a group of children from Oak Raven elementary school and lost a game of chess to a thirteen-year-old named Carlos Harbert. Confronted by a group of gay-rights protesters outside his hotel, Tyson defused the situation by warmly embracing one of their number, and shook hands with long-time activist Peter Tatchell. Angered by Tyson's dismissal of a reporter in New York as 'a fucking faggot', Tatchell challenged the fighter to make a positive statement in support of lesbian and gay rights, to which Tyson replied, 'I oppose all discrimination against gay people, OK?'

At the weigh-in, tensions mounted. Lewis stood expressionless as he scaled $249^1/_4$ pounds, and then raised both hands high into the air. When it was Tyson's turn, he stood before the cameras in long white shorts, his mouth twisting into a toothy leer, his tongue playing at the air, muscles flexed on his right arm, fingers curled into fists, a gold chain swinging across his flat iron chest, dark tattoos of Che Guevara and Mao Tse-tung and Arthur Ashe all the more pronounced by his stance. 'I am from Brownsville, Brooklyn. I am not afraid of anybody,' he said, after his weight was announced as $234^1/_2$ pounds, a heavy – albeit solidly dispersed – weight for Tyson. 'I am just ready to get it on and crush this guy's skull. This fight is normal to me. It's a fight. It's a party.'

The party guests were all waiting: the rich kids jetting in for the weekend, the hucksters and rip-off merchants, the corporate suits and dealers and sharks, the prostitutes and faces and celebrities, they were all there. Denzel Washington, LL Cool J, Leonardo Di Caprio, Tyra Banks, Samuel L. Jackson, Morgan Freeman, Val Kilmer, Cuba Gooding Jr, Jack Nicholson, Warren Beatty – all hovering beside their ringside seats, the make-believe action heroes gathering together for real suffering and bloodshed.

Tyson took the opening round, boxing in a composed fashion and outjabbing Lewis. But that had been it. From the second round on, Lewis tore the former king apart, mastering Tyson with an electrifying jab and performing with such precision and authority that Tyson seemed to lapse into a state of hypnosis. 'I'm hurt,' he would whisper to his trainer, Ronnie Shields. At the end of the third round, an exhausted and demoralised Tyson confided, 'That's it, I'm done,' but still got up to accept the further beating Lewis had in store for him. Lewis's natural trepidation waned, and the delivery of his heavy artillery became more cruelly pronounced. The punishment Tyson took was as devastating as any a man had endured in heavyweight history: as torturous as the wave of pain which had engulfed Tommy Burns in his loss to Jack Johnson; as murderously persuasive as the bombardments which Joe Louis had rained on Max Schmeling in their Yankee Stadium rematch; and as ruthlessly administered as anything which Tyson himself had been responsible for in his highlight-reel smashing of Tyrell Biggs.

Lewis blistered Tyson's face with a rapier jab, and he took him to places of semi-conscious delirium with the venom of his right cross. But it was the uppercuts which wrecked Tyson. One after another, they brought him stumbling closer and closer towards serious injury, and if the psychological impact of his beating might eventually prove to have a somewhat cathartic effect, the ramifications for his physical well being might even now take some time to emerge.

In the seventh round, it was one of these sickening shots which made Tyson buckle forlornly, his head bowed as though awaiting the drop of the guillotine, his knees somehow wavering only inches above the canvas. The referee, Eddie Cotton, incorrectly ruled a knockdown and sent Lewis to a neutral corner in order to administer a count to the damaged challenger. It was said, immediately after the slaughter, that Lewis had had to contend with a further opponent in Cotton, but the referee's mistimed intrusion simply prolonged Tyson's suffering.

In the eighth, Lewis pummelled Tyson some more, and when a long right landed against the side of Tyson's jaw with all the impact of a juggernaut crashing into a scooter, it seemed to stamp permanent disfigurement upon Tyson's clouded features. As Tyson crumpled in slow motion, Lewis nudged a shoulder into his face, perhaps out of instinct, perhaps in a subtle plea for his victim to go down and stay down. He need not have bothered. Tyson had been turned into a bloodied mess, a small animal discarded after a term of wretched experimentation.

Mike Tyson – the man who had crushed so many fighters and destroyed so many hopes – had been stripped bare. On his way back to the locker room, tattered, torn, all bumpy and gored, Denzel Washington grabbed his arm and pumped it, screaming words of consolation and pride. Behind him, in the crowd, dressed in a black cowboy hat and white suit, stood Michael Spinks, quietly familiar with all that Tyson was now going through: he too had once walked that lonely walk, and he too knew how it felt when the fighting days were over and the longest round of all began.

Tampa, Florida, 11 June 2002

I could see why Tucker had chosen Tampa over Vegas. Maybe he would miss the fast life, but Vegas wasn't the place to clear your head after another broken marriage. Besides,

November 1986: Mike Tyson (*left*) destroys Trevor Berbick in two rounds
to capture the WBC heavyweight title.

September 1998:
Mitch 'Blood' Green
at Gleason's Gym in
Brooklyn, preparing
for his bout with
Brian Nix.

May 1986:
Tyson rips into
Mitch Green, but has
to travel the distance
for only the second
time in 21 fights.

December 1986: James 'Bonecrusher' Smith (*left*) stuns Tim Witherspoon to take the WBA heavyweight title.

June 2001: Carl 'The Truth' Williams takes a break from his duties as a security guard in New York.

July 1989: Tyson disposes of Carl Williams in a single round, recording the final successful defence of his first reign as world heavyweight champion.

June 2002:
Tony Tucker
soaks up the rays
in Tampa, Florida.

May 1987: Tony Tucker
(*right*) catches James 'Buster'
Douglas with a left en route
to scoring a tenth-round
knockout of Tyson's future
conqueror and seizing the
vacant IBF heavyweight title.

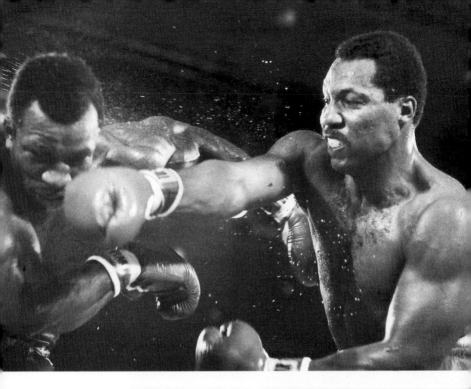

June 1985: Pinklon Thomas (*right*) lands a right cross on the jaw of Mike Weaver in defence of his WBC heavyweight title.

June 2002: Pinklon Thomas relaxes at home in Orlando with daughters Pierra and Patrice.

July 1989: Tyson talks to the press shortly after dispatching
Carl Williams in Atlantic City. Promoter Don King looks on approvingly.

Tampa brought him that little bit nearer to the seventeen-year-old daughter he hadn't seen in five years. Her mother, his first wife, had explained to him that he could 'either have both of us or none of us', and that had been it. They had left with no forwarding address or telephone number, and a piece of Tucker's heart had been broken. In Vegas, his second wife, Kim, left him too, but he still heard from their eight-year-old daughter, Kayla. One day, he promised himself, he would discover a champion, and then he would put his life back together again, reunite himself with his two girls and start all over. Occasionally he would allow himself the luxury to dream, and when he did so, he saw himself as Hollywood's next hero.

Tucker cut a striking figure. Lewis and the Klitschko brothers, the three super-heavyweights of the day, were all bigger on paper than Tucker, but Tucker was no less impressive. He looked strong enough to raise a bus above his head with his own vast hands. With his huge biceps and designer shades, he still looked the part. A Kangol hat covered most of the wiry grey hairs around his ears, and his black moustache and beard were neatly trimmed. He could have been Samuel L. Jackson's cousin.

My eyes were drawn to the scar tissue on his right knuckles where the operation to mend his broken hand had left an indelible reminder of what might have been. In Tucker's own mind, he had paved the way for Tyson's losses to Douglas and Lewis. 'Look at both those fights,' he would argue. 'And then look at my fight with Tyson. Look what I did to Tyson with no right hand, and then look at what Douglas and Lewis did with good hands.' They all had excuses, the men Tyson

had beaten. Trevor Berbick blamed the shadowy figures who
had had him doped; Pinklon Thomas protested that a torn
glove had interrupted what he unwittingly described as the
'monotony' of their fight; Larry Holmes had not been given
enough time to prepare; Carl Williams had blamed that old
chestnut, 'politics'. In comparison, Tucker's plea had some
credibility.

In the warm afternoon haze, we were talking about Tyson
again. Just as defeat had left Tucker in a state of despair, so
there now lay the potential for Tyson to come apart at the
seams in the wake of his own destruction. But as acutely as
Tucker felt the resonance of his loss to Tyson, he felt compas-
sion too – a fighter's love – for his former conqueror.

'You said you felt sad watching Tyson lose last Saturday
night, and I was wondering why that was,' I said to him.

'Because whereas Tyson once looked invincible, now he
looked pitiful. You feel sorry for him, man.' His words trailed
off temporarily and the smile left his face. 'I think that once
he got in there and he saw that line of security guards in the
ring separating him from Lennox . . . he probably said to
himself, "Maybe I'm over my head." He wasn't ready for that
fight. But I'll tell you why I was sad – Tyson just gave up
against Lewis after a couple of rounds, that's why. You see him
with both his eyes busted up, his nose bleeding and then all
that talk afterwards where he said all his stuff had been just
an act, and I felt sorry for him. He wasn't ready for that fight.
I think he'll retire now. I think he *should* retire man, because
right now he's not gonna get the respect or the money that
he's been used to. I'm talking about his stature and the kind
of respect he was getting back in the days when he was fight-

ing me, compared to now. I mean, back then he could fight tomato cans and make millions. Now if he fights them, he'll get half a million, maybe a million dollars. I think that'll be kind of a slap in the face for him. If you offered him a million dollars to fight Joe Blow next month, he gonna think you're crazy! Mike Tyson?! Are you crazy?' He laughed out loud again, his voice ringing loudly in treble tone as his shoulders rocked. 'He wouldn't fight *you* for half a million! That's why he should retire; because he ain't gonna get the kind of money that he's used to no more. He ain't gonna get no more *respect*, man. He got knocked *out!*' He looked at me, almost puzzled, as if I hadn't seen the fight or heard what had happened, and then he said, 'If he asked me, I'd tell Mike Tyson to get into some kind of charity, be in a position where he can help people. He needs to retire now and get his outside life together . . . just be himself, go to churches, talk to people. *Put to use some of the experiences you got.* He's got a lot of experiences out on the street, and from being with people. *You will always have the name of being a world champion, Mike, you know? Now give something back to others.* But then I hear about these other things, and . . . I mean, I don't really know what's going on in his outside life, but I'm always reading in the papers about something. Rape charges. Assault charges. I can just see the kind of stuff he's gonna get into, man. When you're used to the kind of money and lifestyle he's been used to, he just won't be able to be a regular kind of guy with everybody else.' He stared at me through his shades, muscles twitching on his arms, hands spread wide. 'No man, he's gonna be a target.'

We talked some more about boxing and women and Tyson and broken hands and aeroplanes and Lemuel Steeples, and then Tucker would crack himself up with a one-liner, and every so often cough his way through a faint bout of slurring. I remembered watching him fight Tyson on television. It was my first trip to America, and I was a wide-eyed teenager in New York, enthralled by Tucker's refusal to submit and certain he had what it took to rebound from his first loss and earn himself a rematch. Sitting opposite him now I felt strangely nostalgic.

I told him I had admired his defiance that night, and he grinned again and shrugged, and said softly, 'Yeah, well, I would have done things differently if I'd had a chance, but with all the things going on . . . it crushed me, man. I was almost suicidal. My whole life was a mess.'

I told him I thought it was strange that he should want Tyson to retire when he was still thinking about a comeback of his own. But he just shrugged that off: fighting again was just a faint possibility.

'Let me go back to doing some training and seeing how I feel. I'm not thinking about going straight for a title. I was just thinking about fighting some guys from here in Tampa, just having some fun actually. Just to see how I feel, to see what happens, you know . . .'

While Tucker was aiming for success as a professional trainer, he was also scratching a living working with competitors on the Toughman circuit – a rough and ready travelling show which crossed the country offering ready cash to local bruisers and bad boys willing to knock lumps out of each other. There were few rules and the risk of injury was high.

Outside in the sun, we talked some more beside a friend's car. Tony was doing his Samuel Jackson thing, assuring me of recent and successful surgery on his eye, that it had been only a scratched retina – the effects of which were not irreversible. He had known there was a problem for some time. 'I never gave a fuck though, because I'm a fighter, a diehard, a gladiator. Anything can happen to me, I don't care what it is, but by God I'm gonna knock you out eventually,' he roared, before releasing more piercing laughter. 'But hell no, man, I wouldn't really have continued to fight if there had been a serious chance of me going blind. That was just my senses telling me to fight on when the doctor gave me the news. Hell no, I still wanna be able to look at pussy as I grow older!' More laughter, high-pitched and raucous, his shoulders heaving and his chest rising. 'I don't ever wanna go blind, man. In five years' time I see myself lying on the beach, just looking at naked women all day long. I'm just gonna lie on the beach posing. Do they have any naked beaches in London? Man, I'd never wanna go blind.'

I didn't want to see him fight again. And if I'd had the resources, I would have happily opened a nudist beach in London, if that were what it took to distract Tucker from any sense of unfinished business in the ring. But no one takes kindly to being told what to do, not least professional boxers, so I kept my feelings to myself and smiled as he cackled at the prospect of a retirement spent lounging on the sand, beautiful naked ladies surrounding him for as far as his damaged eyes could see. His laughter was still ringing in my ears as I left Tampa, but all I could really feel for him was a tinge of sadness, because as certainly as Tyson, Tony Tucker was still lost.

Four: My Name Is Mister Pink

Children of the Ghetto

A COMMON LINE TROTTED OUT BY TYSON AS HE SOUGHT TO defend himself against charges of misbehaviour was that those who condemned him were ignorant of his past. Put in his shoes, how well would they have coped with what life in the ghetto had thrown at him?

Tyson's childhood was far from sweet. The bigger-name supermarket chains weren't exactly begging for planning permission to open branches in his neighbourhood streets of Bedford-Stuyvesant, and there were more kids running around his block with home-made zip-guns than there were playing junior-league baseball on balmy afternoons. But whereas the ten-year-old Tyson robbed local shops of candy and coats, the ten-year-old Pinklon Thomas had already stopped drinking and was now hooked on heroin. If there was a man alive qualified to comment on Tyson's situation, it was Pinklon Thomas. And he did.

Growing up in Pontiac, Michigan, had been every bit as fast for Thomas as those early years in New York had been for Tyson. By the time he was a teenager, Thomas was already transfixed by the drug dealer's lifestyle and all the superfly fads of the day. The trappings didn't ensnare him, he ran willingly towards them thrilled by the wardrobes of fur and velvet and frills, and enraptured by the dealers and pimps with their jewels and brooches and chunky gold rings.

Like Tyson, Thomas was bigger than all the other kids in his year, and easily impressed by self-styled badasses. Thomas snubbed the kids his own age, and hung out with an older crowd that operated in an underworld of vice. For most of his teenaged years, he spent his time hanging with pimps, chasing fixes and flaking out in front of Blaxploitation movies. He wore fedoras and zoot suits, injected heroin and smoked crack, flitting in and out of alternate states of chemically induced nirvana and mindless misery. By the age of fourteen, he was spending $150 a day on his habit. By sixteen, he had worked as a pimp, been involved in an armed robbery and enjoyed the dubious honour of having a contract out on his life.

Unlike Tucker, who snorted coke out of boredom, or Tim Witherspoon, who smoked a few spliffs at house parties in South Philly, or Tyson himself, who would light a joint, wax lyrical about the Grateful Dead and fail urine tests in Detroit, drugs came before boxing in the life of Pinklon Thomas.

In November 1977, he moved away from Pontiac to stay with relatives in Seattle, Washington. His neighbour was friends with an elderly Hispanic man who worked in parks and restoration by day, and ran a boxing gym by night. Although by now Thomas had made a minor name for himself on the streets, he had never seriously entertained any ambitions about fighting. Like a lot of kids he adored

Muhammad Ali, and like a lot of kids, his dad had given him a pair of boxing gloves for his fifth birthday. But so far his only real acquaintance with boxing had come in the eighth grade, when a teacher who moonlighted as a referee had taught him how to skip rope and taken him to King Solomon's Gym in downtown Detroit.

Confident in his own street reputation, Thomas walked into the Seattle gym one evening, brazenly lied that he came from the same Brewster Projects in Detroit that had spawned Joe Louis, and fabricated a tale about his athletic background that included fifteen amateur fights, each won by spectacular knockout. The tale did not meet with the wide-eyed admiration Thomas had expected. The gym proprietor shuffled off to the side of the room, returned with a pair of battered old sparring gloves and told the boy to hit the heavy bag. With a smirk, Thomas laced the gloves on, strutted over to the nearest bag and began pounding it with his fists, releasing exaggerated snarls, dipping his chin, rolling his shoulders and whooping at his imaginary opponent. After thirty seconds, his arms began to burn. After the first minute, his breath was coming through in short, jagged gasps. After the second, he was reduced to prodding the bag with pain-wracked arms while his chest heaved under the strain. Eventually, he spun away, walked out of the gym and vomited on the sidewalk. On the streets of Pontiac he had been a big, scary guy who would fight anyone who messed with his drugs or his women or threatened his wallet. But as far as boxing was concerned, he was a nobody.

Two months later, and after some intense tuition in the gym, Thomas fought for the first time as a heavyweight at the Tacoma Golden Gloves tournament. He lost a decision to an experienced fighter and former inmate of Wallah-Wallah Penitentiary named Tommy Thomas. Disappointed by his defeat but quietly encouraged by having been competitive against his more practised adversary, Thomas approached his namesake in the shower room after their bout and told him, 'I'll get you at the Seattle Golden Gloves in two weeks' time, man!' The ex-con placed his bar of soap on the stand beside him, wiped the water from his eyes and glared at Pinklon for a moment. Then his face broke into a smile and he said, 'Nah man, you hit too damned hard. I'm going back down to light-heavyweight for that one!' Sure enough, two weeks later, Tommy Thomas was crowned Seattle Golden Gloves champion at light-heavyweight. Pinklon Thomas, a kid with eleven years of heroin abuse on his résumé, became the tournament winner at heavyweight.

After just six amateur bouts, Thomas turned professional, winning a six-round decision over Ken Arlt in Seattle. He continued to campaign as a novice within the confines of Washington state before venturing to Las Vegas in the summer of 1979. There he won another decision, this time over a well-travelled veteran named Leroy Caldwell. By and large he made steady progress. He displayed obvious ability, but had acquired a reputation as a slow starter with a stamina problem, and it wasn't until August 1982 that he sent a loud message to his rivals. Preparing in Philadelphia under the instruction of George Benton, Thomas was being lined up to box an opponent named Jeff Shelby on a Don King-promoted 'Night of the Young Heavyweights' show when he was offered a fight against James 'Quick' Tillis on network television. There was a catch: the fight was in two days' time.

Tillis was no pushover – he had only one loss on his record, and that was in a title fight for Mike Weaver's WBA championship ten months earlier – but Thomas accepted the match. In his twentieth outing as a paid athlete, Thomas was on top of his game, catching up with Tillis and knocking the self-styled 'Fighting Cowboy' out in eight rounds. Thomas would later describe this as the most memorable moment of his career. Four years later, Tillis would prove his resilience by becoming the first man ever to last the distance with Tyson.

The next year, Thomas battled the hard-hitting Afrikaner Gerrie Coetzee to a draw in Atlantic City. Four victories later, he was challenging Tim Witherspoon for the WBC heavyweight championship of the world.

Entourages and Excess

Thomas took a pride in his profession. Like Tyson, he studied the careers of his predecessors and strived to cultivate his skills rather than take them for granted. He considered it important to refine his technique, sharpening his vaunted jab and attempting to execute combinations with precision. He soon had observers wondering whether at long last there was a serious threat to Larry Holmes – that era's pre-eminent heavyweight – on the horizon.

Thomas's professional approach didn't stop once he stepped out of the ring. Unlike the majority of his peers, Thomas abhorred entourages – wasteful packs of do-nothings who collected pay cheques in return for guarding volume-control dials on stereo systems and lollopping around hotel corridors with huge chips on their shoulders.

Tyson would bring the phenomenon to its apogee, but plenty of fighters from Thomas's era had provided blueprints for such indulgence. Tim Witherspoon, the man Thomas challenged for the WBC title in August 1984, was a talented, undisciplined fighter with a personality that was jovial enough out of the ring, but the build-up to every fight saw him hopelessly caught up in clichéd trash talk. Prior to the only defeat he had suffered before meeting Thomas – a controversial decision to Holmes the previous year – Witherspoon had been warned by Holmes about King's habit of upsetting his fighters on payday. He had responded by questioning Holmes' relationship with his mother.

'It's difficult to say who was the most extravagant of the lot, because there's a difference between Tyson, who squandered a lot of money on cars, jewellery and women, and a soft touch like Witherspoon, who was really the heavyweight champion of poor money management,' said Bernard Fernandez, boxing writer for Witherspoon's hometown newspaper, the *Philadelphia Daily News*. 'Everyone who ever came across Tim had some kind of sob story, some tale to tell about how down on their luck they were. Tim would give them all money, but nobody ever paid him back. He won a lawsuit against King and got a million dollars, and yet a year later they cut off his phone because he couldn't pay his bills.'

Witherspoon was not the only fighter to learn the hard way about hangers-on. At the time of his defeat to Tyson, Tony Tucker's camp had been minimal. But by the time he fought Lennox Lewis in 1993, he had inherited many of the minions left unemployed by Tyson's incarceration in Indiana. They succeeded in turning Tucker from a quietly inoffensive good guy into a bad-mouthed boor. Tucker and his sidekicks gesticulated wildly at an impassive Lewis during their weigh-ins, swaying, posturing and baiting the British fighter, until the Tucker camp left the stage singing 'London Bridge is falling down.' 'They'll all be shouting in his corner like fools when the fight starts,' said Lewis when the fuss had died down and the Tucker crowd had departed. 'But he'll be the one taking all the punches.'

Pinklon Thomas was different. He travelled with a crew of four, and not once accepted the overtures of those who bragged of can't-lose deals, or cousins whose voices and names and faces he failed to recognise. 'Why do I need anyone else?' he would ask. 'The attraction for some of those other fighters was to hear how great they were the whole time. They wanted somebody to buff them up. They're around them saying, "Man, I wanna be there for you. I wanna be your Bundini Brown. I wanna be this, I wanna do that." But all they're really doing is trying to get that free trip with you, that free vacation to Vegas. They wanna be in your corner, get their faces on TV. That's what's happening. And then one day, when it's all over, they'll just leave you.'

Thomas had made such a prophecy back in August 1984, directly to Tim Witherspoon. He had found Witherspoon's spectacular camp arrangements highly amusing. Witherspoon arrived in Vegas ten days before the WBC title fight with an entourage of thirty, and occupied an entire floor of the Riviera Hotel. Thomas arrived a little later with two sparring partners, a cutsman, and his trainer Angelo

Dundee. A week before the fight, Thomas and his sparring partners were out on an early-morning run when they came across a line of fifteen men, standing in the middle of whom, with arms crossed and a sneer on his lips, was Witherspoon. Witherspoon threw some jibes at Thomas, and Thomas replied in kind. It was par for the course, and Thomas accepted it. They were fighters, after all. They didn't have to hate each other to hit each other, but when it came down to it, boxing involved hurting another human being; the exchange of insults, the psychological warfare and the parading of nerve and bombast like big cats staking their territorial claims was a natural precursor to the fights themselves.

But then the Witherspoon entourage closed in around Thomas. The two fighters weren't in the whirring artificiality of Vegas any more, but in Pontiac's red-light district, or the South Philly ghetto, gearing up for something which ran deep into the pasts of both men. Thomas stepped into the centre of the circle that had formed around him, raised a forefinger and pointed at each of the Witherspoon camp in turn, before finally settling to a halt in front of his thickly built rival. 'Tim,' he said softly, 'let me tell you something. When this fight is over with, everybody here around you is gonna be gone, except for you. Man, they won't get out of here fast enough when this is all over.'

If there was one man to whom this prophecy failed to apply, it was Mike Tyson. The extra appendages attached themselves early on in Tyson's championship reign, and displayed a ruthless ability to lodge themselves like barnacles upon the craggy rock face of his career. They zeroed in on him, praised him, backslapped him and robbed him all in one deft movement. Under the guise of pompous titles, the clever ones were even able to go about their purse-skimming and false procurement with unwitting approval from the man himself.

Yet, Tyson's market value suffered far less than any other heavyweight of his era in the wake of defeat. The demands on his loyalty and largesse only intensified after he lost to Buster Douglas. By the 1990s, the man who had once claimed that, 'I never wanted all the cars and the mansions and all the other stuff. There's only so much money you can spend,' was becoming increasingly reckless with his earnings. In March 1991, he spent in excess of $180,000 during one shopping trip alone, purchasing an emerald- and diamond-studded Cartier Panther each for Don King and his old friends and by now acting co-managers John Horne and Rory Holloway. Discharged from his Indiana cell in March 1995, Tyson celebrated by purchasing four Rolls-Royces, ten BMWs, several Bentleys and two mansions at more than $3m apiece. A month later, while in Vegas as a spectator for a heavyweight double-header featuring Tucker against Bruce Seldon, and Golden Oldie Larry Holmes against longtime sparring partner Oliver McCall, Tyson spent several hours shopping at the Forum Shopping Arcade in Caesar's Palace, spending over $200,000 on jewellery, Armani suits and Versace shirts – all for his entourage. It was soon calculated that between 1995 and 1997, Tyson had earned $112m and spent $115m – a mind-blowing feat, including the following expenses: $4.5m on automobiles and motorcycles; $500,000 on rare pigeons and wild cats; $450,000 on a birthday party and $310,000 on lawn care for his multitude of homes; regular monthly payments including in excess of $7,500 on pager and mobile-phone bills; $95,000 on jewellery and clothing; and $237,000 pocket money.

Within three years, Tyson had fired King. With him went Horne and Holloway. The two had become the fighter's official co-managers, though it was clear King had called all the shots. (One sports-industry executive remarked after dealing with Horne and Holloway during negotiations with Tyson that 'to call them naive would be an upgrade'.) Between the date of his professional debut in 1985 to the day Tyson ridded himself of King, the champion had earned the sum of $187m. Now, in 1998, he had little to show for such gargantuan wealth other than a host of lawsuits.

'Throughout his career, Tyson had been able to buy friends and live that lavish lifestyle of his,' said Larry Merchant. 'He always had a sense that no matter how fast he spent his money, someone would always be coming around the corner to give him some more. Nothing about that situation ever changed.'

Others did not enjoy the luxury of rejuvenated wealth each time they blew their bank account. When Tim Witherspoon lost out to Pinklon Thomas – his can opener of a right hand outsmarted in a duel with Thomas's spearing jab – it was only a matter of time before he was left with nothing. Witherspoon would protest to anyone who would listen that his fall from grace was the fault of others, but Thomas for one did not sympathise. Thomas never liked playing the role of victim. He had his fair share of weaknesses and grievances, but he neither asked for nor expected sympathy. A day after he dethroned Witherspoon by boxing his way to a decision,

Thomas listened to his beaten opponent grumble about being short-changed by King, and quietly shook his head.

Orlando, Florida, June 2002

'Well, let me tell you what Tim Witherspoon got upset about, and then you tell me if I'm right or wrong,' said Thomas over a coffee on a sticky afternoon. 'I mean, Witherspoon had some nerve to get mad at Don after that fight. He said Don stole two hundred thousand dollars from his purse. Now, he got into Vegas ten days before the fight, and he had thirty people with him. That's fifteen rooms gotta be paid for, their food's gotta be paid for, they're chargin' everything at the hotel to his room, and then when all's said and done he notices there's a hundred thousand off. And Don says, "Well damn, what you expect me to do – take care of *everybody*?! If you're saying somebody gotta take care of them, why don't you take care of them?" That's what happened, but Tim Witherspoon always liked to make it sound like Don took the money off him. Look, Don is a shrewd businessman, you know. Don knows how to make money. Don takes care of business. Don fucks everyone. But they all do it – Bob Arum, the Duvas, everyone – they'll just do it in a different kind of way. I've been screwed by all of them, but everyone's gonna get paid something, you know? That's how it's always worked. This is a business. And you've gotta accept the business, man.'

Minutes later, I was sitting beside Thomas in his Volvo saloon, driving through the humidity and the avenues of palm trees crawling with dragon lizards. He sported a lean physique, narrow waist and hard chest, and a face which bordered on the gaunt. He had always cared too much for his outward physical appearance to spend much time at the dinner table. Both on winning the title, and then losing it to Trevor Berbick, he had entered the ring in tip-top physical condition, his body well defined, legs in fine trim, stomach flat and ironed, muscular shoulders rippling softly, no loose flesh hanging from his cheeks or breasts, no unsightly paunch bulging over the waistband of pink-trimmed shorts. When he retired, far from breathing a sigh of relief and letting it all go, Thomas became obsessed with his fitness regime. He mapped out intricate exercise programmes, specially formulated diets and daily workout routines which incorporated six-mile runs as well as numerous circuits of press-ups, sit-ups and bench presses within the confines of a garage he had converted into his own private gym on Sunset Terrace Drive.

For all the bad that had festered in the early years of Thomas's life, there was much to admire about the way things had panned out for him. I was relieved that here was a story every bit as hopeful as I could have wished for – a break in the grim monotony of former champions frittering away their savings and embarking on listless, life-threatening comebacks. Thomas knew he could never win a championship again, that there was no million-dollar payday just two or three fights around the corner, that the public didn't yearn for his return. He had refused to cling to irrational ambitions and futile regrets. He knew there was no point wishing he had kept away from the smack, or pulled out of the Berbick fight while divorce proceedings from his first wife were finalised, or abandoned preparations for his fight with Tyson after suffering a dislocated shoulder in training camp. These things were all in the past. They had happened, and he had moved on. He had concentrated on building a future, and he had found it in a career so well suited to his experiences that he would declare, 'There's nothing else I could do better than this.'

With one hand on the steering wheel, his left arm lying across the base of the open driver's window and his body eased back in its seat, he was a picture of contentment, humming along to Motown ballads. Every once in a while he made a call: to Angelo Dundee in Miami; to another old Tyson foe, James Bonecrusher Smith, who was busying himself at home in North Carolina with a variety of enterprises. 'Hey Bone, I've got some of those energy drinks you sent over. Man, I'm gonna get home and make myself a few of them shakes before giving myself a real good workout,' Thomas sung as he switched lanes and headed towards the intersection. Then he called his wife, DJ, who worked for an engineering firm during the day and attended evening classes in real estate, and his two youngest daughters, Pierra and Patrice, who were at home raiding the fridge in their parents' absence.

Like his old friends and adversaries, the experience of fighting Tyson had had a marked impact on the direction of Thomas's life. Things had eventually turned out for the best, but his memories of Tyson weren't great ones, which probably added to the satisfaction he had taken from watching Tyson take a systematic thumping at Lewis's fists the previous Saturday night. He had prepared for that evening with care, firing up the barbecue in his back garden, chilling some jugs of soft drink in buckets of ice, and then settling back to watch a man who had once whispered 'suck my fucking dick' into his ear take a fearful hiding.

Thomas's own fight with Tyson had occurred fifteen years earlier. Having lost his WBC title to the cumbersome but more motivated Berbick, Thomas had returned with three bland victories. He was widely considered 'shot', a fighter bereft of reflexes or sharpness of mind. He had undergone surgery to correct a detached retina, and after one of his comeback wins, the referee had lamented, 'I had to stop it, Pink, you were even making me look bad!'

But the memory of what he had once exhibited in the ring lent a certain amount of interest to his bout with Tyson – an event which at the time seemed more notable for the emerging presence of Robyn Givens in Tyson's life. Bizarrely, when one recalls the actress's elfin beauty, Thomas decided at the final press conference that it would be a good idea to call Tyson a 'faggot'. And if his fate had not been sealed by this unwise remark, it certainly was by the time he promised to 'snatch the gold right of your mouth with this' as he waggled his left hand under Tyson's nose.

We parked outside Thomas's home in the early afternoon, but before we entered his house Thomas introduced me to the Galloway family, who lived across the street. One of their sons had needed to shed some weight to qualify for the air force. With the help of his converted gym, the old fighter managed to strip the boy of forty pounds in three months. The younger son was severely afflicted with autism. The Galloways had founded a charity named STARS, and desperately needed publicity for their cause. Thomas stepped up to the plate and offered his services.

When we returned to Thomas's home a mutt named Missy came to greet us, and Thomas patted her head and adjusted

the paisley handkerchief tied around her neck before leading her outside and into the back garden. 'Make us up some
of Bone's drinks, Patrice,' he called out, leaving his briefcase
on a hallway chair and kissing his youngest daughter on the
forehead. 'We got original flavour, tropical fruit, banana, you
name it . . . give me one of those original ones, Patrice.'
Patrice made the drinks, spooning heaps of brick-coloured
powder and ice cubes into a blender, before emptying the
combined mixture into two tall glasses and handing me one
and her father the other. 'They're revolting,' she whispered,
and she wasn't lying.

The girls and I shot some pool on burgundy baize,
American rules and then English rules, while Thomas tried
to make sense of a Sponge-Bob double-bill on the television,
all the time tapping a video cassette on his knee and waiting patiently for our games to end. When the cartoon
finished, he sat his daughters either side of him on a leather
sofa, and put the video into the machine. Then he picked
up the remote controls and for the next thirty minutes we
all watched him battle to remain upright against Tyson.

It was strange watching Tyson pummel Thomas while
Pinklon and his girls sat inches away from me, but the old
champ was neither mad nor particularly bitter. He just
watched his downfall with a smile on his face, protesting
half-heartedly on the odd occasion, more resigned than upset.
Tyson shellacked him in the first round, but Thomas
remained upright thanks to his always dependable chin and
the reawakening of his once-dominant jab. Until the end of
the fifth, he gave a fair account of himself, upsetting Tyson's
rhythm and flashing the left in the young bull's face. He'd

taken Dundee's instructions to heart: whenever Tyson moved in close and the two clinched, he stuck out his elbows to stymie the flood of hooks the young champion sought to plant into his sides. But it was never going to be enough.

The girls laughed at their daddy's untidy mop of sweat-soaked hair, neatly shaved to the skull now, receding and grey. They weren't yet born when the tape had been made; the fight was too far in the past for them to be worried by the punishment he had had to absorb, so they just joked about his hair. In the sixth round their daddy succumbed to a landslide of punches which almost wrenched his head clean off his shoulders.

I hadn't seen the fight since it had been transmitted on ITV about six hours after the event on a bright May morning in 1987. The newspaper listings had invited audiences to 'watch Tyson eat Thomas for breakfast', and so with a plate of toast on my lap and a mug of sweet tea in my hands, I had done just that. Thomas danced mournfully into the ring, hustled his way through the rounds and then collapsed in the sixth from an unstoppable eighteen-shot burst. 'He's a killer', yelled one of the headlines the following morning.

The fight ended but the tape kept running, and beside me Thomas grinned proudly as Larry Merchant and Sugar Ray Leonard praised the efforts of a gallant and hurt loser.

'I like Mike Tyson,' giggled Pierra.

'Yeah, I was sad to see him lose to Lennox Lewis,' said Patrice, clearing away our glasses.

Thomas arched his eyebrows and laughed, stood up from the sofa and questioned their sanity. They just tittered together some more. It was no big deal; their daddy hadn't come to any serious harm against Tyson, so there were no grudges to bear. And Tyson was kind of cute, after all, so why not root for him against the big, lumbering Englishman named Lennox? It was history, same as their daddy's old habits. Which was why they hadn't fidgeted or squirmed when the pre-fight broadcast had contained a segment on his drug-riddled past, including footage of a needle sinking into an exposed arm, and then their daddy himself, muttering about addiction and rehabilitation.

Rehab

After Tyson, Thomas's career effectively came to an end. His defeat had been a crushing one, and was followed soon after by an equally miserable stoppage against Evander Holyfield. Thomas had shaved his head for that fight, and with a droopy moustache and tired patchwork around his eyes, he looked like an old man while being pounded for seven unsavoury rounds. There was worse to follow. Dejected and depressed by his sliding career, Thomas returned to the comfort of the syringe. He saw out New Year's Eve 1988 drinking and smoking crack in Liberty City, a crime hole in northwest Miami. He grew a straggly beard and his eyes and face sunk into the depths of his skull. In five days he emptied his bank account of $7,000. When he turned up in Dundee's gym one afternoon talking nonsense and barely able to keep his eyes open, his old trainer ordered him out of his life until he accepted professional help and cleaned himself up.

And that, with no mean amount of will-power, is what Pinklon Thomas set about doing. It was a bumpy, treacherous road. By the end of '89, he had travelled away from the Miami faces who knew him as a favoured customer and checked himself into a rehabilitation programme at the Eastwood Residential Clinic in Oak Park, Michigan. He had grown tired of being tired. He had been addicted to heroin at ten years of age, and then the crack pipes not long afterwards. It was time to cleanse himself once and for all.

The first week of his twenty-eight-day programme was the most difficult. Cold turkey, group therapy and the bare effort to keep clean were hard to handle, but by the beginning of the second week he had begun to gain a little weight and the colour started to return to his sallow features. Thomas began thinking about the fruits of recovery: a new lease on life, fresh hopes and dreams for the future, a chance to rebuild. He felt so elated by his improvement that by the halfway point he was raring to leave. He was told to stay with it, that he was going through what had been popularly termed the 'fourteen-day syndrome'. Everyone felt good after staying clean for the first two weeks. A lot of people thought they had cracked it. A lot of people were wrong.

'Why you gonna leave?' one of the other clients asked him.

'Look, I'm all right,' he replied.

'Where you gonna go?'

'Back to Miami.'

'What you gonna do down there?'

'I don't know man, play country music or something! I've just gotta get the hell outta here. This place is driving me crazy, and I'm OK now!'

'Man, you don't wanna go yet. Why don't you just stick around for the twenty-eight days?'

'I've gotta get outta here.'

'No man, you need to stay until the twenty-eight days are over.'

But Thomas was convinced the treatment and the therapy had already worked. He was OK again. Then his therapist talked to him, asked him for one last favour, pressed a cassette into his hand and said, 'Just listen to this tape once, and then if you wanna go, go.' Thomas nodded, and an hour later he went up to his room and put on the tape: James Cleveland on one side and Patti La Belle on the other. He sat and listened. It was snowing outside, and he looked out of his window.

'I was in a phase of my life where I felt I was all by myself. Nobody else cares. It's just you and nobody else. I'd call out to God, but you know how it is sometimes; you just say to yourself, "You ain't getting no answer from him!" But then I just had this feeling that I was in the right place. Man, I really broke down. There were tears coming down my face. I went downstairs and told everybody I was staying until the end.'

When the twenty-eight days were over, Thomas still pursued impossible ambitions in the ring, but he also signed up for a programme which involved visiting schools and talking about substance abuse. He'd taken the first step towards a kind of redemption. Dressed in boxing robe and trunks, he visited first-graders and inserted a gumshield before starting his lectures. His words stumbled through the protective plate and the kids yelled for him to pull it out of his mouth, and still he kept on talking until he knew he had their undivided attention. And then, eventually, he was away, talking about respect for teachers and parents, their plans for the long summer holidays, about returning to school the next term to do a little better than the term before, and most of all keeping away from the junk offered to them on the street corner. He went to elementary schools, high schools, colleges and treatment centres, and he'd always call a couple of the best listeners up from their desks and let them hold his belts, encouraging them to hoist the trophies up in the air and imagine themselves as champions.

In 1993, Thomas retired from the ring for good and focused his attentions completely on his school lectures and a small amateur boxing programme he had set up in Orlando. In addition he taught white-collar boxing and organised fitness classes for a group of tae kwon do enthusiasts. A few speaking engagements and public appearances on the side helped keep him busy, but even all these activities failed to fill up half the time he felt he had to offer. He was growing bored.

A chance meeting with a local businessman who had formed an alternative coalition to fight drugs and crime in the community looked like it might lead to a breakthrough. Thomas was asked to address various meetings and seminars. It was an improvement, and every day Thomas would urge himself on with the repeated commands: 'Don't get too bored, don't get too lonely, don't get too angry and don't get too tired.' But it still chipped away at his resolve. He needed something more tangibly productive. He found himself driving around Orlando one morning, agitated and increasingly despondent, and the little orders of encouragement he had written down for himself just weren't doing the trick any more. He stopped at a payphone and called his friend. 'Pink, I'm in a meeting now, but come down here in about an hour, because I've got just the job for you,' came the voice at the other end of the line.

The job in question appeared perfect for Thomas, although actually filling the vacancy wasn't going to be a straightforward process. The Center for Drug-Free Living on the outskirts of Orlando was a relatively new manifestation of what had once been just another institute for young offenders. Although the occupants were there on a court-ordered detention, the emphasis was more on crime prevention and rehabilitation than long-term sentencing. With his experiences, Thomas felt he had a great deal to offer the centre's young inmates, but he was told that it was unlikely he would get a full-time job without a degree. 'Oh I've got a degree all right,' Thomas told the personnel officer, 'you just need to arrange an interview for me, and I'll show everyone what qualifications I have.'

The following morning, Thomas placed his championship belts on the front passenger seat beside him as he drove to an interview with the centre's directors, stopping off en route to buy himself a new tie. The interview began at 9 a.m. Thomas sat himself down on an uncomfortable wooden seat in front of the panel, and began talking. By 9.35 his interviewers had barely got a word in, and still he talked, spilling his guts to them about his boxing career, his life, the drugs, the rehabs, the losses and the triumphs. He talked until just short of 10 a.m., at which point a grandfather clock in a corner of the room began to strike.

Dong! Thomas's eyes froze and he affected a state of

hypnosis. *Dong!* He rose to his feet, and stepped backwards, his eyes unmoving, staring at a blank spot on the wall behind the panel. *Dong!* His eyes didn't flicker, but his torso bent and his limbs danced, and he slipped into one of the most passionate shadowboxing routines he had ever performed. He knifed the air with his jab and shot his right hands; he stepped to the side and countered invisible enemies with arcing left hooks, grabbing them, twisting them, bending, turning, manoeuvring. *Dong! Dong! Dong!* And then when the final chime sounded and the clock lapsed back into its barely audible breathing pattern, he sat down abruptly, his eyes back to normal and a look of apology on his face. 'Please don't worry,' he said softly. 'I'm perfectly all right until I hear a bell. When I hear a bell, I just kinda lose it.'

He smiled at the directors and loosened his tie. A few of them smiled back, and a few of them looked blankly at each other and played with their pencils. 'OK Mr Thomas,' said the governor. 'Why don't you just stay seated while we go away for ten minutes and talk about things?'

'OK,' said Thomas, and when they came back, they hired him.

Within months of beginning work at the centre, Thomas had helped to set up a project named Midnight Basketball. The operation lasted for two years, and during that time kids from the inner city knew there was always an alternative to running the streets at night: a captive, protected environment on the basketball courts of outer Orlando, where Thomas and his assistants would take it in turns to supervise hoop games right through till daybreak. Mister Pink, as he became known to his young charges, had begun to make his mark.

'Gotta keep my mind and body fit at all times,' he explained to me on the drive back to my hotel. 'Especially when it comes to the kids I teach at the drug rehabilitation programme. They run like reindeer, man. They don't know how to get tired. They say to me, "Yo, Pink, how come you run so slow?" So I tell them, "Well, I run slow, but I run long, you know?" I have to use my experience on them. See, the first thing that happens when a new intake of kids comes in, is that some of them might recognise me from the pictures that are stuck on the walls. Then they find out who I was, that I fought Mike Tyson; it usually takes them a couple of weeks to find that out. They respect me, and I respect them. They get to hear stories from the other kids. Mostly they talk to me about being a champion, and about fighting Mike Tyson. All the time man, it's Mike Tyson this and Mike Tyson that. But you know what I do now, man? I use Mike Tyson's story as a lesson for them all.'

He dropped me off outside my hotel and drove away without an apparent care in the world, window down, violet skies on the horizon, the Commodores singing love songs on the radio. I showered and switched the TV on in my bedroom. Beers were going for a dollar a bottle in the hotel bar, so for the next hour I drank cold Budweisers while a man in a ten-gallon hat taught a group of over-fifties how to line dance.

The next day Thomas picked me up on the way to work. When we reached the centre he left his jacket in the back of the Volvo before escorting me through the security entrances. In each section of the building we passed through, kids in coloured T-shirts played table tennis, queued in corridors or grouped together for team talks with supervisors and key workers. Their colours symbolised their house or their behavioural state. They wore bright green and burgundy, orange and turquoise, and they were called Eagles and Antelopes, Falcons, Buffalo, Dolphins and Cougars. If they had messed up, they were on 'contract' and they wore yellow, and they weren't allowed TV or pool cues or telephone calls or outdoor activities; and if they wore black they were mentors, and they were Pinklon's shining examples of how to do the right thing.

'My name is Mister Pink, and I've had a great day. I collected my friend here from England on the way to work, and this afternoon I intend to give myself a real good workout. I'm hoping all you guys will be joining me too. I intend to have a great afternoon.'

Thomas sat forward in his fold-up chair, rubbing his hands together and glancing from one side of the room to the other as a group of thirty kids formed a semi-circle in front of him. One by one they repeated the exercise, beginning with their names, before describing their days so far, sometimes mumbling incoherently between chews of gum, sometimes with a drill sergeant's bark, sometimes softly and eloquently. When he felt like it, Mister Pink would interject and ask for more information, admonishing the sullen and encouraging the shy.

'Sometimes, you know, we have our differences, but then I just jump right on 'em. See, a lot of the others who have come to work at the centre with all their degrees and qualifications have to leave before long, because the kids can be a problem. They get belligerent, they need to be restrained. Sometimes they get physical, but I know how to wrap 'em up, you know? I say to them, "Either I'm gonna get through to you, or you're gonna get through to me, but either way we're gonna get it right." All they're interested in at first is the boxing aspect to who I am, but as they delve deeper and deeper, they realise more about who I am and the problems I had in the past. Most of all though, they see me as a fighter.'

Afterwards, those who didn't wear yellow were allowed outside, into a modest area of grass and tarmac surrounded by high walls and perimeter fences. Most of them scattered to the farthest ends of the area to peer over the walls and out at life beyond. A few waited by the doors in their running kit for Mister Pink, who had changed into shorts and sneakers and a dark pink shirt. Then they started running, lap after lap, first Mister Pink and one of the mentors, then trailing behind them a chubby kid with glasses and a small Hispanic boy and a gangly crew-cut kid with thick arms. Mister Pink ran slow but he ran long, and one by one his companions dropped by the side, doubled up, and stretched themselves out on the dry grass, wheezing and gasping for breath. At the end of twelve laps, only the mentor remained by his side, and Mister Pink's shirt had darkened with sweat.

In the afternoon, Mister Pink crossed the complex and took me into the adjacent building, where we met a different group of kids, who were all coming to the end of their stretches inside. They were attentive and cheered by Mister Pink's presence.

'My name is Mister Pink, and I'm still having a great day,' said Pinklon Thomas, all smiles, rubbing his hands, elbows resting on kneecaps. The kids hung on his every word. 'A lot of you have been asking me about the fight last weekend, and I'm glad about that. See, that was such an easy fight for me to call because I knew that Lennox had been busy training, eating and drinking boxing, and Mike hadn't. See, what better demonstration of success do you need to have? Mike's been drinking alcohol, smoking, playing with women, messing around with all kinds of garbage, while Lennox has been eating right, working hard and going to bed early. You don't think that made a difference in the fight? Sure it did. And you guys have to do the same thing, because the ones who mess around and follow the crowd are the ones who will be back in this situation before the end of the year. Live clean, do the right thing, do you understand? So what if you can make a quick buck selling garbage on the streets? Keep away from the junk, man. What's more beneficial – making two hundred dollars selling garbage, or giving five dollars to a guy on the street who needs a bath and something to eat? You know the answer to that. And if any one of you can show me one thing that's positive about just the thought of using drugs, I'll lick concrete. You can't do it, and you know why? It can't be done.'

Once the session was over Mister Pink took the kids out into the yard and handed them pieces of blank paper and little pencils. He asked them to draw 'conflict cartoons': scenes from their lives which might help to explain their troubled circumstances. Almost every one of them drew images of fathers hitting sons, of kids running from the police, of mothers smoking joints the size of rocket launchers. A window opened in one of the hotel rooms towering above the perimeter wall. The kids dropped their pencils and grabbed each other and pointed, but the shutter quickly came down. They groaned and returned to their work. Mister Pink laughed quietly to himself and shook his head. 'Last week there were these two girls staying in that hotel, and when they saw the boys down here and knew they were incarcerated, they lifted their tops and exposed their breasts. That's why the kids are always happy to do their work out here in the yard.'

Some of the kids came up to me later. 'He can be hardcore but he's pretty cool,' said the gangly one who had tried to keep up with Mister Pink on the running track earlier.

'He fought Tyson, right? Was he a good fighter?' asked another.

'Yes,' I said. 'He was a very good fighter. You shouldn't just think of him as someone who lost to Mike Tyson. He beat some good fighters.'

'Only ones we ever heard of were Tyson and Holyfield,' said the boy.

'Well, one day, ask him to tell you about some of the others,' I suggested. 'Ask him about Tim Witherspoon and Mike Weaver.'

Late into the evening, and the kids had all gone to bed. Thomas spent some time in the staff area, chatting with nurses and counsellors. He leafed through some files, placed a handful neatly into his briefcase and threw an apple core into the wastebasket. A woman on night duty wrapped a cardigan snugly around her shoulders, and then Thomas bade them all a good night. We made our way back through the security doors, and then out into the open again, where the air remained humid and still.

'I guess a lot of the kids look to Tyson as some kind of a role model,' I suggested. 'You know, the me-against-the-world type of attitude.'

'In some ways they do relate to him,' he replied, starting the engine up and checking his mirrors. 'But I just gather them back in and remind them of what's what.'

'But you don't have much sympathy for Tyson.'

Thomas grinned and then looked thoughtfully out of his window, shifting uneasily in his seat. 'Well, let me put it like this . . .' he began, and then he had to think some more, still that rueful look on his face. 'I don't want it to sound like I'm really cold, because I don't wish no bad on nobody, man. Just because Mike was in my field and I fought him, doesn't mean I wish bad on him. But I just don't have no respect for him, for what he did to Holyfield, the way he has conducted himself in a lot of those interviews he did – especially the ones with women. I mean, all that stuff made me lose respect for him completely.

'See, I know his personality, because I deal with kids like him every day, you know? They're not as hard as Mike, I know, but in many ways they're just like him. On the inside I believe Mike is soft like a kid. He's got a heart, you've just gotta know how to get to it. And very few people have been able to do that, because he's constantly surrounded himself with guys who really are protecting him for their own interests. The greatest thing that Mike could do would be to get involved in something outside of boxing. And unfortunately he's got a felony charge against him, so it's gonna be real difficult for him. But whatever he does, it won't matter how much money he has put away, he'll need to stay busy. You know, he don't do well with idle time. Nobody do, man. Nobody do. He'll go stir crazy.'

Idle time was what Thomas himself continued to fear the most. If there was no idle time, there was no possibility of succumbing to the afflictions of the past. Right now, Thomas had come through it all. His family and his work were his life. They were everything to him; Pacquana in Michigan, Delana in Georgia, DJ and Patrice and Pierra at home with him in Orlando, and Pinklon III at college in Ohio.

'Don't think I take pleasure from Mike's circumstances,' he said. 'As a matter of fact, when Mike got sent down I was ready to go behind the wall so that I could talk to him. I know where Mike's at, man. And I know this: whatever it is he decides to do with his life, all the people who are now making a lot of money off him are gonna have to help out, because he's just not gonna be able to do it on his own.'

'But that's what you managed to do,' I said. 'You had people in rehab help you through it all, but when it came down to it, it was you. You made the decision to put that stuff behind you.'

The lights were red. Thomas pursed his lips, chewed at his mouth with his teeth like Ali used to do and tapped his fingers on the steering wheel. 'Well, it'll be hard for him,' he sighed. 'I mean, it's still hard for me too, you know, because there's always someone out there trying to make you do something you know you shouldn't.'

'Carl Williams said they were still trying to persuade him to fight again,' I said. 'He said those kind of temptations made him angry.'

'Well, sometimes, you know, it doesn't make me mad, it actually makes me feel good – that people still know you and still want to see you fight. But I've never been offered the kind of bucks that would have had me jumping on the table and quitting my job for. But I know when I fly out to Vegas in September for Oscar De La Hoya and Fernando Vargas, I'll get some offers. Oh yeah, I always get some offers when I go to Vegas. You know how it goes – if you sit in a barber shop long enough, you gonna get a haircut!' He chuckled and signalled right.

The bus station was only yards away now, and it was almost time to say goodbye. 'I've been tempted with garbage so many times since my twenty-eight days were over,' he admitted. 'I know if I take my butt into an environment where this stuff's going on – if I stay there long enough, someone gonna start pushing junk in my face. I don't go. I've passed the test so many times now. But the thing is, I just don't wanna be a part of that ever again.'

For now though, Mister Pink was part of something else, something that was even more important than fighting Mike Tyson. He was making a positive impact on people's lives, and establishing the kind of appreciation and respect that ultimately had eluded him in his days as a champion boxer. And the person who made me realise this more than anyone else was a teenager named Cheryl.

Earlier that day, after working with the boys in the yard, Thomas let out a deep sigh and said, 'OK, we'll check on the girls for a while, but not for long because they can break your balls.' The girls lived in a separate block. They were Cougars or Dolphins. We joined the Cougars for ten minutes, and one particularly brassy girl with matted brown hair and dimples on her face came up to us both. She spotted my notepad and Biro and blurted, 'Who the hell are you, his secretary?' The next instant she'd forgotten all about me; for here was Mister Pink.

'Mister Pink! How're you doin' Mister Pink?!' The room shook with the force of her vocal cords; jet pilots encounter less turbulence flying through the tropics. 'Mister Pink! Mister Pink, I have a question.'

'Yes, Cheryl, what's your question?'

'Mister Pink?!'

'Yes Cheryl.'

'Mister Pink, you're so cool they should put up a billboard with your face on it.'

'Well thank you, Cheryl. But what would I be endorsing on the billboard?'

Cheryl thought about this quite intensely before announcing, 'Us, Mister Pink. The Cougars. There'd be a picture of you on the front, Mister Pink, and then the Cougars all lined up behind you.'

'But what would the billboard say, Cheryl?'

'It would say . . . it would say . . .' We waited as Cheryl racked her brains again, knuckles white against her hips. 'It would say, "Mister Pink".'

'That's it?'

'That's it. What else would it need to say? Just, "Mister Pink".'

'Well thank you, Cheryl.'

'You're welcome, Mister Pink.' Then Cheryl turned her attention back to me, jabbed a thumb in my direction and glanced at Mister Pink once more. 'Now, like I said – what do I call your new secretary?'

Five: The Deacon and the Baddest Man

Philadelphia, Pennsylvania, 13 June 2002

THE PAMPHLET IN MY HAND WELCOMED ME TO THE FAITH TEMPLE Church of God in Christ, 'Where the Table is spread and The Feast of the Lord is going on'.

The morning's service had yet to begin, but a small group of virtuous souls – ladies in their Sunday hats and men in dark suits – sat in a corner of the church receiving instruction from the pastor's understudy, a plump man with little white curls on the sides of his balding head, eyes occasionally scanning the pews from behind thin spectacles.

In the South Philly ghetto, the streets were lined with buildings shrouded in the yellowed stain of decay, rows of little tobacco-brown homes as foreboding as South American barrios. Upon tattered porches, under broken windows and beside empty parks, women drank bourbon on doorsteps and men swaggered to nowhere. Shopkeepers sold their wares from behind barred shutters and padlocked cage doors, men with bare feet snoozed against walls beneath drooping felt hats, and African cab drivers locked their doors and leaned left and right, anxious to avoid wrong turnings.

But it was a Sunday morning, and while the good attended church in their polished shoes and sober hats, the bad guys slept on benches and inside the clapped-out wrecks they parked on the street.

Three rows in front of me, shoulders fitted snugly inside his jacket, a dusty sprinkling of grey in his hair, a young reverend responded to one of the understudy's questions, and the rest of the scripture students nodded their heads in approval. A lady dressed in black and silver turned and smiled, then opened the catch to her handbag in preparation for what would be the first of five collections that morning. 'Mmm-mmm . . . the Lord is here,' she said quietly, and as she snapped her bag shut and rubbed two dollar bills between her thumb and forefinger, the reverend shifted in his seat and gave first her, and then me, a welcoming smile of his own.

Smokin' Joe and the Butterfly

The reverend was born in September 1960, to Joe and Florence Frazier, and his name was Marvis. Like Tony Tucker, he too had grown up around boxing; and his own father had been every bit as influential as Bob Tucker.

Joe Frazier moved from Beaufort, South Carolina, to Philadelphia the year baby Marvis was born, in a bid to find a life away from the cotton fields. He packed meat in a slaughterhouse, and took up boxing at a local club. Life was hard. Amateur boxing didn't pay the bills and washing conveyor belts of animal carcasses held little promise, but Joe had his eye on a prize and his vision never faltered. Sometimes at night, before clocking off from his shift at the factory, Joe banged his hands against sides of meat, splintering ribs and punching great dents into the gleaming flesh. Some years later, he would be approached by an out-of-work actor and asked to talk about these days of hardship. Inspired by the guts of a mob-strongman-cum-prizefighter named Chuck Wepner, but also to a significant degree by Smokin' Joe, Sylvester Stallone wrote a script that would become *Rocky*. His lead character, Rocky Balboa, hailed from Philadelphia. He worked as a minder for a local crime boss and moon-lighted as a heavyweight, and when he trained for his shot at the world title, he thumped fists against raw flanks hang-ing from the ceiling of an abattoir.

Before Marvis's fourth birthday, Joe Frazier lost two deci-sions to a bulky yet nimble opponent named Buster Mathis, and with it the heavyweight berth on the US Olympic team bound for Tokyo. He remained on the team as a reserve though, and when Mathis had to pull out with an injury, it was Joe who represented his country. Frazier stormed his way to the gold medal, returning home to a hero's welcome and a consortium of businessmen named Cloverlay, Inc., which would oversee the launch of his professional career.

In 1967, having refused on religious grounds to be drafted into the army for service in Vietnam, Muhammad Ali was stripped of the world heavyweight championship and forced into what would amount to three years of exile from the sport. He escaped a prison sentence but trod a minefield of public opinion. The politicians, the military hierarchy and much of middle America condemned him as a coward and a traitor; the students, hippies and Muslim activists lauded him as their hero.

With the world championship left dormant, the job of finding someone to fill Ali's shoes was left to the multiplicity of organisations that mismanaged boxing's alphabet soup. The WBA, which had three years earlier withdrawn their recognition of Ali as world champion after he had officially disclosed his ties with the Nation of Islam, wanted to pool the world's leading eight heavyweights into an elimination tournament to decide his successor. Frazier, however, under the guidance of manager Yank Durham, could not see the sense in having to prove himself against three opponents in order to contest the title when it was he who already sat firmly in the number-one contender's position. Durham announced that Frazier would take no part in the WBA tourney, and instead received validation from the then powerful New York State Athletic Commission for his man to tackle old amateur rival Mathis for their version of the crown.

In March 1968, an eleventh-round knockout of Mathis in New York saw the dawn of Joe Frazier's time at the top, a seven-year period of smoke and flame which would leave his name indelibly marked on the pages of boxing history. Smokin' Joe made four successful defences of his title, and then in February 1970 faced off with Jimmy Ellis, the winner of the WBA tournament. Ellis was a close friend of Ali's, a stylish, mild-mannered fighter who had begun his pro career as a middleweight. At the end of four destructive rounds with Smokin' Joe, Ellis retired in his corner and Frazier was pronounced undisputed heavyweight champion of the world.

While there was no longer any official dispute over

Frazier's status, one important figure mounted a typically voluble campaign to disparage his standing as world champion. Freed from his contentious exile, Ali had moved from the lecture halls of college campuses back into the ring, and was doing his colourful best to whip up a frenzy of public interest in a showdown between himself and the man he accused of being the temporary custodian of his rightful laurels. Frazier relished the challenge. In November 1970 he dusted off the world light-heavyweight champion Bob Foster in two rounds and soon after signed to meet Ali in New York. The promotion was labelled, with perfect simplicity, 'The Fight'.

Ali–Frazier marked the first occasion on which two undefeated champions were to meet for the world heavyweight crown. Although corporate and political forces had relieved Ali of his title in '67, no man had ever defeated him in the ring. Ali and Frazier was a pairing like none the division had seen before: the elegance and artistry of Ali versus the perpetual aggression of Frazier; Frazier's deadweight hooks against Ali's florid stream of jabs; the beauty and wit of Ali matched with the blue-collared austerity of Frazier.

In the build-up to the fight, Ali did a lot of talking. He branded Frazier as ignorant, a dumb black man, a white man's black man, and a whole lot more. Sometimes he was funny, and Frazier would grin and promise he would soon be laughing himself when he plucked the wings off the butterfly. But sometimes the jokes went too far and Frazier would quietly fume. The anger never fully subsided.

Though cut from a different cloth, Ali and Frazier were both religious men, the crescent and the cross of heavyweight boxing. Ali spoke of his beliefs with defensive indignation; the subject of faith prompted only Frazier's exhilaration. Ali tried lecturing the predominantly white Anglo-Saxon media on the importance of the Muslim's diet and the teachings of Elijah Muhammad; Frazier dressed himself and young Marvis in pinstripe suits and went to church in South Philly. The father and son would be photographed in their seats on Sunday mornings, bearded Joe listening pensively to the preachers while Marvis smiled sheepishly and stared at his reflection on buffed toecaps.

The first Ali–Frazier fight was perhaps the most momentous in boxing history. It was more than a boxing match; it was an event which stirred the passions of writers and artists, historians and generals and presidents. On a cold March evening in 1971, beautiful black women in furs mingled with aged hacks in Panamas, pimps mixed with politicians, Hollywood femme fatales caroused with dope dealers in long velvet gowns. Madison Square Garden was filled with the sparkle of jewelled fingers, the smell of cigar smoke and leather, the sounds of rising expectation and the jangle of nerves as the two giants entered the arena.

For fifteen rounds they boxed out of their skins, Ali in red velvet and Frazier in iridescent green and gold sequins. Frazier absorbed the torrent of jabs, and Ali rode with the hooks. They took each other to the edge in their relentless desire to win, their refusal to give in. With everything delicately poised at the start of the last round, Frazier clubbed his tormentor with a rolling hook as Ali stepped back along the ropes, and then with another just as Ali seemed to be on the way down. Ali fell, but as the turning Frazier glanced over his shoulder, the fallen man shook his head and rose to his feet quickly. Ali's jaw was broken and swollen to the size of a melon, and Frazier's face was riddled with welts and lumps. Somehow they fought on until the final bell, and then minutes later Frazier was proclaimed the winner.

Whatever heartache and ill fortune awaited Smokin' Joe from that point on, it was he who had had his arm raised in triumph. Pride played a big role in Joe's life, not only in what he had achieved, but in all that the Frazier name was to represent; much of that legacy came about as a result of the victory over Ali. Even as a shy ten-year-old, Marvis had a sense of what his daddy had accomplished, and he knew then that he too wanted a taste of his father's glory, an opportunity one day to continue the Frazier heritage in the ring.

Times would never be as good again for Joe. He repelled the challenges of Terry Daniels and Ron Stander the following year, but in 1973, in Kingston, Jamaica, he was crushed by the devastating uppercuts of George Foreman. Later that year he fought Ali again and lost a decision, and his star faded. But in 1974 Ali shocked Foreman in Kinshasa, Zaire, knocking the seemingly indestructible champion out in eight rounds. In 1975, Ali and Frazier signed to meet for a third and final time.

It was October when Ali met Frazier in the infamous 'Thrilla in Manila', two ageing warriors clashing in the searing humidity of the Philippines capital, two great rivals reaching the sunset of their careers. What they put themselves through was agony. Marvis was a teenaged amateur by now, and he had flown to the Far East to be at his father's side.

Ali meanwhile whacked a toy ape at a press conference and swore he would get the gorilla in Manila.

Ali and Smokin' Joe fought beyond the realms of desperation, their bodies wilting under the heat and the lashing of their tortured fists. By the middle rounds Ali's speed dwindled and his fluidity evaporated, and Frazier's vision was obscured by grotesque, hanging cliffs of contusions. Their lungs dried and burnt, their limbs numbed, the two flailed at each other, bumped each other, silently begged for the other to yield. But even as Frazier's advances subsided into a pained, geriatric scuffle, and Ali's movement became the same cumbersome parody of men he usually taunted for their immobility, neither would resign.

At the end of the fourteenth round, the two slumped in their corners. Ali would later describe his exhaustion as the closest thing to death he had ever experienced. Frazier could barely see the fingers of his cornermen as they worked on the injuries covering his face. Ali dropped his head, his eyes devoid of their usual shine, chest heaving and a ripple of fat falling over the waistband of his shorts. And then, as the world watched, Smokin' Joe's trainer, Eddie Futch, signalled to the referee Carlos Padilla that he would not allow his fighter to come out for the final round. Life was more important than that.

Even after a defeat which would rankle for years, Smokin' Joe's valour would be written in stone, and pride in the Frazier name would not subside. Ali would never float so gracefully around a ring again, while Manila would mark the last time Frazier would fight for the world title.

Little Smoke

In 1976, Frazier shaved his head for a rematch with the still-formidable Foreman and lost pitifully in five rounds. But as one point of the Frazier line paled, another began to glow. In Philadelphia, the Frazier family had spawned a number of hopeful young fighters inspired by Joe's success. But of all the many cousins who benefited from the tutelage of the family patriarch and old sages like George Benton and Sam Hickman, the sixteen-year-old Marvis represented the family's greatest chance of having the Frazier name once again inscribed on the heavyweight championship belt.

Aged sixteen, Marvis adopted the nickname 'Little Smoke', ran up thirteen straight victories as an amateur and talked the talk. While Joe would always be open about his extra-marital dalliances, he remained a committed Christian. It took a little longer than he had hoped for Marvis to get the message. Church, for Marvis, was a routine to be endured. 'In my own life, I was a scambooger,' he would admit. 'Growing up, I had a brand-new car at sixteen, I was digging the scene with my gang of friends, had all the honeys around me, all the parties, all the wine and the women and the song. My main thing back then was that I was Joe Frazier's son, and I was undefeated. And all the time I was at home getting ready to go out with my friends, my sister Jacqui was running around the house saying, "Marvis, don't you know that the Bible says this, and the Bible says that?" She was preaching and stuff, leaving me notes and excerpts from the Bible on my mirror and all over the place. I was like, "Shut up and get outta my face, I know who God is!" But I didn't. I really didn't know who God was.'

While his sister chased him with her bible, Marvis pursued the good life and glory, and with his daddy temporarily retired, attention focused on his own career. In 1979 the Fraziers returned to the Far East, and inside an arena in Yokohama, Japan, Marvis captured the world amateur heavy-weight title. Shortly after his return home, James Broad knocked him cold in a round at the Olympic trials. His fifty-eight-fight amateur career, during which he'd lost only twice, was over.

Marvis's success as an amateur had come as a result of several factors. To begin with, the privately educated young-ster had been a decorated sportsman at school. While his natural athletic ability alone couldn't guarantee success, it provided him with a solid basis from which to cultivate the crueller technicalities of the game. But for all the hardship and pain fighters went through, the amateur code and its three-round bouts were far removed from the gruelling, bloody longevity of a professional contest.

Marvis turned pro in 1980. In the August edition of *The Ring* he posed for the cover holding his father's gold medal, while Joe leaned over his left shoulder with a dark frown on his face. In September, Marvis launched his career with a three-round stoppage of Roger Troupe at the Felt Forum in New York. The following summer, he made the cover of *Sports Illustrated*, standing beside his daddy in their family gym back in Philly, gloved hands on hips, unsmiling, above the caption, 'Chip off the Old Champ?' It was the same picture he would later place proudly on the back of his busi-ness cards.

The speed with which the media caught on to Marvis was

matched only by his father's desire to see him shoot up the rankings. This was in stark contrast to the manner in which Bob Tucker was managing his own son's career, but it was Joe Frazier's belief that Marvis had already served an ample apprenticeship as an amateur. Also behind Joe's wish for Marvis to move swiftly was mild concern about a pinched nerve, which his son had blamed for the surprise knockout defeat to Broad. Whether in training or at rest, Marvis would experience intermittent pain in his neck. Though doctors could find nothing that would immediately endanger his career, Joe suspected the affliction would rule out a long-term campaign as a fighter. First though, Joe needed persuading that his own fighting days were done; in December 1981, with Marvis six wins into his journey towards the title, the old man made an unfortunate comeback that ended immediately after he fought to a draw with Floyd 'Jumbo' Cummings in Chicago.

While Marvis took a sabbatical to watch his father prepare for the Cummings fight, a pair of other relationships began to blossom in his life. He'd had plenty of girlfriends over the years – he was Joe Frazier's boy – but now he had fallen in love, and the object of his affections was driving him crazy. She didn't care who he was. Worse still, she insisted that if she were to agree to a date, he would first have to accompany her to church. 'I thought to myself, "Yeah, I'll go to church with her and then I'll get what I want,"' Frazier recalled. 'But while I was busy chasing her, the spirit of God was soon chasing after me!'

One Sunday the heart-struck Marvis escorted Daralyn to her church and stood in the congregation, counting the minutes and pondering where he would take her for lunch and what flowers he should buy before dropping her off home. He paid the minister only sporadic attention at first, but when the clergyman spoke of something he described as the wages of sin, Marvis snapped out of his daydreaming.

'The penalty for sinning is death,' warned the minister, 'but the gift from God is eternal life. There are only two places you can go when you die. The first is heaven, a place described in the Bible as a place of peace and a place of joy. The other is hell, a place of torment and a place of darkness. God forbid that you have not made Christ the Lord of your life by the time you die.'

The minister had caught Marvis's attention but he had yet to convert him. *God, get this guy out of here,* Marvis thought, trying hard not to let Daralyn see his cynicism. *This is nothing but a fairy tale.* As far as Marvis was concerned, if he and his homeboys ever arrived in hell they would just have to put the Devil's fire out.

'I know we've got some sceptics here,' cried the minister, searching for a Doubting Thomas. 'I know we've got some people here who don't believe that hell might be their destiny, so let's pretend for a second that you're right if that's the way you think. Let's pretend that there is no heaven and hell, that none of it exists. Even if that's the case, what's wrong with treating your neighbour the way he wants to be treated? What's wrong with being fair and forthright?'

The preacher stepped down from his pulpit and moved towards the central aisle of his church. Marvis could not help smiling. 'You see,' continued the minister, taking one

1998: During his one-year suspension from boxing after biting the ear of Evander Holyfield, Tyson busies himself with guest appearances on the Worldwide Wrestling Federation circuit.

July 1986: Marvis Frazier is annihilated in 30 seconds by Tyson
at his most destructive.

June 2002: Frazier at his offices in Philadelphia, shortly after Sunday service.

Larry Holmes, world heavyweight champion from 1978 to 1985, shares a few laughs with promoter Don King. Their relationship would not always be so convivial.

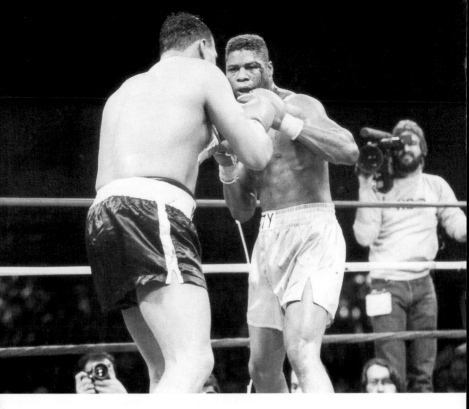

March 1987: Tyrell Biggs (*right*) suffers a badly cut eye and a few rocky moments before turning the tables on David Bey and securing his title fight with Tyson.

November 2003: Biggs (*left*) at training camp in Fort Worth, Texas, with Kirk Johnson's sparring partner Ray Austin.

April 1985: Tony Tubbs (*right*) outhustles old rival Greg Page to take the WBA heavyweight title.

November 2003: A wheelchair-bound Greg Page, surrounded by members of his family.

November 2003:
Tony Tubbs outside
his home in Cincinnati.

November 1996: In a major upset, Tyson is brought down to earth
with a bump by Evander Holyfield.

painstaking step after another, 'Christians have treats, have fun, go on vacation. They do pretty much what everybody else does. But what they always do is make sure they do what the Bible tells them to do.' He stopped beside Marvis's pew and looked sternly into the young fighter's eyes. 'That doesn't seem too bad now, does it?'

'No,' replied Marvis. 'That don't seem too bad.' *Get this guy out of here, someone, please!* The minister paused for a moment and studied Marvis hard, as though he could read his mind. 'But what if I am right and you are wrong, and there is a heaven and there is a hell?' Marvis smiled nervously but gave no answer. 'Where will you stand on Judgment Day? What will you say to God when He asks you about where you placed His son in your life? Did you accept His son or reject him?'

Marvis still had no answer, but he sweated inside his suit. *Man*, he thought, *I wish this guy would shut up.*

The minister made an abrupt about-turn and retreated to his altar. He smacked his hands together and faced his parishioners. 'Right,' he said eventually, 'I want any of you who accept Christ to come up to the altar now.'

Marvis was tempted. The minister's words had nagged away at him, undermining his defiance. He didn't want to stay back on his own, and he didn't want Daralyn to be disappointed in him, but he was still reluctant to step forward and be counted amongst the minister's flock. His mother Florence went to church, his sister Jacqui went to church. Surely, he figured, he was covered by their prayers and equipped with a permanent excuse note?

'And for all those of you who think Grandma's coming to

church to save you from hell – no!' cried the minister. 'This is a personal relationship between you and Jesus Christ. Grandma won't be saving you from him, that's for certain!'

'So I walked up to him straight away,' Marvis told me in a small office above the family gym in Philadelphia. 'And I've been close to God ever since.'

Exhilarated by a faith reignited, Marvis continued with his career. He added three wins to his record in 1982 and at the beginning of 1983, with only three years' pro experience under his belt, decided it was time to make a move. In April he took on Broad – his old amateur conqueror, who had compiled a pro record of 12–0 and harboured title aspirations of his own. While it was Marvis getting all the copy in the magazines and newspapers, the much bigger, heavier Broad held a distinct psychological advantage. Minutes before he was called to the ring that night, Marvis knelt down in his changing room and said a prayer. His elbows on the locker-room table, eyes closed tight, he prayed for the safety of himself and his opponent and asked for God's guidance. A tingling feeling pulsated throughout his body, a few seconds of convulsive shivering and then serenity. Never before had Frazier felt the tangible sense of a higher power. This, in his mind, was the final proof of God's presence in his life. Implementing the busy efficiency and smart techniques he had learned as an amateur, Marvis outboxed Broad and won a decision which helped him break into the world's top ten. Two months later, back in Atlantic City, he faced Britain's enigmatic veteran, Joe Bugner. Bugner had been beaten by Ali twice and by Smokin' Joe too, but neither one had come close to knocking him out. Marvis also beat Bugner by decision.

The boxing world had become ever more fractured by political dissent and the overblown egos of despotic commissioners. For twenty years the sport had been ruled by the Caracas-based WBA and its Mexican rivals at the WBC, with each organisation sanctioning its own title fights. The IBF was created in 1983 in a bid to offer an alternative US power base. For the media and the fans this was bad news, but to Larry Holmes it was a godsend.

Holmes had held the WBC title since 1978, and as a result of his victories over men who would proceed to take it in turns holding the WBA belt, he was considered the real heavyweight champion of the world. Displeased, however, both with his promoter Don King and the WBC (whose decisions seemed often to coincide with King's interests), Holmes saw the IBF as a way out. He relinquished his WBC belt willingly and grabbed the IBF's new trinket.

At the time, Holmes boasted a record of 46–0, only three steps away from Rocky Marciano's final stats of 49–0. Marciano's was heavyweight championship history's only unblemished résumé and an achievement Holmes was desperate to surpass. Holmes, guided at this point by a Muslim businessman named Murad Muhammad, was being advised to pick his opposition carefully. At thirty-three he was approaching the downside to his career and saw little need to accept the challenges of seasoned, top contenders like Greg Page and Tony Tubbs, or indeed a rematch with Tim Witherspoon, who had come desperately close that year to relieving him of his title. It was Muhammad who suggested that Marvis Frazier would be a more suitable opponent.

In his heart, Holmes pitied Marvis. He had no great desire to face a ten-fight novice, no matter what claims were made for Marvis's impressive bloodline. Although Holmes' time had not come during the ferocious years of the mid-seventies, when Ali and Frazier and Foreman had ruled, he had been on the periphery of the scene, slowly making a name for himself in the background by working as Ali's chief sparring partner in Zaire prior to the Foreman fight. He had absorbed as much as he could from the great heavyweights of the era. In 1980 he had had to puncture the helpless shell of Ali, a man he loved dearly; now, three years on, he was to face the son of Smokin' Joe. For Holmes, Marvis was still the skinny, bashful teenager who had travelled across the world to watch his daddy fight. The kid just wasn't big enough to be a fully-fledged heavyweight. Marvis's supporters had the same doubts, but they hoped age would catch up with Holmes on the night. Still, Joe Frazier thought his son was as ready as he would ever be. On the evening of 25 November 1983, Holmes pulverised the poor youngster, outmanoeuvring him, outboxing him, dominating him, destroying him in fifty-seven seconds.

The manner of Marvis's loss was shattering. None of the experts had picked him to win, and most had questioned the wisdom of his being allowed anywhere near a man like Holmes so soon into his career. Nevertheless, his beating was frightening. Holmes would concede years later that he had sought to make brisk work of the young challenger so as not to prolong his distress. Joe, the pundits said, should advise his brave son to call it a day; it would be better if Marvis returned home to Philadelphia and helped his father work with their other fighters. But Marvis was not to be deterred. He was too proud for his own good, too haunted by his loss to Holmes to quit on such a glum note, and too determined to please his pop.

'Losing to Larry Holmes showed me the true analogy of my father,' he would explain. 'Even though I was knocked down and beaten up, my father was still there for me and he still loved me. That fight showed me that there were many different aspects of life where you could also get knocked down, but the ones who love you will still be there support- ing you. Many of us have what I call the Burger King syndrome, where the slogan is "You've gotta have it your way." In life, we always try to have things go our way, even though we know that can't always be the case. It's when things don't go your way that you see who the people are that truly love you.'

Marvis continued boxing. The following year he put together a run of six victories. In one of his bravest perform- ances, he overcame a knockdown and cracked jaw at the heavy fists of James Bonecrusher Smith to capture a ten- round decision. Back in the picture after this modest run of success, the Fraziers received an offer for Marvis to become Mike Tyson's twenty-fifth opponent.

Glens Falls, New York, July 1986

Of all the men to whom Tyson's would be compared, it was Joe Frazier's name which cropped up the most often. Both were relatively small heavyweights, under six feet tall and seldom weighing more than 225 pounds. Each had sought to perfect the art of working his way in close, enabling them to pound a taller opponent's body, bring his arms down and then zero in with shots to the head. There were minor differences. Frazier's heavy hooks came in rolling, incessant waves, whilst Tyson's were sharper and usually the precursors to rapid-fire combinations. But essentially Joe and Tyson were developed from the same prototype.

Joe Frazier had mixed emotions about Tyson's rising status in boxing. He admired Tyson's relentlessness and no-nonsense approach to what the youngster called 'the hurt business', but he strongly rejected any suggestion that the budding superstar might be the next Joe Frazier. The joints in Joe's legs may have rusted and the vigour of youth waned, but inside him beat the heart of a fighter still. Unable now to fight Tyson himself, it seemed Joe was hell bent on Marvis doing the job for him. For this fight, Joe took sole charge of his son's training.

'As great a fighter as Joe was, he was a very one-dimensional trainer who just didn't recognise other fighters' strengths,' recalled Bernard Fernandez. 'No matter who he trained, Joe would have them winging hooks. He tried to make Marvis into himself instead of concentrating on Marvis's strengths. Marvis was completely different to Joe, but he always wanted to try and do what his father wanted him to do.'

Joe told reporters that the Fraziers had jumped at the chance to take the fight. It was a great opportunity, and Joe claimed to have no doubts whatsoever that the more experienced Marvis could take the young Tyson. 'Tyson's got a big shock coming,' promised Joe. 'He's still a big baby. Now he's gonna see a real man facing him in the ring.'

'Marvis would not do any trash-talking, but Joe did,' remembered Fernandez. 'Joe kept saying how Marvis was gonna do this and Marvis was gonna do that, and even though Marvis himself never said anything at all, Tyson was just getting more and more irate. Very soon, all Tyson wanted to do was rip Marvis's head off.'

At this early stage of his career, Tyson had never sunk into the back-alley profanity that would soon become his trademark. Indeed, it was strange for some observers to hear Joe talk in such a way. He had been the target of Ali's invective in the seventies, the stooge to Ali's comedy routines and a victim of his crueller racial taunts, but throughout it all he had remained poker-faced. Now it seemed as though Joe was playing Ali and Tyson was playing Joe, and ultimately the one who would get hurt by it all was Marvis.

'The slick, stylish amateur Frazier . . . might have given Tyson fits with his lateral movement and pesky left jab,' said a report in *The Ring*, 'but the pro version, a replica of his father, former heavyweight king Joe Frazier, didn't have a chance. Under the guidance (some say misguidance) of the man he calls Pop, Marvis had developed into a mauler, one who matched his father's tremendous intensity and heart, but lacked his crippling left hook. In nearly every bout, "Little Smoke" would charge forward with his gun drawn, but with no ammunition in the clip. In bouts with inferior opponents, his natural talent was enough to lead him to victory. But against Tyson he looked like he was trying to pistol whip a man holding a machine-gun . . . Tyson would indeed be spectacular, horrifyingly so . . .'

At Glens Falls Tyson glided into Marvis at the opening

bell of their fight. The previous month he had been taken the distance for only the first and second occasions in his career, against the sly James Tillis and the wily Mitch Green, but his sixth sense for an opponent's weakness immediately locked on to Marvis's trepidation. Under threat while the bell still reverberated at ringside, Marvis covered up and was driven back to the ropes by three blazing jabs. He scuttled from left to right, but was met by Tyson's swarming blows at every turn. He moved into a corner, elbows locked to protect his face, and he was doomed.

The first shot of the combination probably knocked Marvis out, a right uppercut thrown with such speed and precision that he never had a chance to avoid it. It connected with his jaw, springing his head back violently. As his eyes rolled and his legs dipped, he looked certain to collapse to the floor, only to be jerked upright by another thunderous uppercut and then a dramatic spray of hooks and right hands. Marvis crumpled slowly to his knees, his head bowed in unconsciousness, a man beaten savagely into compliance in thirty seconds.

For the second time in his career, Marvis had been annihilated by an opponent who had claims to being one of the greatest heavyweights of all time, but for some a bad taste lingered in the mouth. Why had Joe Frazier encouraged the whole affair to proceed in the first place? Larry Merchant, a former editor at the *Philadelphia Daily News* and now a commentator for HBO, thought the match made sense for Tyson; his management needed an opponent who could help restore Tyson's image as a young destroyer after the bouts with Tillis and Green. But Fernandez suspected that Joe had woefully underestimated his son's opponent, and Steve Farhood – at the time an editor at *KO* – felt all along that Marvis had no business sharing a ring with the undefeated prospect under any circumstances.

'Marvis was always a great guy,' Farhood told me. 'He was an all-round nice kid, but he was such a small heavyweight. For me, it was almost criminal for Joe to push that fight. It was so obvious that Marvis had no chance of winning, but his father just couldn't let go. Because of Joe, Marvis had to go through with being blown away in such brutal fashion. I almost believe that really what was going on was that Joe wanted to live vicariously through Marvis and fight Tyson himself. Joe really wanted to prove that he could have beaten Tyson, and if it had been a few years earlier, he probably would have called for that fight to happen.'

Though he was not as angry as Farhood, Fernandez was equally suspicious of Joe's motives. Almost ten years later he ghosted an article on Joe Frazier's behalf for *The Ring*, entitled 'How I Would Have Whupped Mike Tyson'. 'I still think I can handle myself,' said Frazier in the piece. 'Give me some time to prepare and I'd give Michael all he could handle. I mean, right now. If I was a younger age, back when I was on top, I don't see where I'd have a problem beating him . . . I don't think he makes it through the sixth round.'

Smokin' Joe was always adamant that he had done no wrong. In 1999, when he was asked by Eric Raskin in a *KO* magazine interview if he should have handled Marvis's career differently, he replied: 'I think I did it right. Marvis had the neck problem and the eye problem. We had to move him because his career couldn't be that long. Marvis won all his fights, then just lost to guys that everybody else lost to; Michael and Larry. I knew what I had to do for him to be moved in the right direction. I took my shot. But that's the fight game.'

The loss to Tyson played heavily on Marvis's mind. He had wanted desperately to win for his pop; instead all he'd wound up with was half a minute on Tyson's highlight reel. Fernandez, the boxing beat writer in Marvis's hometown, compared the young Frazier's reaction to that of Floyd Patterson after losing to Sonny Liston in 1962 and Gerry Cooney after falling to Holmes twenty years later. 'He was ashamed of himself,' said Fernandez. 'He wanted to hide away. He was embarrassed, even though there was no shame in losing to either Larry Holmes or Mike Tyson.'

Marvis did not retire immediately. He knocked out Tommy Fischer in two rounds and won a decision against Robert Evans, but would fight just once more before finally bringing the curtain down on his professional boxing career.

In October 1988, Fernandez went to Las Vegas to cover Sugar Ray Leonard's contest with Donny Lalonde for the WBC super-middleweight and light-heavyweight titles. He was staying in town for a few days because two nights later Leonard's great rival Thomas 'The Hitman' Hearns was fighting James 'The Heat' Kinchen. Sandwiched between the Leonard and Hearns bouts was a small club show in nearby Tucson, Arizona, featuring Marvis Frazier against Phil Brown. When he heard that Marvis had announced this would be his final fight, Fernandez called his paper back in Philadelphia and told them to save some space for a report of the young Frazier's farewell to the sport.

Inside a tiny arena in Tucson, Fernandez was one of only two ringside press for the show. In the corner opposite Frazier stood Brown, a tall heavyweight who had once knocked out Marvis's cousin, Rodney, and become the first man to take Britain's hard-hitting Frank Bruno the distance. When the fight started, a cameraman stood up on the ring apron to record the proceedings for a local cable station, blocking the view of a tattooed choir of Hell's Angels. Marvis and Brown started fighting, and the bikers started yelling. At the bell for the second round, Marvis and Brown came out to box, and the bikers returned from the concession stands armed with hot dogs and cups of beer. Marvis and Brown threw jabs, and the bikers hurled their food. Beer dripped from the cameraman's hair, and the referee kicked relish and onion from the floor. As the round-card girls dived for cover under the ring, Marvis and Brown boxed on and mustard smeared the cameraman's lens. At the end of ten rounds, Marvis was announced the winner. He embraced Brown and smiled, oblivious to the mayhem around him.

The Deacon

In the years which followed Marvis's low-profile finale, he made the transition from fighter to civilian with relative ease. As a Frazier he could not altogether abandon the fight game, but the majority of his time was spent as an evangelist, travelling to ghettos and jails across America and the Caribbean. The word 'Bible', he would tell the convicts he spoke to, was really an abbreviation for, 'Basic Instructions Before Leaving Earth'. Smokin' Joe renamed him 'The Deacon'. Marvis would continue to polish the raw talent of young Philly fighters in the gym, but he had accepted a higher calling.

When Tyson was sentenced to six years' imprisonment for the rape of Desiree Washington, Marvis sent him a poem. Tyson didn't reply, but that didn't deter Marvis. Some months later, Marvis's gospel journeys took him to Indiana. He went to the penitentiary which housed the former world champion, and asked the guard on duty to let Tyson know that he had come calling. Ushered into an exercise yard, he waited for several minutes before Tyson appeared.

'When he heard it was me, he came outside,' Marvis would recount. 'He came up to me and we embraced. "Man, I appreciate you coming here and the poem you sent me," he said. He was pleased to see me. Look, unless there's been some very nasty stuff going on, the majority of guys in this sport – especially heavyweights – once that last bell sounds, the first thing they do is embrace each other. We're all friends really, most of us. There's respect there. That's what Tyson and I felt for each other. We're not trying to kill somebody. Sometimes, Mike took it to the extreme. Sometimes it was real, sometimes it wasn't. But I really believe that he felt if he could remove all the obstacles in his way inside the boxing ring, then his life would also become easier. We talked for an hour or so in the yard, and I believed there was still goodness in his heart.'

In 1995, Tyson, newly converted to Islam, stepped meekly from the penitentiary gates surrounded by a ton of security beef in fedora hats. At the same time, Marvis began ministerial work in his church. Though many wondered whether Tyson would continue to fight, given his loss of weight and lack of boxing training while inside, he never really had a choice. Marvis, meanwhile, aimed for a master's degree at Philadelphia's Center for Urban Theological Studies. As the Tyson comeback began, Smokin' Joe felt certain that Tyson would blaze a trail towards the championship once again. Marvis was not so sure.

The Frazier family's boxing programme took a fresh boost after the Atlanta Olympics of '96, when they signed a bronze-medal-winning lightweight named Terrance Cauthen to a professional contract. Joe had long been scathing about the forces which controlled the sport and their lack of first-hand experience. He would question promoters' and trainers' knowledge of the game, joke that they had probably experienced no fights and lost six of them and then sit back disgruntled, nursing his aching ankles and the chip on his shoulder.

Marvis's office sat adjacent to his father's, a dimly lit room on the second floor of a corner building at the top of North Broad Street, and along from this office was another for a sister, Natasha, who handled various secretarial duties. From the large window in her room, the Fraziers could look down at the gymnasium floor and watch their charges at work, skipping rope, pounding heavy bags and sparring in one of the rings. In the seventies the gym had been a bustling den of activity. Film crews and reporters from all four corners of the earth would queue to see the great Smokin' Joe at work in his strategic command centre, and fighters from Pennsylvania, New York and New Jersey would make it their business to further their education in the care of some of Philadelphia's most sagacious masters. In time, as Joe and then Marvis faded from the limelight, the gym grew quiet. The murals remained – huge pastels of Joe surrounded by Marvis and his cousins, all booted and gloved, and of Joe warring with Ali. And even though the halcyon days had long passed, some of the old faces who had stood by Joe's side in the early years of smoke would return to the gym on weekday mornings, sit on top of dusty benches and rolls of carpet and amuse each other with tales from the past. Yank Durham was dead, but there was Sam Hickman, stick thin, with white hair and glasses, who would talk about Joe's fights with Oscar Bonavena and Jerry Quarry, his taste for 'bangers and beer' acquired after the trip to London to fight old Bugner, and the leggy 'Knockouts' – Joe's backing group – with their wild Afros. There was another, a heavy-set man with a round, pockmarked face whom they all referred to as Number Four; he would sit in the background, his features creasing as he laughed and wallowed in the nostalgia of it all.

There was never any danger of the Fraziers' relationship cooling, even to the degree of Bob and Tony Tucker's. In his office, Marvis decorated the walls and shelves with his daddy: framed poster-sized copies of *Life* magazine covers featuring Joe and the Butterfly in tuxedos; portraits of Joe in charcoal, bronzes of Joe, trophies won by Joe, statuettes of Joe, murals of Joe, canvas paintings of Joe, black-and-white stills of Joe. 'People always ask what it was like growing up in the shadow of my father,' Marvis would admit to *Sports Illustrated*. 'I always thought of it as standing in a great light.'

Lacking the financial muscle of America's promotional juggernauts, however, the Fraziers struggled to retain the services of their pro signings. When Terrance Cauthen lost for the first time, he was wooed by another promoter and jumped ship. A young heavyweight named Derek Bryant, a man Marvis described as the most naturally gifted fighter he had ever worked with, left them too. 'Sometimes', sighed Marvis, 'fighters are like street women, always wanting to see if things are better on the other side of the road.' Very soon, the most high-profile athlete on the Fraziers' books was Marvis's sister Jacqui, the sibling who had thumped the Bible in his presence as a teenager. Now a qualified attorney, she was cashing in on the expansion of women's boxing by fighting one of Ali's daughters, Laila. Marvis took on the responsibility of training Jacqui, and in June 2001 she battled the daughter of her daddy's fiercest rival at the Turning Stone casino in New York. She lost by decision after six dramatic rounds, but by now Marvis had been ordained as a Baptist minister and his appearances in a fighter's corner were becoming less frequent. 'You may not get that car, you may not get that promotion. Hey, you may get knocked out by Mike Tyson,' he told *Sports Illustrated*. 'But when God mixes our lives up, he makes sure to put some good in there as well. Right now, my life is full of the good.'

In God's Game

In his prime, Tyson seemed an unlikely convert to Islam. While he was still world champion, Don King had arranged for him to be baptised at the hands of the Reverend Jesse Jackson. A month into his prison sentence Tyson's closest confidant and most frequent visitor was a Baptist minister from Indianapolis named Reverend Charles Williams. Tyson would attend Williams's weekly chapel services and engage in discussions about religion, history and literature, and afterwards Williams would voice his belief in the fighter's innocence to the awaiting press. 'Mike Tyson is innocent of any wrongdoing,' the minister would insist. 'And he really knows how to treat a lady. I've asked him for advice on relationships myself many times.'

Clearly Tyson tired of dispensing pearls of wisdom to the excitable Williams, for within a year a new mentor, Dr Muhammad Sideeq, had taken the reverend's place. Tyson had been courted by the Black Muslims for some time – he may have been contemplating an allegiance to Islam before prison; and the Muslims were his most vocal supporters on the day he was sentenced. 'You bring a hawk into a chicken yard and wonder why the chicken got ate up?' shrieked Louis Farrakhan, the Nation of Islam's leader, at a convention held in Chicago shortly after Tyson's incarceration. Occasionally mopping at the streaks of perspiration on his caramel skin, he added, 'All these fine foxes just parading in front of Mike, and so Mike's eyes begin to dance like a hungry man looking at a Wendy's beefburger or something ... and you wanna see if this is as good as it looks.' To wild applause, Farrakhan reached out with his hands and grabbed at imaginary objects before him. 'How could she be out at one a.m.? Who did she tell? How did she get out?' A voice in the audience corrects one of his statements and he chuckles. 'Two a.m.? That's even worse! Well now, you gonna sit with Mike in his limo? You know – Honest Mike?! She wanna get an autograph for her father at two a.m.? She says she said, "No

Mike, no!"' He mopped himself furiously again and dropped the smile as he looked out at his congregation, male and female sentries in gendarme hats and tunics standing solemnly behind him, hands clasped over the buckles of their shining belts. 'I mean, how many times, sisters, have you said "No", when you meant "Yes" all along?' Howls of support, and Farrakhan's voice rose. 'You see,' he bellowed, 'you're not dealing with a man that don't know you this time, and the damned deceitful games that you play!'

Sideeq connected with Tyson more than Williams had managed. The Muslim scholar talked to him about a wide range of subjects, and pressed for 'upbeat, positive Muslims' to pay the boxer regular visits. Among those who rallied to Tyson's side was a trio of former light-heavyweight title-holders – Eddie Mustafa Muhammad, Dwight Muhammad Qawi and Matthew Saad Muhammad – as well as a wealthy Wall Street banker named Aziz Munir. Tyson's adoption of Islam was completed by the end of 1993, and upon his release two years later, he emerged from the Indiana Youth Center in black robes and a white skullcap, to be escorted immediately to the Islamic Society of North America in the middle of a nine-car convoy.

Tyson, who was rumoured at this stage to be contemplating changing his name to Malik Abdul-Aziz, was joined for this low-key pilgrimage by Muhammad Ali. On being ushered to a downstairs dining-room at the centre, Tyson took Ali's tray from his trembling hands, sat him down at a table and poured him tea. After a light meal and conversation stilted by the effects of Ali's Parkinson's disease, Tyson bowed towards Mecca, prayed, read aloud several passages from the Koran and then caught a morning flight home to Southington, Ohio.

Although he bowed to Mecca after dispatching the wretched Peter McNeeley and the marginally better Buster Mathis Junior the year of his release, the clearest evidence of Tyson's ties to Islam came on the night of his rematch with the muscle-bound Englishman, Frank Bruno, in March 1996. After three rounds of effortless choreography, in which Bruno, the WBC champion, had been reduced to a wreck, blood dribbling from a deep wound above his eye, Tyson, cheered on by scores of bow-tied brethren from the Nation of Islam, collapsed to his knees, repeatedly bowed in reverence to Allah and basked in the apparent rediscovery of his undying powers. It was eight months before his defeat to the self-styled 'God's Warrior', Evander Holyfield.

'I would say that Mike was misguided by the Muslims,' Marvis Frazier would tell me. 'Obviously I believe Christianity is the way, and I believe when Mike fought Evander, God used that fight to show us all once again the analogy of David and Goliath. Here was Evander, a Christian man, while Mike, the Muslim, was supposed to be the invincible one. Everyone was saying that there was no way in the world Evander could beat Mike, but instead Evander just showed the whole world what he could do with the power of God.'

'Isn't that rather arrogant?' I asked. 'Not only to say that one faith is higher than another, but also to suppose that any god would choose to spread his message through a prize-fight? That would be hard for some people to comprehend.'

'Well, a lot of people have had problems with reconciling

me being a professional fighter when I was younger, and also a man of God,' said Marvis. 'They just spoke about the brutality of boxing. That's all they concentrated on. But me, I never viewed boxing as anything other than a sport. Yes, it's also a business and it's a rough game, but it ain't about killing – it's about competition. And the way I handled that was to point out to them the story of the rooster in the Bible, because in the Bible God used a rooster to speak to Peter. He told Peter that before the rooster crowed twice, he would deny Him thrice. So if God can use a rooster to talk to Peter and a mule to talk to a prophet, why can't He use a fighter to speak to people? God can choose anybody to do anything He wants, so who is man to say He can't?'

'But to suggest that Mike has been misguided and that you are on the right track . . .' I offered weakly.

'Well, I don't hold anything against him for choosing what he chose. I believe if you're really a brother, you gonna be a brother always. Whether that brother's white, black, Asian, Oriental, no matter to me. Even if he's a Muslim, I'm still gonna be a brother to him. God himself says that love is the greatest gift that any of us has. So if you like chocolate ice cream and I like vanilla, I'm not gonna argue with you. I'll stay true to what I'm holding on to, but I can still love you like a brother.'

Philadelphia, Pennsylvania, 13 June 2002

It was the mother of all church services, over three hours of foot-stomping and hand-clapping, dispersed among several angry sermons by the pastor, Dr Samuel Prince Fulton.

Marvis stood by the pastor's side throughout the service, and when he sang his eyes became wet. Six months earlier, Daralyn had passed away, leaving behind a heartbroken husband and two teenaged daughters. 'People are looking at me and saying, "How is he doing it? How is he continuing to march on? How is his family able to sustain themselves and not fall apart? How is he not throwing himself off at the deep end?"' He said in tones muffled by despair. 'Well, it's because of nothing except through the spirit of God.'

Before Dr Fulton finished, he called up an elderly lady from the front pew – who, through the power of Jesus, he claimed, had been cured of her limp. Then he spoke of his own battles with cancer and a conversation with God that he could not fully disclose to his flock. A lady in the choir rattled some cymbals each time he paused.

Later, we sat in the shadowy interior of Marvis's office while his daughters played a golfing game on Natasha's computer, and a distant relative was brought in by a worried mother to receive a pep talk before his exams. Maybe Smokin' Joe had not been mistaken after all. They had taken their chances against Holmes and then Tyson, and they had missed the jackpot, but it wasn't just about winning, it was about representing their name with honour. It didn't matter that Marvis had fallen in the ring, or that his cousins had never made it to the big leagues. What mattered was pride. Honour. Respect. For a while in the late eighties, the Fraziers had managed a fierce young banger named Bert Cooper, even granting him use of the word 'smoke'. It was a shame when Smokin' Bert lost to Reggie Gross and then to Carl Williams, but they didn't cut him loose. But then he began

dabbling with the wrong crowd and hanging with drug dealers, and they wouldn't have any of it – no associate of the
Fraziers was getting mixed up with such things. Honour,
being a man, was of more value than a perfect record.

'When we look at the majority of our youth today, there
is a certain apathy there,' Marvis sighed. 'They think that to
be a man means to go with all that slang they speak: *Yo, I'm
dope, I'm fly, I'm def, I'm slammin', you kickin', keep goin' on
the DL* . . . They think talking like that makes them a man.
Other guys think it means having a bunch of rings on their
fingers, putting a watch on their wrists and a beeper on their
sides. Some guys believe it's having a bunch of cars. *I've got
a BMW! I've got a four-by-four!* Other guys, it's like, *I've got
Mary, I've got Betty, I've got Lucy, I've got Lollie! I've got a little
Khalil, a little Jalil.* You know, some people think that's what
it takes to being a man. I was lucky enough to have a father
who showed me what it meant to be a man. When Mike
Tyson won the title for the first time, his father wasn't there.
But he had Bill Cayton, Jim Jacobs, Cus D'Amato, Kevin
Rooney . . . and these people were not there for him when
it came to fighting Lennox Lewis. These were really the
people who were there for him throughout his life, who struc-
tured him, who he knew he could trust, who loved him and
motivated him. There was no way Mike Tyson could have
won that fight with Lennox without any of those people
around him any more.'

Already, only a week after Tyson's fight with Lewis, the
pugilist's hangover was subsiding, and he was making noises
about revenge that belied his immediate magnanimity in
defeat. Tyson, it was true, needed a second fight with Lewis,

or more correctly, another money-spinner, to set up his retirement fund. The problem was how to make such a fight plausible in the eyes of the paying public. With each passing
defeat, first to Douglas and then through the two losses to
Holyfield, the number of excuse-makers dwindled. Tyson
was a poster boy for the law of diminishing returns. The
same process had consumed Sonny Liston; seen him lose
twice in suspicious circumstances to Muhammad Ali, retain-
ing less and less of his stony, malevolent aura, until he was
beaten into a mess by the ordinary Leotis Martin.

'A hardy spirit comes before a fall,' said Marvis. 'I'm really
praying for Mike now. I think the Lord saw his arrogance
and decided to humble him. When he said later after the
fight, "Well, that really wasn't me saying and doing those
bad things I was doing" . . . No, man, that was you, and God
humbled you. But I also believe he will come back a better
man for it. And I think he'll come back a better fighter too.'
He spotted my scepticism. 'I believe he will respect people
a bit more now. I remember seeing him just kissing his baby
throughout one of his recent interviews. It seems to me like
he's just looking for love. You see, when he's at the top of
his game everybody's around him, slapping his back.
Everybody loves a winner, but when you lose, you lose alone.'

After we left the gym, Marvis drove me into the town
centre before heading for a Father's Day lunch with his two
girls. It was still Sunday quiet, unclogged roads and couples
sipping cappuccinos in café windows. The next day, he would
be preaching in local community centres, competing with
beepers and Rolexes for the attentions of Philadelphia's
young men.

'Right now, I'm just ready to do whatever the Lord wants me to do with my life, man,' he said as we waited at some lights. 'I don't know why right now, but apparently the Lord has taken my wife away from me for a reason. There's obviously something He wants me to do, or a place that He's trying to take me to, or somebody He wants me to talk to. I'm just all eyes and ears to His spirit, you know? If He's up there saying, "We have work to be done here – who can We send?" I'm right here, saying, "Lord, send me, because wherever it is You want me, I am willing to go."' We closed in on the centre of town, his daughters sitting quietly in the back, gospel music on the radio. 'God has sustained me for all these years, so I know He is on my side. We haven't had any handouts from anybody all this time, we Fraziers, yet God continues to take good care of us.'

Six: Damage

Mike Tyson: The Power and the Fury

THE LAST THING A FIGHTER LOSES, SO THEY SAY, IS HIS PUNCH. Which was fortunate for Tyson, given the general slide in his boxing skills. The ability to blast another man senseless with one punch had in the end prevented his humiliation at the hands of François 'The White Buffalo' Botha in January 1999. It had also helped fuel speculation in otherwise sane minds that he presented a serious threat to Lewis in 2002. And it still enabled him to unleash highlight-reel, X-rated entertainment upon the poor saps lined up to restore a fresh illusion of invincibility. The reflexes had faded, the foot movement had deteriorated and the jab had been shelved, but those single bullets could still inspire fear.

In the early days, his combination of speed and power had been shocking. According to Steve Farhood, 'Tyson was like a wind-up toy; he hit people and knocked them out.' 'I won't let Tyson bully me,' promised Tyson's eighth opponent, Michael 'Jack' Johnson, before the pair clashed in Atlantic City on 9 September 1985. 'How will he react when I land my best punches? That's the sixty-four-thousand-dollar question.' Tyson's answer was a two-fisted slaughter which saw the lanky, dreadlocked Johnson hit so hard that when he collapsed in the opening round, the referee Frank Cappuccino immediately called for a doctor, who bent to pick five of the man's teeth off the canvas before sending the stricken fighter to hospital.

In his next fight, 9 October, Tyson took on Donnie Long, who had lasted the distance with former world champion John Tate and ranked contender James Broad. Donnie was long gone in 88 seconds. Fight number twelve, 13 November, Tyson met Eddie 'The Towering Inferno' Richardson in Richardson's hometown of Houston, Texas. Richardson was six foot six tall, very confident, and had won twelve of fourteen contests. His fires were put out in 77 seconds. He described taking Tyson's punches as like 'getting in the way of a runaway truck'. Sammy Scaff became Tyson's fourteenth victim on 6 December at the Felt Forum in New York. Destroyed in 79 seconds, he was quick to explain that he had 'never been hit so hard in my life'. Two days after Christmas, Mark Young from Charlotte, North Carolina, declared, 'I ain't in the mood to show any seasonal goodwill,' and rushed Tyson at the opening bell. Basted and roasted in 70 seconds, he could only mutter, 'I went out with the intention of testing his chin . . . and then he hit me.'

The following year Tyson took on a better class of competition. On 21 February 1986 he hammered Jesse 'The Boogieman' Ferguson in six rounds. It was in the immediate aftermath of this latest carnage that Tyson made his infamous remark about punching nose-bones into brains. 'There is somewhat of a comic book quality about Tyson's fights,' wrote Nigel Collins in *The Ring.* 'When he hits opponents they just don't fall or slump to the mat. They fly across the ring, often bouncing off the floor or ropes before crashing to the canvas. It's a little like watching Popeye belt Brutus, or Batman plaster the Penguin. The violence is so exaggerated, it seems slightly surreal.' Madison Square Garden, 13 June; Reggie Gross had an 18–4 record. 'You wanna fight on?' cried the referee Johnny Lobianco, when Gross protested against his stoppage in the opening round. 'Youse can't even walk right now!'

By the time Tyson had reached contender status in the latter half of '86, the only puncher among the heavyweight division's three reigning champions was the WBA title holder, Tim Witherspoon. Tyson's initial target, WBC champion Trevor Berbick, was a strong spoiler but no great shakes as a hitter, and the IBF titlist Michael Spinks was a former undisputed light-heavyweight champion who lacked genuine heavyweight power. Witherspoon was a defensive specialist, but also possessed an overhand right that caused considerable damage when bounced off another man's jaw. The only other major-league bangers among the world's top heavyweights were James 'Bonecrusher' Smith and Frank Bruno. Each would soon match his own vaunted power shots against both Witherspoon's and Tyson's in world championship matches.

In July 1986 Witherspoon left Frank Bruno a sorry, lumped-up heap in the eleventh round. He was scheduled to make his next defence against the man he had beaten for the title, Tony Tubbs, at Madison Square Garden five months later. Tubbs pulled out a week before the fight with a shoulder injury, and Don King called in 'Bonecrusher' Smith as a replacement challenger. At first Witherspoon protested the change in opponent, but when King turned the screw the champion relented.

'I knew I had to knock Tim out,' Smith told me. And he did just that, bludgeoning Witherspoon to the mat three times, in the process becoming the first college graduate to reign as world heavyweight champion. 'I could hit,' sighed Smith happily, clenching and unclenching his big fists in front of me. 'And when I hit you, you stayed hit.'

When he fought Tyson in March 1987, however, he did a lot less hitting and plenty of holding. Intimidated by Tyson's reputation, and intent on not being knocked out, the Bonecrusher clutched ribs and arms and sides for eleven stultifying rounds. In the last round he finally opened up with a single right that jolted Tyson's head back. But that shot, and the wild combination that followed, wasn't enough to prevent his defeat.

Bruno would not receive his opportunity against Tyson for another two years. After losing to Witherspoon, he'd been rebuilt within the space of four fights in 1987 – against a faded but still crafty James 'Quick' Tillis; a tired Reggie Gross; an ageing Joe Bugner; and worst of all, sandwiched between the Tillis and Gross bouts, an obliteration of the downright incompetent Chuck Gardner. Forget the Rumble in the Jungle or the Thrilla in Manila. Bruno's one-round demolition of Gardner in Calais was the Farce in France. An opponent who had about as much innate boxing ability as Freddie Starr, Bruno's sparring partner during the pantomime season, was no preparation for Mike Tyson.

By the time Tyson and Bruno teed off against each other in February 1989, Tyson's world was well into its downward spiral. He was being driven berserk by marital woes and tangled business affairs, and the love affair with the press that had been born the night he hammered Trevor Berbick back into the realms of mediocrity had long since dissipated.

Tyson was never what some fight people would call 'a cutie' in the ring. His purpose and methods were blunt. He came to take care of business, without frills or bells or hoops or spangles. But along with the tunnel-vision instilled in him by D'Amato there had been an immaculate composition to his destructive style. Now he had become the thug-warrior; a churlish, livid young man with an XXXL-sized chip on his shoulder, who could not be assuaged simply by beating another man stupid.

For the Bruno fight, Tyson shaved the sides of his head to the bone and stalked the ring petulantly as the MC announced both fighters. At the bell, HBO's Larry Merchant elected to inform his audience that 'the fastest KO in heavyweight [title] history [is] fifty-five seconds . . .' Dressed in blood-red velvet shorts, Bruno tentatively prodded with his jab and then hit the mat – almost out of nerves, it seemed – as Tyson tore into him. When he got up, Tyson came at him again. But Bruno stood his ground: he clipped the champion on the head with a brace of left hooks. The BBC's Harry Carpenter went into an orgasm of hysteria.

As the fight wore on, Tyson became a buzzsaw of elbows and butts and clubbing hooks to body and head that ripped seams of blood across Bruno's lips and below his nose. Between rounds he would thrust gloves upon hips, in emulation of old fighters like Ad Wolgast and Battling Nelson, whom he had seen in D'Amato's scrapbooks and Cayton's old fight films. And in the fifth round he drenched Bruno with blows that left the Londoner sagging and gasping on the ropes, his neck almost torn from its shoulders and his head flapping in the night air. Bruno's trainer Terry Lawless hurled a towel stained with the gruesome evidence of the challenger's valour into the ring.

Bruno had taken his punishment, but the distress he suffered at the time was largely physical. Ultimately, he was able to achieve his lifelong goal: to become a world champion. The consequences of his beating by Tyson could have been much worse, as Tyrell Biggs might attest.

Fort Worth, Texas, October 2003

On a secluded industrial estate five miles away from the centre of Fort Worth, the Southside Boxing Club lay between a weightlifting gym, an auto-repairs station and a roadside diner selling three-dollar fajitas to mechanics and lorry drivers.

I had come here to meet Tyrell Biggs, and the task of pinning him down had been an arduous one. Like Tony Tucker, Biggs lived a nomadic existence, moving about the country often and at short notice. He had grown up in Philadelphia, but moved to Atlanta and across South Carolina with his elder brother Xavier, taken small training assignments in Ohio and temporarily settled in California. He now divided his time between the Texan cities of Dallas and Fort Worth. In Fort Worth he had fallen in love with a local girl and then taken casual employment as a chauffeur and odd-job man for the Canadian heavyweight contender, Kirk Johnson, who was currently training for a world-title elimi-nator against Vitali Klitschko. 'As a matter of fact,' Biggs insisted, 'I'm really the camp coordinator.'

Biggs was a tall, graceful stylist, the classic Ali clone. A gifted athlete with steady legs and a jab longer than a trombone, he had turned to boxing after reasonable success shooting hoops at college. It proved to be a good choice, at least for as long as he remained in the amateurs. In 1984 the Olympic Games were hosted by Los Angeles, and with the Cubans and Soviets boycotting in revenge for America's no-show in Moscow four years earlier, there were high expectations for the team.

As the Games approached, the super-heavyweight Biggs encountered Tyson for the first time. Vaguely aware of the teenager's reputation, Biggs watched him lose two decisions to Henry Tillman in a box-off for the squad's heavyweight berth. Despite losing to Tillman, Tyson had remained a fixture on the team as an alternate.

A popular ringleader amongst the American boxers, Biggs was a ladies' man who liked to party. He snorted coke and knew how to chat a girl up, and at every opportunity he was supposed to have poked fun at Tyson's awkwardness and immaturity. The final straw for Tyson was reportedly Biggs's refusal to let him join the rest of the team for a night out on the town, voicing concerns that Tyson's ugliness would frighten away the girls.

For three years Tyson seethed when Biggs's name was mentioned, the humiliation of that moment embedded in his consciousness. As if Biggs could do himself no more favours, he went on record with previously unmentioned accounts of Tyson's abusive behaviour towards women. Maybe Biggs believed in his own ability to dissect Tyson in the boxing ring; if so, his confidence was difficult to share, for it was clear that as undefeated world champion Tyson could no longer be ridiculed without the certainty of painful retribution.

Biggs tells it differently today. He says there was never a bad word or feeling exchanged between the pair, but that a small problem had stemmed from Tyson's desire to box for the super-heavyweight slot on the team. Getting down to 201 pounds was taking a toll on Tyson's ever-maturing body, and he fancied his chances more as a full-strength opponent for Biggs than a weight-drained one for Tillman. But the US Amateur Boxing Federation felt Biggs was the superior bet at the top weight – he was bigger, taller and far more experienced in international competition, while the opposition at heavyweight was not so tough.

The alternates were never called upon. Tillman and Biggs both won gold; so too did Mark Breland, Meldrick Taylor and Pernell Whitaker – each of whom would surpass Tillman and Biggs by becoming world champions as professionals. In the light-heavyweight division, Evander Holyfield was comfortably winning his semi-final with New Zealand's Kevin Barry when a shot fired momentarily after the referee had called for a break resulted in a disqualification loss. He had to settle for the bronze. Biggs, like many of his teammates, was snapped up by Main Events after the Games. Boxing salivated at the thought of Biggs and Tyson meeting as pros: together they were supposed to rekindle the kind of heavyweight rivalry not seen since the days of Ali and Frazier. And it was easy to guess which fighter would play whom. People who had missed the days of Ali could be excused for wishing they had been born earlier, but the notion that Biggs was anything more than a hazy prototype of the Louisville Lip was purely fictitious.

Dancing in the Footsteps of a Giant

Until a twenty-two-year-old Cassius Clay pirouetted around Sonny Liston in Miami Beach, the heavyweight division had for the most part been ruled by hulking brawlers and murderous punchers. Jack Johnson exhibited science and technique but lacked the young Clay's fluidity, and though Ezzard Charles used his slippery skills to outbox bigger, older men like Jersey Joe Walcott and a badly shop-worn Joe Louis, he lacked the audacity of Clay's ballet-dancer act. The others were a mixture of granite hardmen and heavy-handed assassins, men like Jack Dempsey, Rocky Marciano and Liston, whose sole aim from the first peal of the bell was to separate any opponent as quickly as possible from his senses.

'Muhammad was the first big guy capable of such movement,' was the opinion of Ali's trainer, the revered Angelo Dundee. 'Up until he came along, heavyweights were just considered to be big, clumsy punchers. Muhammad was so smooth, so fluid, it was like admiring a beautiful picture. He had everything, but it was his movement which would help set an opponent up. He was too quick for an opponent to read him.'

Ali – as Clay soon became – was a heavyweight Sugar Ray Robinson; a multi-dimensional fighter who could box sweetly, move deftly and change direction in a split second, sharp-shoot in combination and effortlessly dictate the tempo of a fight. But the classic Ali manoeuvre, and the one which many who came after him would copy, was the shuffle and dance behind the long, leaping left hand, circling an opponent until he had been reduced to impotence, forced to turn in increasingly restricted circles.

'I was spoilt,' said Dundee. 'I had Willie Pastrano, then Muhammad, and then Sugar Ray Leonard, so when anyone talks about speed and movement – oh boy! But movement is a four-way combination: it's about going forward, moving backward, and from side to side. It's also about balance. But most importantly of all, it's about being able to do something whilst you're employing that movement. If you're just moving around the ring, looking pretty but not doing anything else, it's a waste. That's what a lot of the guys who came after Muhammad did, but it was a mistake all along for them to try to imitate him. No fighter can do what another fighter does. Fighters should watch each other and try to apply certain things, but never imitate.'

For a number of heavyweights who followed Ali – significantly Tyrell Biggs – it was the simpler aspects of Ali's game, the circular containment of what was perceived to be an opponent's one-dimensional threat, that they sought to emulate. Against early, less risky opposition, these tactics resulted in some aesthetically pleasing performances, but there were three vital issues the dancing men overlooked.

It was not Ali's movement alone which subdued Liston,

but also the psychological warfare and rock-solid self-belief in his superiority. Movement would have borne little fruit for Ali against the smouldering intensity of Joe Frazier, had it not been accompanied by a frighteningly impervious resolve. And movement had been virtually forfeited against the terrifying fists of George Foreman, as Ali instead opted for the risky rope-a-dope game, lying on the ropes while Foreman expended all his energy pulverising Ali's arms and ribs with hammer blows.

The second issue which the movers forgot was the obvious gap in class between the men on whom the new age of dancers had honed their skills of evasion and the likes of Mike Tyson. It felt good to shimmy and float and probe with the left hand while their feet made like Fred Astaire against opponents with all the firepower of Ginger Rogers. Dancing one's way to victory against Tyson was another proposition altogether.

The final and perhaps most crucial oversight was the mistaken belief that the danger posed by a fighter like Tyson lay only in his bristling armoury. For just as Ali had fortitude and bravery and guile to back up his smooth agility, Tyson's power was enhanced tenfold by the blazing speed with which he could employ it. It was speed that allowed him to realise his full, catastrophic potential.

'Tyson had the speed too, but it was offensive speed instead of defensive speed,' said Dundee. 'He'd slide in to your right, clinch, and then get you with a clubbing hook to the kidneys, and if you bent over in pain he'd get you with a follow-up, devastating uppercut. He had the speed to do these things, but a lot of guys didn't realise this until they got into the ring with him. He was quick and small, and he would slide in on you and use his speed to overwhelming advantage.'

For all the beauty of Biggs's left hand and the grace with which he could circumnavigate a ring, his fate was almost certainly sealed even before his professional debut. Biggs was damaged goods. Not the kind of damage inflicted by the heavy, battering fists of a Bonecrusher or a Bruno, but the psychological impairment caused by freebasing cocaine. When in only his fifteenth pro contest he challenged Tyson for the world championship in October 1987 it was to a backdrop of barely concealed whispers from his own team that he was a wacko, a headcase whose chips needed to be cashed in before some no-name came along and beat him. Introduced to coke by the jocks at college, Biggs quickly became addicted. He went through times that even he referred to as 'pretty rough' prior to the Olympics. When he won the gold medal, Biggs partied and bathed in the adulation and capped the evening off with some lines. And when he turned pro at Madison Square Garden and found himself being lustily booed by a crowd made restless by a poky affair with Mike Evans, he sought solace in some tin foil, a cigarette lighter and a crystal of crack.

Although a successful stint in rehab heralded the beginning of a nineteen-year (and counting) period of sobriety, Biggs would freely admit to the press that the monkey would never be off his back. 'It will always be there,' he would explain. 'I will never recover. I will always have to take each day as it comes. But God willing, I'll get by.'

Getting himself back on his feet and away from drugs was a victory in itself, but Biggs had been left with a lingering need to prove himself more than just a nimble, quick-fisted Ali impersonator. He wanted to show everyone his competitive streak, particularly his trainers Lou Duva – who had been in the business long enough to have rubbed shoulders with Rocky Marciano – and George Benton, a wily old middleweight from Philadelphia who had come of age during the 1960s and early '70s when men from the City of Brotherly Love almost monopolised the division's world rankings. Biggs's first opportunity to do something special came in his ninth outing, when he crossed the path of Jeff Sims, an experienced fighter from Miami Beach with a quirky reputation.

'I knew that fight was gonna be tough because of the way Sims' attitude was and the fact he was kinda crazy!' Biggs remembered. 'He wanted to intimidate me. I knew he was gonna do that, but I wasn't gonna get into it. I had my mind made up that I was gonna whip him no matter what, just because of the way he was.' In the second round of the fight, Sims nailed Biggs's collarbone with a right cross. The pain which swept through his body was extraordinary. Even on television viewers could see that serious damage had been caused by the blow, and as Biggs grimaced and dropped his right hand, agonising defeat looked certain to follow. 'You know something's wrong,' said Biggs as he recalled the return to his corner and the looks on Duva and Benton's faces. 'But you don't wanna think that way. I didn't wanna say to myself, "Oh shit, he's broken my collarbone." I knew it was somethin'. I knew it was probably that, but I just didn't wanna think it. I told George and Lou that I couldn't move my right arm. And what did they say? "Well shit, Tyrell, just use the left hand!"

Well, as you probably know, I had a pretty good left hand – at least, I thought it was pretty good anyhow, and I thought I could beat him with just that. Which is what I did.'

It's a double-edged sword though, proving yourself in adversity, especially early on in your career. You got back on your feet after being knocked down? *What were you doing on the floor in the first place?* You ignored the pain of a broken collarbone? *How could you let a guy like Sims land that kind of shot on you anyway?* But for a short while Biggs was happy with what he had achieved. He later described the approval and admiration in his trainers' expressions as the highlight of his pro career.

A year later he would have to undergo a similar examination of his heart. On the undercard of the Tyson–Smith bout in Las Vegas, Biggs was matched with a stubby former contender named David Bey. 'He was from Philadelphia, like me, so there was a sort of pride thing going on there straight away . . .' Bey may have been proud, but his skills had never been more than basic; he had come up short in previous bouts with Larry Holmes and Trevor Berbick. His one-dimensional style should have made the fight the ideal opportunity for Biggs to showcase his Ali ingredients before the Vegas crowd and help to build up an impending challenge to Tyson that May. Instead, Bey thumped short right hands and hooks through Biggs's guard, roughed him up and slashed him above the eyebrows with cuffing blows to the face. His rhythm offset by Bey's awkward willingness to rumble, and bleeding profusely, Biggs was on the verge of being stopped when a last-gasp assault drove his opponent back into the ropes. Biggs let fly with wide blows to Bey's fleshy sides before bringing in the head shots. Biggs gritted his teeth and bled while his fists flew; Bey covered up, endured for a time and then eventually wilted as the crowd rose to its feet and applauded the turnaround.

Once again, the criticisms outweighed the kudos. Biggs had shown heart, a second wind, an ability to win against the odds. But he had been beaten on and wounded and nearly knocked out by an over-the-hill, balding old man who should not have been able to strike his backside with the proverbial handful of rice. Such was the gravity of Biggs's eye injuries, his fight with Tyson was pushed back to October, and in May Tyson feasted instead on Pinklon Thomas.

'None of those problems with my collarbone or eyes played on my mind at all when the time came to fight,' Biggs assured me in Texas. 'My thing was to just give Tyson a boxing lesson like he'd never forget. But then, as we got into the fight, things just happened where that wasn't gonna be the case . . .' Come October, Tyson vs. Biggs in the Atlantic City Convention Center was billed as 'The Clash for the Crown'. No one thought it was going to be Ali–Frazier any more. Biggs was a seven-to-one underdog. The bookmakers just couldn't make a case for him after two near misses against opponents who would have been unceremoniously shredded had they found themselves up against Tyson.

Still, Biggs looked good before the fight. He was tall and groomed and carried himself well, and when he held a Rolex wrist before Tyson at an early press conference he seemed confident enough. But by the weigh-in some suspected a slip in his resolve. A reporter from a British newspaper even claimed that the challenger had turned grey with fear after finding himself in close proximity to Tyson's naked, rhinoceros-like torso.

Today, Biggs will say that he gave Tyson a lesson in the finer arts of prizefighting for the opening round at least, and he may be right. He jabbed Tyson's head back and danced his circles. But after the first round Biggs suffered a slow-motion slaughter, his body dissected by a Tyson at his most vicious, his craggy eyebrows flayed open by the harsh brush of Tyson's forearms and laces. By the third round, he knew he could not and would not survive, let alone win.

Biggs's tracksuit and hairstyle before the fight had been Carl Lewis; his face by the time of the fateful seventh was strictly Picasso. The resistance was squeezed out of him by every weapon in Tyson's repertoire, until he was dropped heavily twice. The second time he toppled like a condemned building, his head coming to rest in a corner, legs bent up before him, eyes glazed, cheeks puffy with punishment and blood smudged across the white satin of his shorts as Duva and King screamed obscenities at each other.

'Every time I hit him, he made noises like a woman crying,' mocked Tyson afterwards. But even Tyson could disgust Tyson, and fifteen years later he told a reporter, 'I'm sorry for what I said that night. If I had a chance to speak to Biggs again, I'd tell him so. I never should have said those things that I did.'

Fort Worth, Texas, October 2003

There was something odd about Biggs playing the part of chauffeur, bagman, cheerleader or even camp coordinator for Kirk Johnson, but there had been numerous precedents in heavyweight boxing and they had been set by men vastly more accomplished than either Biggs or his chubby employer from Nova Scotia. John L. Sullivan had rallied behind the white man's call for Jim Jeffries to return to arms and rid the sport of its glowering, provocative black boogieman, Jack Johnson. In turn, Johnson had snootily offered his counsel to several of Joe Louis's rivals, while Louis himself had been a regular fixture in the camp of Sonny Liston.

Biggs may have been Johnson's driver, but despite living in Fort Worth his knowledge of the area was suspect. He arrived late that afternoon at the Southside Boxing Club, clad in a scruffy tracksuit, the soft overflow of his belly pushing at his sleeveless top. His big, wide face broke into a huge smile as he acknowledged Johnson and his trainer Curtis Cokes in mid-ring and shook hands with Johnson's sparring partner Ray Austin, a tall stylist from Cleveland with a swollen left eye.

When Austin stepped into the ring to spar, David Banner rapped about niggers and whores on Johnson's stereo system, and Biggs rested chin on hand and sporadically offered mellow, polite encouragement. 'I always joke with Kirk', he said to me, 'that if I'd had the power he possesses, I sure would have become heavyweight champion of the world.'

'But does he have the jab you had, Tyrell?' I asked.

He smiled sheepishly and ran a finger through the dyed copper tinge of his hair. 'Well, he got a pretty good jab there.' Johnson and Austin sparred for three rounds, while Cokes – a former world welterweight champion – studied their moves. A flunky videotaped their efforts and made me swear not to report what I witnessed. (Heaven forbid that the

Klitschko camp might discover that Johnson actually threw some punches in sparring.)

Biggs had teamed up with Johnson a few years earlier. As far back as 1988, after Biggs had lost for the second time – on cuts to Italy's Francesco Damiani, the same man he had beaten for Olympic gold – he had received a call from Johnson's co-manager Kenny Lillien, asking whether he would be interested in helping to bring the young Canadian amateur along. Biggs agreed and helped out occasionally as Johnson prepared for the '92 Olympics in Barcelona (where he was eliminated in the quarter-finals), but he still had several years to go before he could get fighting out of his own system. In 1989 Biggs, now managed by a racehorse breeder named Leslie Roncari who had never seen him box before, took a fight with the lumbering, stamina-challenged Gary Mason in London. Recovering from the flu, Biggs almost boxed Mason to a standstill, only to collapse from a short right hand in the seventh. In 1990 he accepted a bout with an up-and-coming Riddick Bowe, surprising Bowe with a whistling left hook before submitting to the younger man's superior strength and arsenal in the eighth. A year later he was annihilated in three rounds by the rapidly rising Lennox Lewis. Six years on from that one, he fought Larry Donald on a Native Indian reservation in Connecticut. Donald was another Ali impersonator, though not even as good at the act as Biggs had once been. He couldn't punch either, but by now Biggs was a walking accident, and after he was stretched in the second round he had to be hooked up to an intravenous drip while doctors checked on a minor heart ailment. Incredibly, he had one more fight – a gift really, against an overweight, part-time pug from Belize, whom he knocked out in two rounds. And that was it. All over. Back to travelling the country with his suitcase. Until he became reacquainted with Johnson.

Johnson had taken a liking to Biggs. Truth be told, Biggs owed his appearance on the Canadian's payroll to Johnson's charity. There had been a time when he had been allowed to spar with Johnson, but now Cokes didn't want anything to go wrong in the gym and he forbade Biggs from sparring any further. He could get in the ring with Johnson and show him a few moves if he wished, but there would be no more full-contact engagement. It may have hurt Biggs's feelings, but his pride seemed to remain intact. 'Probably now . . . well, it's possible we could spar next week,' he whispered to me as Cokes ordered the two heavyweights in the ring to separate from a clinch, but I knew there was no such possibility. 'Depends how things go. I want to start working out and getting some things together, you know? If they're willing for me to box, I'm ready to box. But really, I suppose . . .' He glanced at the floor, train-track scars above his right eye and the smattering of stitch marks on his left; gloomy, fleshy reminders of Bey and Tyson. 'I suppose I'm really just here to do some driving.' He supposed right. As Cokes had already explained to me, 'Hell, Kirk gets a kick out of Biggs being around, but we won't ever be using him for boxing any more.'

Biggs was eager to please those around him. He offered Johnson cherubic beams of approval, and whenever he felt the fighter's attention was his, he snapped out his left hand and suggested that the jab be fired 'like a pistol', twitching his forefinger back as though pressing a trigger as the left fist recoiled against thin air. 'Been pretty much living out of a suitcase ever since I started boxing,' he recounted to me in his Barry White bass. 'Philadelphia's my home, but even when I was younger, I always said I wanted to settle down anywhere other than where I came up. When I started boxing I was travelling for the very first time. I got the experience of seeing new places, getting a feel for it and having a better idea about where it is I'd like to go.'

'So Fort Worth is the place?' I asked.

'It just worked out that way. Came here a few years back to help Kirk out in camp. Curtis don't like it much here, but it's quiet and Kirk doesn't like being troubled when he's in training like he can be back in Dallas. I didn't plan to stay. But I met an Oriental lady who I got kinda close with, started hanging out together and we're still together, so . . . always did just wanna settle down really, find myself a wife, have a family, nothing out of the ordinary, you know . . .'

A buzzer ended the sparring session and Biggs broke off to unlace Austin's gloves and find him a fresh towel. 'Biggs, you be takin' Ray back to the hotel?' Johnson asked. A couple of the guys from the neighbouring gymnasium stepped inside and asked Johnson to pose for a picture. 'Get a picture of Biggs too. Hey, Biggs, over here man. Come and get your picture took. This is Tyrell Biggs, man. Remember him?'

'The thing is . . .' Biggs continued, when he rejoined me at the back of the room while Austin took himself off for a shower, 'this is my nineteenth year of being sober, and ever since I got sober, the main thing I had to be able to do was adjust and be able to change. That's what I've done. I've been able to adjust to whatever predicaments I've been in. So dealing with moving around and living like this has never been a problem.'

'You don't worry too much about what might have been? You don't think about the way you were supposed to be Ali and Tyson was going to be Frazier, and you were going to be a superstar?'

'Well, you can always look back and second-guess. Monday-morning quarterback, right? But shit . . . I don't care to do that.' The smile left his face and he appeared to think hard about something that was bothering him. 'I heard a lot about that Ali and Frazier stuff, but it didn't really stick in my mind at all. Ali was a guy who I liked a lot because his style was so different from all the other fighters. That attracted me a lot, I don't mind saying. I also admired Joe Frazier as well. I trained at Joe Frazier's when I was coming up. I liked Joe and all his family a lot, and I hope they felt the same way about me – I always thought they did. It's just that the way I was built . . . I felt better fighting Ali's style. But as far as Joe's determination and left hook . . . well, I picked up a lot of stuff from him too. When I took on this boxing thing, I just wanted to fight and be successful . . . don't take a lot of punishment. That was pretty much my only view . . . didn't see myself as the next Ali, even if other people said stuff like that . . . wanted to be the best I could be. Yeah, I expected me and Tyson to have a rivalry. Just like I expected to give him a boxing lesson. I never thought he ever was gonna be able to outbox me. And the time I was coming up, I couldn't help but think it would be Tyson I'd have to beat if I was gonna become champion, because there was nobody else. Tyson, when he was coming up . . . the ferocity, knocking everybody out . . . he was really, really busy. He was fighting every three weeks, whereas me – I was fighting every three months. Still, I knew what would happen. I knew that so long as I kept on winning, I would have to fight him. I think all the talk that went on about him wanting to get revenge on me for making him an outcast was a bunch of hype. As far as I'm concerned, it was all fabricated. We were pretty cool together in camp, as far as I was concerned.'

'You really felt that you were going to beat him?'

'Sure. I'm a competitor. I always believe I'm gonna win.'

'No doubts at all?'

'Well, I was 15–0 when I fought him, and I had an amateur record of 118–7. Maybe I should have been 20–0 as a pro before we met, but . . .'

'You were happy with the first round?'

'I had fun in the beginning.'

'And then things changed.'

'The way he was elbowing me and using his head . . . I guess his hand speed surprised me too. I knew he could hit, but I didn't know he could hit so damn fast.' Biggs shook his head ruefully. His beating had been different to the others Tyson administered in those days. For most of them, it had been quick – almost too quick for them to have to concern themselves with the small matter of pain. And even for those who gave Tyson rounds, it hadn't been so bad: Pinklon Thomas's briefly rejuvenated skills had kept him safe before everything caved in in the sixth; Bonecrusher Smith knew he was too far behind on points to win a decision, but his grappling game nullified Tyson's advances and there had been no prolonged beating. But Biggs – Biggs was tortured slowly. Even Tyson himself was to admit that he could have ended it all as early as the third round. He didn't, because he wanted Biggs's misery to continue. And what made it worse was that Biggs knew it. He knew it was over, that the cause was lost when Tyson just walked through his trombone jab and began the pulverisation of his body and mind.

'I kinda wanted to bang back at him for whatever reason,' Biggs explained. 'I wanted to get into more of a slugging thing with him, which played more into his game. And that's why the fight went the way it did.'

'So you knew what was coming?'

'I knew.'

'How soon did you know?'

'Probably around the third or fourth round. Probably . . . I knew I wasn't gonna be able to keep it up.'

'He said recently that he was sorry he said those things about you, you know . . . crying like a woman.'

'He did? Well, it's been a long time ago. What can you do?'

'You never see him any more? Never bump into him at the fights?'

'Haven't seen him since the year we fought. But I was up in California that November, a month after the fight, because I was dating this lady. And he was dating her sister! One evening I was coming up to her house to collect her, and who do I see walking down the path? Mike Tyson! We were kind of, "Hey there, how're you doin'?"'

'Did you stop and talk?'

'We spoke a little, then kept going. He was pretty friendly at that time. You've just gotta catch him at a good time, and then he's the coolest guy you'll ever wanna know. I guess when you . . . when you guys from the press . . . when you're around him, he has this whole dark side going on.'

'He never seems certain what he wants to do.'

'That's something we all go through. I kinda like the idea of doing a lot of things, but life don't always work out the way you want it to. I kinda like the idea of coaching the amateurs, taking some kids to the Olympics. I also like to do speaking work for kids with drug and alcohol abuse. I do that whenever I can. I'm involved with the AA, go on the lecture circuit and help out with several causes, as a matter of fact. And I still follow boxing today too, not just with Kirk. I'm pretty happy with my life. You deal with what life gives you. That's all I can do. I mean, it can be sad remembering I never won the title, that I never did beat Mike Tyson, but it's all been and done now. What good will it do if I walk around thinking about it? I was good at this sport one time, but it's been and gone. Tell the truth, I probably never stopped wanting to change the past, wanting to be the champ, until I stopped fighting for good. I made a big transition when I came off the drugs, and I'm doing the same thing now in retirement. It's something we've all had to go through. Some guys just can't leave it alone because of the money, their egos. Boxing, for boxers, is addictive. But I'm OK about it now.'

Biggs was keeping his head above water, surviving, getting by. He was doing what most of the rest of the world did, scrimping and saving and earning a few dollars here and there, but if his stay in Fort Worth was going to be anything more than temporary, he would soon need to think about other sources of income. Eight weeks later Johnson turned up at Madison Square Garden, droopy-eyed and hog-fat, and when his destruction at the sailing fists of Vitali Klitschko had ended in the second round, he was already on the same boardwalk of regret that Biggs had trod before him.

'This boxing game is fun,' Biggs had told me. 'But only for as long as you're good. When you stop being good, it ain't so fun no more.'

Seven: Generation Found

A Bug on the Windscreen

IN THE BEGINNING, BEFORE HE BECAME MIDDLE AMERICA'S Candyman, Tyson was loved. He was excitement, high-voltage night-time entertainment, an eighties icon. But what the media loved him for the most was his obliteration of the so-called 'Lost Generation' – the wasters who had clogged the arteries of the heavyweight division with their lethargy and indifference, and who had neglected their skills for the good life. Almost to a man, the eighties era of lost heavy-weights wallowed in the kind of junk-food binge Colonel Sanders would have prayed for. They grew fat, whiling away the days between scooping alphabet titles by loafing around their living-rooms and raiding the refrigerator. When eventually their turn came to roll with Mike Tyson, the ceremony at the scales would display more jiggling flesh than a photo shoot at a Hugh Hefner pool party.

If there was one outstanding candidate for the Lost Generation's poster boy, it was Tony Tubbs: a gifted amateur, one of the jewels in Muhammad Ali's boxing team, but perhaps the most vulnerable of them all. 'For three and a half minutes he gave Tyson a boxing lesson,' Larry Merchant told me, though he omitted to follow up with his oft-quoted remark, that by the fight's end 'TNT' Tony had become 'nothing more than a fat bug on the windscreen of Tyson's career'.

'He basically squandered his talent with drink, drugs, food – a lot of food – and a worrying lack of dedication,' said Bernard Fernandez. 'When Riddick Bowe was on the way up, he fought Tubbs in Atlantic City when Tubbs was basically just an old, fat has-been. There were more than a few of us there who thought Tubbs schooled him, even though they gave Bowe the decision. You could see it then – what Tubbs could have been, if only he had kept his mouth shut and not shovelled so much food into it.'

Cincinnati, Ohio, November 2003

He kept smacking me lightly on the side of the knee whenever a point needed to be emphasised. Then his conversation would slowly peter out, only to change direction as disconcertingly as he would decide to swing his car into the fast lane.

If the ageing process had hit Tony Tubbs hard, his ski hat and clothes disguised it well. In fact, if anything he looked like he had dropped a few pounds since his heyday. His speech, despite its unpredictable course, was reasonably clear and much lighter than the rasping glee of Tony Tucker or the husky, low enunciation of Tyrell Biggs.

'It bothered me when they laughed at my weight,' he said. 'People talking about how you look fat makes you feel like you're less than a person. You know, man, you doin' the best you can do . . . I mean, everybody can't be built like Holyfield or Schwarzenegger. Everybody got certain genes that are gonna make them a certain way. It's like all the media wanted to talk about was, "Whoa, he's gainin' weight, he's gainin' weight . . . he's doin' this, that and the other." Hey, I can walk around at two-forty, two-fifty and feel good. But no, the press always just wanted to talk bad about you. Kept going on about my weight, and I just kept goin' on, knocking folks out, and they don't care about that. Makes you angry.'

We drove through Cincinnati's projects, past acres of dereliction and towards Tubbs's home in the middle-class suburb of College Hill, a four-bedroom house he had purchased after winning the WBA heavyweight title in 1985, and the wisest investment of his life. Cincinnati had its boxing history too. It was the home of Ezzard Charles, the Cincinnati Flash, world heavyweight champion from 1949 to 1951. When the Brown Bomber Joe Louis retired, Charles whipped Jersey Joe Walcott twice; and when Louis launched his inevitable return, a shadow of the fighter he once had been, Charles whipped him too. And although Walcott took him out with one of the biggest shots in the sport's history third time around, Charles nearly ripped Rocky Marciano's nose clean off in '54 before it all went wrong for him in the eighth. Charles was a popular champion and a well-liked man. When he was the champ, he mingled in the neighbourhood and talked to the street kids. Cincinnati named a drive after him.

'There should be a Tony Tubbs Drive down there some time pretty soon,' Tubbs joked, but he wasn't without recognition in his hometown. At least, not from the kids on the street. 'Right now,' he said, leaning into the steering wheel and gesturing out towards the streets and shop doorways shrouded in autumnal gloom, 'there's always these young kids here in my neighbourhood who try to bother me. But I don't never let them get out of line where they don't give me my respect, know what I'm saying? Lot of them think they can just go around, do this and that, but I don't ever give them a chance because I always keep a pair of boxing gloves in the trunk.'

Until the day he died from a brain seizure that led to his pick-up truck careering into an electricity pylon, the kids in Knoxville, Tennessee had treated 'Big' John Tate mercilessly too. Big John had held the WBA title six years before big Tony, and he also had failed to hold on to it for long. A decade later, bloated and deluded, he chased a fight with Mike Tyson. The implausible hunt brought him to England, where he dropped a decision to a tattooed Liverpudlian named Noel Quarless, and at 281 pounds broke the record for the heaviest man to box in a British ring. Before he died, back home in Knoxville, he stole cinder blocks from convenience stores and slept rough. His mental state crumbled and the kids poked him and laughed, holding their noses away from his unwashed body and mocking his tattered clothing. Tate had had no answer to their cruelty.

'You take the gloves with you wherever you go?' I asked.

'Sure,' laughed Tubbs. 'And if the kids get too far out of line with me, I stop the car, get out there and smack 'em around a little bit! Hey, I may be in my late forties, but I've still got the speed! Some of the bigger kids . . . they try and take me on thinkin' they can handle this old man, but I give them a whupping!' We approached a steep rise, and Tubbs pointed out a dilapidated building that used to be a gym. 'Sometimes, you know . . . after I've given them their whupping, I try and tell them if they got into boxing properly rather than hanging on the streets, they could maybe become pretty good fighters themselves. Man, you never know what tomorrow might bring. Thing is with me man, I love Cincinnati but I hate Cincinnati, because the longer I'm here the more I'm bound to find an incident.'

He was right. Over the years he'd found plenty: driving under the influence of alcohol, driving without a seatbelt (some habits were evidently harder to break than others), possession of narcotics, intent to supply crack cocaine (frequently to undercover police officers who knew they could count on him for a felony disorder when things got dull down at the station) and failure to pay child support. Extending his stays in Cincinnati did Tony Tubbs no favours, but a stint spent training one Preston Hartzog – nephew of the actor John Goodman – in Bogalusa, Louisiana, had recently come to an end. Tubbs was still looking for fights. In the meantime he had moved back in with his parents. The place was crowded: he was sharing the same roof as a sixteen-year-old son named after his deceased younger brother, Derek, as well as his parents and an uncle with kidney disease.

'When I'm away from Cincinnati I can get things done, man,' he said, slowly slipping into another distorted conversation. 'I can get things moving. But this place stays the same. We've got two kids out here right now, good fighters; one's gotten lazy since leaving the Olympics and the other's going to court for some sexual act or whatever. This is not really a fight town any more. Detroit's a fight town. I'd like to go to Detroit. There's too many temptations here. I'm gonna get me a fighter that's gonna be a champion. Cincinnati's always been the town that I came back to relax and do what I wanna do, then go back to my job. I don't ever wanna get caught up in some of that other shit again. It's very tempting though. Matter of fact, way I feel right now, I'm about ready to get out of here again.'

In College Hill, Tubbs's neighbours were sweeping leaves off their driveways while barking dogs chased after mangled tennis balls. Tubbs ambled over to help his father unload a truck, shifting boxes and old tables to make room in the garage for the latest batch of second-hand furniture and boxes of bric-a-brac. In the yard, sunken in mud track, lay evidence of the Tubbs school of motoring: one vehicle fresh off a full-contact sparring session with a lamppost, another appeared to have been rammed by a Great White.

Roger Tubbs was an imposing man, taller than Tony and just as broad, with a dapper white moustache and hands as big as baseball gloves. Tubbs senior had sired between seventeen and twenty-three kids, depending on whom you spoke to, and fewer than half of them called his wife Leola 'Mom'. Leola Tubbs was pretty formidable in her own right, welcoming me into her home with a familiar and enveloping clench before ordering her brother Greg to give me a guided tour while she hurried off to an appointment in town.

If Elvis's interior designer had freelanced in the early eighties, the Tubbs household had surely commissioned him. As they entered the front door, guests were greeted by a coat of arms which appeared to show a pair of purple beavers munching their way through a sheaf of pink foliage. Covering the floors of two reception rooms lay a lurid, shagpile carpet. Leola's brother stepped over to a print of some waterfalls that held pride of place over an electric fireplace, and pulled a switch. 'Get a kick out of this every time,' he chuckled. As the picture lit up, tiny crocodile heads suddenly emerged from the foreground and a metallic sound of trickling water emanated.

'Four bedrooms upstairs, one downstairs,' he continued. 'And then right here we have some of Tony's trophies.' We stood in front of a cabinet containing some old belts and awards from Tubbs's amateur days. A framed poster of 'Tony Tubbs – W.B.A. Heavyweight Champion of the World' sat beside a sofa with gold-leaf armrests, and a pair of dusty gloves hung from a hook on the wall above it.

Even though Tubbs's moment in the sun had come in 1985, the cellar was clearly more a homage to *Saturday Night Fever* than to old-school rap. Why a diorama of wooden deer occupied one corner of the room remained something of a mystery. Greg turned just enough lights on for me to get the full effect. In a nearby alcove, cordoned off from the rest of the room by three ancient ropes that were badly frayed, scarlet and amber lights flickered down upon a disco floor. 'When he was the champ, Tony would have parties here all the time,' said Uncle Greg. 'We'd have celebrities and all sorts. Tony would stand in his boxing ring before the music began, and he'd grab a microphone and tell jokes, sing a few songs, just have a lot of fun, you know what I'm saying? We'd have singers, musicians, actresses, people from the fight game, they'd all come to Tony's parties, and Tony loved being the host. They were pretty cool, those times.'

'It doesn't look like this room's been used in a while.'

'Not for a long time. But I'm gonna start fixing it up next week, get it all nice and cleaned up before I move on again. It'd be nice to have some more parties in here. Maybe the next party could be in honour of one of his sisters. They're mostly school teachers, but one's into real estate. All doing well for themselves. Maybe they're gonna want to come back next year for a visit. That would be a good time for a party.'

'Tony's younger brother,' I asked. 'How long ago did he die?'

Uncle Greg took me back upstairs and showed me a picture of 'D' resting on top of a cabinet. 'He was sixteen, I believe, so that must have been twenty-five years ago. Nineteen seventy-eight. I'm sure it was seventy-eight.' D was a good-looking, strapping young fellow. There was a strong facial resemblance to Tony's own teenaged son, also named Derek. D got into an argument with a man much older than him at a nightclub here in Cincinnati. See, D was big for his age. He could handle himself. When it got down to fighting, D hit the guy and the guy ran away. But later that night, when D left the club, the guy came back and shot him dead.'

I sat before Tubbs in the kitchen, one of Leola's freshly baked seven-flavour cakes sitting between us in its cardboard container. He drank a glass of Sprite and delicately peeled away the casing before taking a knife to the cake's soft, sugar-sprinkled surface. Next door, Derek lay on his bed listening to music and Uncle Greg watched soap operas on a fuzzy TV screen. Upstairs, Roger was taking a siesta, and we all shivered slightly against the cold. Unless you pressed him continuously, Tubbs would jump from one subject to another, quick bursts of animation that were usually short lived. I knew he felt closed in, suffocated, by his inability to make a living from anything other than boxing and by the hopelessness of avoiding trouble in Cincinnati. I wanted him to take me back to '85, when he was the champion and the beautiful people came to his house to listen to him sing and tell bad jokes in his disco cellar. 'Man,' he sighed. 'The championship of the world – that was something I'd wanted ever since I was a kid.'

When he was young he had been a short, tubby child who wanted to run with the Cincinnati gangs. The gang-bangers had laughed at him, but he would not be dissuaded. He knew they met at night, under the street lamps, where they fought each other and their rivals for dollars and infamy. He met them there, on the sidewalks, and did not shy away from any of them. 'Once I got used to taking the pain, got used to getting hit in the mouth . . . busted nose . . . man, it was all easy after that. And when I seen that they was tryin' out for the local boxing team at St Mark's, I came down there to try my hand at it.'

What followed was not only a path to a title, but an intense rivalry that would bring together the families of Tony Tubbs and Greg Page, a sneaky customer from Louisville, Kentucky, who would one day be anointed by another Louisville resident, Muhammad Ali, as his 'heir apparent'. Tubbs ended up fighting and losing to Page in his very first amateur contest.

'I think Greg might have had about nine under his belt by then,' said Tubbs. 'Then, every time there was a tournament, it was always me and Greg in the top two. We was fighting for this tournament and that tournament, the Golden Gloves . . . when it was all over, Greg beat me four out of seven.'

The Tubbses and Pages went back a long way. Uncle Greg was best friends with one of Page's uncles, and Leola knew Page's parents. Later, Tubbs's half-brother Nate would date Page's ex-wife Brenda. Shortly after Tubbs challenged Mike Tyson in Tokyo, in March 1988, Nate was hired as a punch bag for Tyson. By then Page was Tyson's chief sparring partner, but unlike Nate he didn't seek to be friends with his employer. Today, Leola Tubbs still stays in touch with the Page household, asks if they need anything, while Page himself watches reruns of *Bewitched* and *Sanford and Son* on lonely mid-afternoons, the world drifting by outside his window as he sits at home in his wheelchair.

'Four out of seven,' sighed Tubbs, slicing himself ever-narrower slivers of cake, and playing with the moist crumbs between his thumb and forefinger. 'I said, "Damn . . . I know I can beat Greg, but sometimes it's like he's one step ahead of me." We were pretty similar. I had a lot of speed and talent. I could catch and counter, catch and counter. Greg had a lot of movement and a fast jab too. Greg could hit. I'm telling you, he could hit. We was faster than most of the guys we fought, yet the media just loved to get at us both about the weight by the time we were pros. They thought just because we came in a little overweight, we hadn't trained. I was outta the game, they used to say. But I was always fresh . . . always.

'They said Greg was the new Muhammad Ali. And I *knew* Muhammad Ali. Man, Ali was just it for me. I was in his team. He had about seven of us from his team become champions when we became pros. He was beautiful. Man, he could smack the skin right off you with his jab. I just look back at those times and just figure . . . everybody got to live their life how they wanna live their life . . .' I was losing him again, his words falling into whispers, but then he came back to me once more, smiling and offering me more of his mom's cake. Leola's baking clearly had much to answer for.

'Greg was a sensation at one time. He could dance. And pop the jab. I had more than a hundred fights as an amateur . . . Greg was the one I fought the first and the most. But I had the speed to trouble him. And as we got older, Greg never changed his style. I had Odell Hadley change my style a little bit when I turned pro . . . made me become more . . . professional. You never would have thought though, that one day we would end up fighting for the heavyweight championship of the world.

'It was in Buffalo, New York. I took a fifteen-round decision. Fifteen rounds, and they said I was out of shape. I had already knew Greg's style. He knew my old style, but I had changed. I started using feints and counter-punching. Greg was still a straightforward counter-puncher. And he could still hit. He could knock you out with either hand, but Greg never threw left hooks. He would jab and move back, jab and move back, and then try and counter you as you moved in with the right hand. Me and Greg . . . man, that night we fought for the title, I had the speed. After I won, I came back here to Cincinnati, they gave me the key to the city and got a whole lot of kids to walk with me through the streets. Hell, I think that was the best day of my life, and that's something they can never take away from me.

'I just wanna see that belt again . . . I just really feel it. I really do. I wanna see that belt again . . . but me and Greg? They were pretty good times, man. And Greg could dance.'

Louisville, Kentucky, November 2003

'How does that feel?'

'It hurts.'

'No!'

'Yeah, it hurts a lot.'

'Come on, just raise your fist.'

'No. It hurts.'

'Come on. How many times you had this fist raised during your career?'

'Whole bunch of times.'

'See . . .'

'But it hurts a lot.'

The Jewish Hospital lay just off First Avenue and Muhammad Ali Boulevard, and in the Frasier Center for rehabilitation and physiotherapy, a young, neatly groomed man in a crisp, white outfit cajoled Greg Page and pulled at his limbs.

'My leg hurts,' gasped Page, stifling and arching his body in pain.

'Come on, Turtle,' urged one of his daughters.

He wiped at his chin and lips, and when the saliva trickled down his throat, he choked and coughed for a full minute before the discomfort passed.

'Throw a left hook,' the nurse said.

'Can't,' spluttered Page, the tips of the fingers on his left hand trembling with the strain, but unable to form a ball. 'Damn left hand . . . nothing but a lazy bastard.'

On 9 March 2002, Page had boxed for the last time. He was forty-two years old and fighting for a purse of $1,500. That's about $600 after deductions. No one had a gun against his head. He was fighting for a title, but then every fight is for a title these days – it's up to the more discerning fan to work out which one's worth the effort. This fight was for the championship of Kentucky, and it was staged at a dingy restaurant and function room named Peel's Place, which would soon fail its environmental-health inspection. Page and his opponent, a muscle-bound bodybuilder and part-time barman named Dale Crowe, had to change in a building across the street and walk through the evening chill to reach the venue.

In the seventh round, Crowe clobbered Page with a hook. Page tumbled back, then slumped into a sitting position, his head and shoulders flopping against the ring ropes. It took fifteen minutes to determine that he had been badly hurt. Hours later, half of his skull was being removed to relieve pressure on his swelling brain. Already brain-damaged and barely clinging on to life, Page's condition got worse. His kidneys began to fail. The doctors feared imminent cardiac arrest.

He was in a Cincinnati hospital for four weeks. Somehow, he cheated death. Transferred to the Frasier Center in his hometown, he staged a near-miraculous recovery. Three months later he returned home, only to catch pneumonia.

The uncontrollable trickle into his lungs had triggered an infection, and he was back in the Jewish Hospital for a further four weeks before his condition could be stabilised. Now, continuing his rehabilitation as an outpatient, he became close pals with Dale Crowe, appearing with him on Health Channel documentaries and the *Oprah Winfrey Show*, and inviting him over for dinner. And when he finally persuaded Crowe to continue boxing, he was wheeled into the barman's corner, from where he would sit and shout and occasionally summon the strength to bring himself to his feet and strike the air with a lashing fist as Crowe went toe to toe with his opponent.

Late that afternoon, after two hours of physiotherapy which left him exhausted, we drove back to Page's home in a peaceful residential area of the city. In their small front room, his wife Patricia lifted him on to a makeshift cot. He motioned for me to sit next to him in his wheelchair. 'This is my wall of fame,' he spluttered between the hack of his cough and the struggle to swallow the slime in his wind-pipe. 'Everyone in this world that I care about.' Behind the swipe of his hand dozens of photos were fixed to the wall, most of them family snaps of his and Patricia's extended families, but one or two of faces from the fight game – Crowe, Gerry Cooney, Tim Witherspoon (who was raising funds to buy his old rival a specially modified van), even Larry Holmes – whom Page had once labelled 'a chicken-livered coward' for not agreeing to fight him.

When Page's mother returned to Louisville to watch him recuperate, she had been shocked by the experience: the sight of her strong son reduced to a state of dependence, the sentences slowed down by the congealed gunk in his throat, the video images of bone-flap surgery that Page kept putting on the VCR. She could not bear it for long, and before she departed with tears in her eyes she pulled Patricia to the side and whispered, 'He's pathetic. I can't stand it any more.'

But Greg Page would be happy to box on if he could. He told me so. As a kid he had set his heart on a basketball career; 'You can box or you can box,' Daddy Page had barked, so he had boxed, and been pretty successful at it too. He and Tony Tubbs had dominated the regional amateur scene. At Central High School in Louisville he was a popular kid with glistening jheri curls and smart new tracksuits. Patricia – his childhood sweetheart and now his second wife – remembered him walking old folk home and on one occasion chasing after a purse-snatcher who had struck beside the school gates. He never bragged about his sporting exploits; instead he gave motivational talks to kids with learning difficulties. He hated to party, even on the day in December 1984 he knocked out Gerrie Coetzee in South Africa for the WBA title. The only time he ever touched alcohol was when his mother gave him a hot toddy one winter, and he retched at the taste of the stuff. Yes, he would do it all over again if he had to, he repeated. He had no regrets about his boxing.

After he lost his WBA title to Tubbs in April 1985, Page became disillusioned with his profession, and although his chin remained a solid obstacle to fitter men's blows, he failed to win the decisions in important fights that would have provided him with another crack at the big time. He was still a name to reckon with, however: after Tyson wiped out Trevor Berbick, Page was one of the names Don King threw at the

press when they asked the promoter whom the new champion would face in '87. Three years later he was Tyson's sparring partner. At least he'd been given the opportunity to prove
a point to himself. When Tyson returned to Japan to make
the tenth defence of his kingdom against the laborious James
'Buster' Douglas in February 1990, Page went with him.

'I wasn't there to help Mike Tyson,' Page sputtered at home
in Louisville, sinking into the cot and gathering a blanket
around his chin so that only his face appeared above the bed
linen. Now I knew why he was called Turtle. 'I was there to
punish him. They thought it would be hard for me. It wasn't
hard. This is hard. This is the hardest fight of my life right
here, in that wheelchair and in this bed. Tyson was easy
compared to this.' He broke off for a moment, wincing as
he felt it coming: his face darkened and he tried to pick
himself up as the coughing returned. We limply raised his
pillows, and Page squeezed my hand against his side. The
flat, solid shape of the Baclofen Pump sewn beside his rib
cage weighed against my palm. 'This is hard,' he whispered.

When the fit passed, he sucked at the juice bottle thirstily.
'Tyson was a good fighter,' he eventually sighed. 'He knew
the basics. He trained good in the beginning. In Tokyo – my
timing was pretty good out there and Tyson wasn't training
so good. So I said to him, "You'd better start training or
Buster's gonna run over you." He reacted like he was
shocked, punk that he was, said he was gonna knock Buster
out quick and that Buster was nothing. I said, "He's not that
easy. Trust me. I fought him. I know. He's like a train. He's
coming straight for you." But Tyson just laughed, and the
asses in his corner weren't listening.'

The week of the fight, Tyson sparred with Page before news reporters and cameramen. 'He comes charging at me,' recalled Page. 'I throw a jab, then I move away from him. Then he charges me from another direction. Doesn't work. I follow him with another jab. Then I hit him with a double-jab. Then I throw the right hand behind another double-jab, and guess what? Bing!' The right hand sent Tyson scattering to the floor, embarrassed and outwitted by Page's manoeuvre. It wasn't as though Tyson was ignorant of Page's reputation for trickery. Two years earlier, with Tubbs convulsing in front of him, Tyson had rushed to throw another shot even as the Cincinnati Flesh completed a macabre little jig and melted into the canvas. It was in case Tubbs 'had been trying anything cute like Greg Page', Tyson explained later.

'Someone hit the buzzer,' said Page, catching his breath after every few words. 'Ding! Ding! Ding! They ended the round early. Oh man! I just wanted him to get up so I could do it again. They thought I was just gonna be fooling around in there. No. I didn't care about him or his money or his managers or his trainers. I was just trying to knock him out every day. That's all I ever went out there to do.'

Page didn't need any reminding about Mike Tyson. Out in Las Vegas, his first wife remained close friends with the former Iron Man. Whether she had meant to taunt him or not, earlier that year she had sent Page photos from their daughter's birthday party. In one of them grinned Tyson, leering suggestively and running a tongue over the party girl's face.

'Even when we were married, he was in my house more than I was,' Page muttered, drowsy but irate. 'Shouldn't really be saying it, but it's true. She allowed him in . . . I was always away working, trying to make money. How do I feel about him today? I feel he needs somebody to care about him, or else he's in trouble. Cus D'Amato . . . Bill Cayton . . . all gone. Who's left? Who's out there now who cares about Mike Tyson? No one. But then, who's out there now who Mike Tyson himself cares about? Maybe that's the question.'

Cincinnati, Ohio, November 2003

'Were you ever scared?' I asked Tubbs a few days after I had visited the Page family.

'Scared?!'

'Sure, scared . . . doesn't it even scare you now, fighting on the way you're doing, especially after what happened to Greg?'

'Oh, OK . . . now I hear you. Well, I'm never gonna get injured like Greg did. No way . . . I mean, anything can happen to you in that ring, but as far as Greg's injury goes . . . I really think he had an injury before he fought that boy in Kentucky. That kid couldn't beat Greg.'

'Maybe not fifteen years ago,' I ventured.

'No, man, not ever. Greg was winning the fight. He must have had something wrong with him before he got into the ring. Greg knew that kid couldn't beat him. He knew that. He knows that now.'

I doubted if he did. I suspected Greg knew full well that he was old enough and slow enough to have been vulnerable against a lot of guys. But for $1,500, I guess he needed the money.

'Can Greg walk yet?' Tubbs asked.

'No. Not at the moment. He's been out of physiotherapy for too long. Maybe after a few weeks of work he'll be able to walk a little again.'

'He still can't walk?'

'He did for a little while. He's not walking at the moment.'

'Oh.'

'Doesn't that worry you?'

'I don't think about that.'

'OK, were you scared when you fought Tyson?'

'No, man, let me tell you something . . . when you're a champion, what you got to fear? If I do what I'm supposed to do right, you're not gonna hit me and you're not gonna hurt me. And even if I do feel a little bit scared, well I'm just gonna fight better. I had the tools to beat Tyson too. Back then . . . Tyson was the new era. I fought the best guy in our era. No one was better than Tyson back then, but they only gave me three weeks to prepare for Tokyo. He was supposed to fight Tim Witherspoon, but that fight fell out and Don King rang me and told me to take his place. He had a contract with HBO, and he didn't wanna mess it up. I filled in for Tim, and I didn't really have a chance to get ready like I wanted to.'

It was March 1988, Tyson's final defence before his show-down with Michael Spinks in Atlantic City. A fight with Tubbs was never going to be a big sell in the US, but the Japanese had money to spare if it meant King could bring his premier attraction to their capital city. Tubbs was selected for his dura-bility. He had lost just the once in twenty-six fights – a major-ity decision to Tim Witherspoon in January 1986 that had cost him his beloved WBA belt – and been floored only the once, in his thirteenth fight, by one Clarence Hill. For one round Tubbs employed the lateral movement, nimble footwork, quick hands and sharp combinations that belied his pudding-like physique. In the second round he got caught by a left hand thrown so fast you needed an action replay to see it clearly. As Tyson's follow-up volley shot over his head, Tubbs caved in and quivered on the canvas, a slim stream of crimson trickling down the side of his face.

'That first round, man . . . I had him. I outboxed him in the first! Then in the next round he caught me with a left hook, and it hurt me. I should have put my arms out and held him instead of boxing him some more because we only had maybe ten seconds left in the round. Then I could have just come out and hit him with my jab. But Tyson was Tyson back then,' he laughed. 'That was the real Tyson you saw against me, not this guy you see in the ring today who knows he shouldn't be around boxing too much no more because his reflexes have faded. He cut me across the eye. When he knocked me down I started to get up, but Odell [Tubbs's trainer] said that I'd had enough. I had a cut. But shit, once you get hit, man, that's when you're gonna fight. See, a champion's always gonna want to get back up. Once you get hit by a shot, you know about it and you won't get hit by it no more. I always figured if I could take Mike Tyson over four rounds, that would be it for him. I still figure that could have been the way. It could have been a lot different, and Tyson wasn't the only person who made sure things turned out the way they did with my career because Don King has a lot to answer for as well.

Man, if it hadn't been for Don King, a lot of things would have turned out different.'

Sovereigns

A week before Tyson fought Lennox Lewis, King had been a little put out when I asked what his strategy might be for getting back into the big heavyweight picture, given that he controlled neither. 'Get back in? Get back in? How can I get back in, if I've never been out?' It sounded like a chorus written by some dodgy teen band, but before I had a chance to elaborate on the question, he was machine-gunning a tableside gathering of reporters with musings on Sir Winston Churchill, Voltaire, the IRA, Lazarus and 9/11.

No one else in the short and undistinguished lifespan of alphabet titles had made their political complexities work for him as profitably as King. The splintering of the heavyweight championship suited him just fine. It gave him more oppor-tunities to promote more fights as championship matches, to stretch out his arms and grab nearly every top heavyweight contender in the business, and to acquire lucrative TV deals with the big cable companies. If that wasn't enough, King even succeeded in having a number of his signings agree to management deals with his own stepsons, Carl and Eric. By the mid-1980s King exercised a despotic grip over the divi-sion. When King's unification tournament came to a head in August 1987 with Tyson squaring off against Tony Tucker, King's involvement in all things Tyson had widened consid-erably. Although he did not 'own' Tyson at the tournament's outset, King had realised that Tyson was too valuable to ignore.

King was notorious for the way he treated his fighters: his machinations infuriated Greg Page to the point, Page would later admit, where he bought himself a handgun with which to murder his promoter. On several occasions King slashed Tony Tucker's purses in order to make the numbers add up after some fanciful financial forecasts. He leapt over the semi-conscious form of Michael Dokes to embrace Dokes's conqueror, Gerrie Coetzee, a man he had previously lambasted for his Afrikaner roots. But of all King's fighters, Tim Witherspoon suffered the most at his master's hands. In billing 'Terrible Tim' for training expenses after the American had demolished Frank Bruno, King famously added an extra zero to one of the listed charges levied against his fighter's purse. Witherspoon took him to court and successfully sued him to the tune of $1m – a sum that lasted Witherspoon about as long as it took for him to wolf a pair of Big Macs. Years on from these unscrupulous dealings, Larry Holmes even believed he had a quiet, last laugh: he assured me that by attending all of King's publicity events and honorary evenings, he was killing the man who had once coerced him into fighting with a broken hand with the simple weapon of kindness.

Although King had no exclusive deal in place with Tyson after he beat Tucker for the undisputed title, Tyson's co-managers Jim Jacobs and Bill Cayton soon accepted his offers of title defences against Tyrell Biggs and Larry Holmes in Atlantic City. Beyond these two fights, King proposed a world tour of further defences – against Tony Tubbs in Tokyo, Francesco Damiani in Milan, Frank Bruno in London and Adilson Rodriguez in Rio de Janeiro – that would culminate in a triumphal return home for the long-awaited match-up with Michael Spinks. By the time of the Tubbs fight, however, Jacobs was losing his long battle with leukaemia. Jacobs never made it to Tokyo, dying before Tyson returned home. During the funeral, at which Tyson was a pallbearer, King courted the grieving youngster. Back on the east coast, Robyn Givens and her mother-in-law Ruth Roper were demanding access to Tyson's bank accounts and financial records. In Jacobs' will, complete control of Tyson's career was rather presumptuously bequeathed to Cayton. The time was ripe for King to make his move, and he did so not only by buttering up Tyson but by playing Cayton and the Givens–Roper axis off against one another.

On 27 June 1988, Tyson had arguably the finest night of his career, annihilating Michael Spinks in 93 seconds. That evening, before the fight, Cayton had received a letter by fax dismissing him from his management post. Among the letter's claims was that, despite his awareness of the gravity of Jacobs' bad health, Cayton had not kept Tyson properly informed of the situation. Tyson's relationship with Rooney too had become volatile. Rooney insisted that he was the only one who could ensure the young fighter realised all the prophecies D'Amato had made about him. But Rooney was no D'Amato, and Tyson, his ego and defiance growing daily, had become increasingly irritated with the trainer's style of direction. Days after Spinks's destruction, Rooney was handed his marching orders. King was within touching distance of sole control of Tyson's career. For a brief period over the summer, Tyson seemed reconciled to the idea of Cayton staying on board in a watered-down capacity, but the truce was short lived. Cayton was fired for good.

There are those who say that Tyson was ruined by the promoter, bled dry, misguided and robbed of millions. Others would have one believe that all the allegations against King were simply the latest in a long line of racially motivated character assassinations. The former suggest Tyson was nothing more than a gullible schmuck. The latter claim that King was no more manipulative than the next high-flying businessman. Both interpretations are naive.

'For a long time Tyson was going down a particular road, regardless of who was around him,' said Steve Farhood. 'Maybe Don helped speed up the process a little, but the reality is Jim Jacobs and Cus D'Amato created the monster all on their own. They were a hundred per cent successful in making a champion out of Tyson, and part of the adrenalin rush about Mike was his unpredictable behaviour. To blame everything that later happened to him on King is just nonsense. Those who do that are the same people who would have you believe King was responsible for the Holocaust, the Vietnam War and the assassination of John F. Kennedy.'

'But don't you see a pattern there?' Kevin Rooney, Tyson's trainer for his first thirty-five fights, would argue. 'The one thing all these guys who held the title for a few months had in common was King. The one thing that linked all the guys who ended up broke and fat and without any motivation was King.'

Tyson had been accused of sexual and physical assault long before he ever signed with King, but for all their short-comings, D'Amato, Rooney, Jacobs and Cayton had each been mentors in their way. King, however, showed little inclination to become a father figure. Once he had Tyson's name on a contract, he pretty much left the young champion to his own devices. Tyson ran amok at parties with John Horne and Rory Holloway. His training team of 'motivators', hustlers and wannabe gangsters was devoid of the tacticians and wise old-timers who might have nurtured his talent and kept an eye out for him when the gym door slammed closed at night.

Tyson would win two more title fights post-Spinks, before Buster Douglas and Desiree Washington put him out for the count. If he had been matched with anyone moderately better equipped than Frank Bruno or Carl Williams, his demise could easily have arrived sooner.

When a Tyson with his mind on other matters skipped towards Douglas in Japan and ended up on his back in the tenth round, the world saw one of those rare moments when the façade of King's integrity dropped. Infuriated by a slow count administered to Douglas two rounds earlier, King exploded at ringside, berating the WBC's portly president, Jose Sulaiman, and shouting obscenities at the referee. For twenty-four hours King and Tyson tried to deprive Douglas of his victory, and only in the face of a surprising and hostile public backlash did the pair back down. The Douglas fight was one point in Tyson's downfall for which King shared responsibility, for the men in Tyson's corner that night, and the ones who had been charged with looking after his affairs in Tokyo, had been appointed by King himself. The most damning indictment of King's treatment of Tyson, however, would soon prove to be his administration of Tyson's finances.

In May 1991, King was – not for the first time – the subject of an FBI investigation. A King employee, Joseph Maffia, had filed an affidavit with a New York court highlighting multiple instances of alleged purse-skimming. Tyson's name was there in the list of affected fighters.

Tyson responded to the accusations by stating, 'if Don steals every nickel, I'd rather for a black man to steal it than a white man'. King was exonerated of the charges. A year later, residing in an Indiana cell, Tyson had grown no more alarmed. When asked by CBS reporter Ed Bradley whether he felt King had ever taken advantage of him, prisoner no. 922355 replied, 'Everyone uses someone. He uses me, I use him. We've never misused one another. We respect one another. Don is my man. And that's all there is to it.'

Once the court case was over, King desperately tried to gather together the dislodged pieces of the heavyweight jigsaw puzzle that had dropped from his hands when Tyson fell to Douglas. Douglas had lost the titles to Evander Holyfield, who was promoted at the time by Main Events; Holyfield in turn lost to Riddick Bowe, a former Brooklyn neighbour of Tyson's whose affairs were handled by a bois- terous and staunchly independent former radio DJ named Rock Newman. And when Bowe dropped the WBC title in a London dustbin, it was Lewis who fished it out.

At the start of 1993, Bowe and Lewis were the division's rival champions, and King had no hold on either of them. But what he did have was a line-up of retreads and former alphabet champions for whom he could create unlikely title- shot opportunities. By March 1995, when Tyson returned to freedom after four years' imprisonment, the heavyweight division was once more drowning in alphabet soup, in part thanks to the inability of Lewis's and Bowe's managements in delivering a unification match, but also by King's adroit manoeuvres.

Not everything went swimmingly for King. Equipped with fresh evidence of wrongdoing, the FBI took up its pursuit of the promoter with added zeal. In his latter days behind bars, Tyson's queue of visitors had included a colourful mix of individuals seeking to usurp King's sovereignty by acquiring the boxer's services for themselves. Bob Arum made overtures, so too did Rock Newman, and Tyson enjoyed personal visits from Michael Spinks's man Butch Lewis, Razor Ruddock's guy Murad Muhammad, Akbar Muhammad, various other Black Muslim splinter groups, and a convicted fraudster named Harold Rossfields Smith. While King remained the favourite to re-sign the former champion, Tyson's conversion to Islam suggested the Muslim parties were in with a shout. Still, despite a long-running feud with the Muslims – he had once been severely beaten in Nassau for trying to muscle in on Muhammad Ali's final fight – King had worked profitably enough with the group before.

'Mike has no real choice but to box for me,' King chortled. 'I'm the man who made him sixteen million dollars in his last two fights, when he wasn't even champion. How else is he going to pay for more Lamborghinis and Cadillacs? By going to college?'

Tensions surfaced between King and Tyson within hours of the fighter's release. King had arranged a welcoming party for Tyson back home in Southington, Ohio. It was not a success. Not only had King invited a group of press to Tyson's home without the authorisation of Tyson himself, but the lavish banquet he'd provided included dishes of shellfish and pork. Tyson ordered the press out of his home and did not touch the feast. King's confidence sagged a little and, fearful now that Tyson would look elsewhere for a promoter, he begged the fighter to stick by him. With the FBI snapping at his heels, King needed Tyson more than ever.

Within days, Tyson appeared at a press conference in Cleveland, dressed in a boating hat, dark suit and shimmering pink tie. During the course of a seventy-six-second speech, he finally clarified his intentions: 'I will fight again and . . . confirm that Don King will continue to promote my fights. Don is the greatest promoter in the world . . . May Allah bless you.'

Whatever his motivations, King had displayed a certain stubborn loyalty to Tyson that included organising numerous rallies to proclaim the fighter's innocence in the face of rape allegations, and continued throughout the post-fight mayhem that followed Tyson's cannibal act against Evander Holyfield in June 1997. But while King stumbled to find excuses for Tyson's carnivorous assault on Holyfield live on air, Tyson's subsequent twelve-month bar from the sport by the Nevada Commission would set in motion a chain of events that would finally lead to King's fall from grace.

By the end of 1997, the IRS lumbered an inactive Tyson with a monumental tax bill in excess of $12m. In a desperate scramble to keep the fighter sweet, King went to the offices of Showtime, the network to which Tyson was exclusively contracted, but his request for a $5m advance on future Tyson bouts was turned down. There was better news when a $3.5m deal was made with the Worldwide Wrestling Federation (WWF) for Tyson to work as an enforcer at a showpiece wrestling event in Boston the following March. It was a modest but definite step towards alleviating Tyson's debt, but in the process King could not resist pinching a slice of the action for himself; he asked the WWF's overlord, Steve McMahon, for a $300,000 fee for the use of Tyson's likeness in a WWF doll. The rights to Tyson's image, King claimed, were his alone to sell.

This was arguably the catalyst for King's exit. No longer indifferent towards the persistent allegations of his promoter's treachery, Tyson sought the counsel of Irving Azoff and Jeff Wald, a pair of businessmen who had worked with George Foreman during the climax of his fairytale return to the top of heavyweight boxing at the age of forty-five. Tyson concluded that he had had enough of being taken for a mug; he was especially incensed that a Tyson doll could earn King a fortune, given the phenomenal success of WWF merchandise across America.

Tyson rushed to challenge King, and on finding him outside the Bel Air Hotel in Beverly Hills, he issued a stream of insults, shoves and slaps, culminating in a thunderous kick up the backside as King scurried towards the cover of his limousine. On 5 March 1998, the ditching of Don King was formalised. Tyson's lawyers filed a twenty-nine-page lawsuit against the promoter, including accusations that King had duped Tyson into signing complex legal documents, double-dipped from fight purses – including the levying of a $100,000 WBC sanctioning fee for a recent fight that had not fallen under WBC jurisdiction – and generally enriched his own empire at Tyson's expense. The suit concluded with the allegations that between 1995 and 1997 King had stolen over $45m from Tyson's earnings and that nowhere in the offices of DKP were there any serious financial records of Tyson's earnings, but simply numbers on scraps of paper. 'They were ridiculous,' scoffed one of Tyson's attorneys. In total, Tyson's suit sought damages of $100m. In response, King filed a counter-suit.

Four years on, seemingly resigned to the loss of his richest client ever, King looked at me, wide-eyed and innocent. 'So he's suing me for a hundred million dollars and I'm suing him for a hundred and ten. But when you look at what happened between us, he never really spoke to me about what went wrong. He just walked away. It's like having your wife, and you leave home to go to work one day, and when you return you find out she's gone. You don't never get no excuse why she left. There is no accusation or argument, so how do you resolve? In our country you've got the right to face your accuser. You've got due process, the greatest thing that ever existed on this globe, but I ain't never seen Tyson since the day he left me. Never, ever, other than on television. I seen him on television saying, "Hey, you took my money." No, man, I never took your money. OK, here's your accountant and here's your books, you know what I mean? That's what I would have said to him if he had approached me about this.'

Behind the scenes there were rumours that King was using all his resources to draw Tyson back into the fold, but King's words suggested that all bridges had been burned. 'Now I see him saying to people, "No one did anything for me. I'm all alone, Little Lord Fauntleroy. Nobody cares. Nobody does anything for me." No, man, we did a lot for you. We put our reputations on the line for you. He got so carried away, one time he even went on television and said, "Listen, man, I think my community betrayed me. I don't owe my community nothing. I wanna disassociate me from them. Don't get me wrong, I'm with no black struggle." That is totally unacceptable to me. Don't tell me that Tyson can blaspheme like that, against the very community that for right or wrong reasons, when he was convicted of rape, begged, pleaded and gave every way they could for him to have a second chance. He's a liar. He can't do that. He's becoming a walking billboard for the Ku Klux Klan. The Klan can call him their poster boy now, because they could not have a better example of what they've been saying for three hundred years now – that black people are depraved, lazy, rapists, savages, lecherous, that they don't wanna work – all these negative things, and Tyson's become the personification of them all.' He glared at me again, eyes wide and hands open before him. 'He is a traitor to our community,' he surmised. 'And they say a traitor is to be feared worse than a murderer.'

With or without Tyson, King would march on, the sharpest mind in heavyweight boxing, even if his empire had been diminished. Tyson had been his fattest goose, but there were always others waiting in the wings. As King liked to say, history had a way of replenishing itself.

'King is the greatest smoke-and-mirrors act of all time,' said Bernard Fernandez. 'He's the best at using duffle bags stuffed with hundred-dollar bills to tempt guys who traditionally would have been brought up without a pot to piss in. Don dazzles people and draws their attention away from the small print. He's the most effective, ruthless promoter that there's probably ever been.' But King wasn't the only one. As Pinklon Thomas would remark, 'Whether they fucked you hard or fucked you slow, they all fucked you.'

A decade after Tyson had ended Michael Spinks's career, Spinks's manager Butch Lewis, was sharing a rare, quiet moment with King before a show in Atlanta. While King had fallen out with most of the fighters he'd worked with in the past, Lewis and Spinks were still close friends. 'Butch,' sighed King, as the two dwelt on their relationships with their fighters, 'your mistake is that you fall in love with your guys. But when these guys have gone, we'll still be here. You can replace the furniture, but you can't change the house. We're the house, Butch. Do you get it now?'

Cincinnati, Ohio, November 2003

'I know that some of us have been more successful with our money than others,' said Tubbs, running a finger down the flat side of his knife and popping the cake residue into his mouth. He pulled the ski hat from his head and bent forward so he could slap the side of my leg again, baring his teeth in a remorseful grin that spread below his dark moustache. 'But most of us who ended up with nothing were with Don, you know? He was the one in charge of everything. Today I'm thinking, "Wow, when I see how much fighters are making today? Damn!"'

'It's relative though, isn't it? If you're going to blow one million dollars, you're just as likely to blow ten million.'

'No, man, it would be different,' he objected. 'My biggest payday was about half a million dollars, and after taxes I only ended up with two hundred and fifty thousand. That was my biggest payday. I won a million-dollar tournament once, but they only paid me a hundred and seventy thousand! That was crazy.'

'That wasn't King.'

'Still crazy. And anyway, they're getting a lot more than ten million dollars these days. They're getting between twenty-five and forty million!'

'That's inflation,' I offered. 'You can't blame King for pure economics.'

'But I've got some bitterness for Don. We were Don's fighters, most of us guys from the eighties. I think we should have ended up with some franchise or something. I don't care if it was a fast-food store or what, but Don had the money to do something like that for us. We helped him make money, why can't he do the same for us?'

'He did help you make money. Two hundred and fifty thousand dollars is a lot of money to most people.'

'He made us pay taxes on a whole lot of things.'

'Everyone has to pay taxes, Tony.'

'It's not right for us to be used and then don't have nothing left to fall back on.'

'But what about the money you did earn?'

'It weren't a lot of money. By the time we paid taxes on it, and get us a car . . . shit, that's it all gone. Now, if we had a good manager who had shown us how to make good investments . . . but we had no one to do that for us.'

'You could have found yourself an independent adviser,'

I suggested. I knew King was no saint, but he was hardly the only rogue in this business. No one in their right mind would have expected him to hold a grown man's hand and point him in the direction of a decent stockbroker.

Tubbs got to the crux of the problem quicker than I thought he would. 'Man, when I was fighting, I just thought there would never be no end. If I ever needed something, I could always get fights. You know, I got a little bit of property with my mother and all, but it's not like what I should have had. You always miss what you should have had.'

'There were no extravagances?'

'No. I mean, I may have had most of the jewellery and clothes I wanted, stuff like that, but when I started having all my kids, man . . . I couldn't do that no more. Don should stop one day and be looking back on his fighters, man, seeing what we may need. We made him money. Now look where he's at and where we're at, and tell me if that's right. Tyson will be all right. His only problems are when he's in the spotlight. All fighters are survivors, right? But it's all about money, nothing else. Tyson's got multi-millions of dollars man, even if it does seem like somebody's trying to sue him every day. His problem really isn't money or Don, his problem is the spotlight, because somebody's always gonna wanna aggravate him. See, a lot of fighters don't want trouble, but now and then you come across one who don't wanna do nothing else but fight. His problem's aggravation. My problem's money, and Don should have been there more to help.'

'But surely you were aware of his reputation,' I argued. 'Especially back in the days when you were at your best. It was no secret, the way Don liked to do business. He's always been very shrewd. Lots of fighters had complaints about him – Larry Holmes, Tim Witherspoon, even Ali.'

Tubbs thought about that one for a while and tapped me again. 'I was aware,' he said quietly, 'but back then the only way you could become heavyweight champion was by being with Don because Don had all the other heavyweights. He had them all. It was not like it is now. There's really no need for Don King now. But back then . . . back then it was different.'

Later, he drove me back through the outskirts of Cincinnati, laughing in embarrassment at the statistics of his rampant fertility, which would have done his own father justice. Sixteen kids and counting! He was a little sheepish but also a little proud of the numbers. They looked like increasing: he had just been ordered to take a blood test to reveal whether he was the father of a twenty-two-year-old kid he had yet to set eyes on.

Even though he knew he was not the fighter he once had been, he still swore he could be competitive provided he took an opponent past the fourth round. Which would have been troubling enough even if a young Ghanaian named Abraham Okine hadn't recently dispatched him in the eighth round. ('He could never knock me out,' Tubbs said. 'But he did, Tony. He knocked you out.') But it was all irrelevant really. This wasn't a pursuit of former grandeur but something even more morbid. Tubbs had trapped himself, become a slave to the fight game, because there was simply no other way he could afford to maintain himself and his offspring.

'I'm just trying to see if I can take some fights that can take care of this child-support thing going on,' he said. 'See, they're trying to get me to pay up now. I don't have much more time left to give them what they're asking for. Then there's the back payments they're trying to get from me. And I honestly don't know if I can do it without fighting again. I honestly don't. I could sell the house. It's sad, man. I really feel like I should have a pension or something to help me, especially when I paid over a million dollars in taxes. But I've got nothin' comin' to me when I'm older, and I've got a lot of money to find right now, and I don't see the situation changing. Ever.'

Epilogue: The Longest Round

Memphis, Tennessee, February 2003

THEY BROUGHT MIKE TYSON BACK TO THE PERSECUTION CHAMBER of the Pyramid Arena just eight months after his loss to Lennox Lewis. This time though it would be Tyson's turn to administer a world of hurt, to an ex-con from Baton Rouge in Louisiana named Clifford 'The Black Rhino' Etienne. There was money to be made, debts to pay off, illusions to be spun in dreamy old Tennessee: the Tyson carnival was working its way to another meeting with Lewis. Lewis himself was willing, anxious to accommodate Tyson via the rematch clause in their initial fight contract. Usually such stipulations were there for the benefit of the loser, but Tyson was boxing's biggest banker, and Lewis had been hinting at retirement parties and lazy afternoons on Jamaican sands if the match couldn't be made.

Economic compulsions had pushed Tyson into their first fight; he had been on the back of nine months' inactivity and without a victory over a rated contender in more than five years. The beating he had suffered at Lewis's hands was still fresh in his mind. If they were to collide once more, he promised, he would prepare right. 'I felt purified after that fight,' Tyson disclosed. 'It's like he whipped my butt and baptised me at the same time.' But his new-found humility had its limits. 'I might have kissed him after our first fight,' he admitted, 'but I'll crush his head next time!' Before he could do that, though, Tyson wanted a warm-up fight. The opponent he selected, Clifford Etienne, was eminently beatable.

The build-up was, as ever, extraordinary. On 12 January, divorce proceedings at Montgomery County Court in Rockville, Maryland, between Tyson and Monica Turner had come to an end. Tyson had remained in training camp for the duration of the case, but in his absence he had been ordered to pay an estimated sum of $9m to his ex-wife, as well as having to hand over a $4.75m mansion in Farmington, Connecticut, and another residence in Potomac worth $4m. Turner had also acquired custody of the couple's two children, and a percentage of all the fighter's future purses.

If Tyson found the divorce settlement objectionable, he had kept his feelings well hidden. The general mood in his Las Vegas training camp a fortnight before the Etienne match had been light-hearted. Tyson had enlisted the services of another new trainer, the redheaded, bespectacled Freddie Roach. A former pro and protégé of the late Eddie Futch, the onset of Parkinson's disease had failed to stunt Roach's growing reputation as the best young trainer in the business. He had a reputation for softly spoken, low-key relationships with his fighters, which were in contrast to the mentors with whom Tyson had worked as a teenager – the ranting philosopher Teddy Atlas and the simpler though no less excitable Kevin Rooney.

But Tyson's various 'issues' quickly resurfaced. On 15 February, exactly a week before the contest, the former champion was a no-show in training. Rumours began to circulate of the fight's cancellation. Press events were postponed, frantic phone calls were made and Tyson was photographed stepping out of a limousine with a Polynesian warrior insignia tattooed upon the left side of his face. That evening, Tyson contacted Roach and informed him not to bother meeting for their routine 5 a.m. run the next day. He also suspended any rope-skipping and other exercises that would cause further stress to a claimed back injury.

The next morning, Shelly Finkel told the press that Tyson 'might have bronchitis. Mike's been experiencing a bad case of diarrhoea and other temperature trouble.' On the Tuesday, the bout was officially cancelled on the grounds that Tyson had been bed-ridden with the flu. But when Showtime made threatening noises about withholding money and leaked news that it would seriously reconsider any future dealings with the former champion if Tyson's complaints proved to have been exaggerated, Tyson recovered in record time.

Tyson may have been ready to fight again, but his opponent was not. When the match had looked dead and buried, Etienne had consoled himself with a few beers too many. Having broken his monastic preparations, Etienne was no longer in the mood for battle. He insisted that he had been played a fool and wanted no further part of the promotion. By Wednesday morning, however, Tiffany Etienne had persuaded her husband that throwing away the best part of $1m was a little extreme. The fight was back on. Everyone was happy again; Showtime had its main event, the people of Memphis had something to do on a Saturday night, Mrs Etienne could return to her home-decorating catalogues, and on the Friday before the fight Tyson got to grasp the nubile rap star Lil' Kim at a public workout.

And when the official action eventually got underway, it lasted all of 49 seconds – a booming right hand struck Etienne on the side of the face and left him in a sprawling heap on the floor, eyes agog and chest pitching as he struggled to remember what planet he was on.

The Longest Round

Within a few months, it was all coming to a close. Not only for Tyson, but for those who had been able to best him in the ring. By the summer of 2003, Evander Holyfield had won only two of his seven previous contests. That June, Lewis struggled frantically against the hulking Vitali Klitschko before a labyrinth of facial lacerations upon the towering challenger's face eventually saw his lead on the scorecards rendered irrelevant.

Lewis had been out of action for the twelve months separating the Tyson and Klitschko fights. The Tyson rematch seemed ever further away. The real action was now outside the ring. Lewis's business manager Adrian Ogun started filing lawsuits: not only against Tyson, but also Don King for allegedly interfering with their negotiations.

It looked more and more likely that Tyson had had enough. But how was he to set about making a life after boxing when the turbulence in his personal life remained rampant? In an interview on Fox News Tyson appeared to be losing the plot altogether. 'I really wish I did [rape her] now,' he snarled when the subject of Desiree Washington was raised. 'I really do want to rape her and her mama. [Washington] is a lying, reptilian, monstrous young lady.' A day before Lewis nearly came unstuck against Klitschko in Los Angeles, Tyson was arrested on an assault charge after becoming involved in an altercation outside the Marriott Hotel in Brooklyn. A group of drunken idiots had taunted and physically provoked him when he had refused their request for autographs.

On 1 August, Tyson filed for Chapter 11 bankruptcy in New York, disclosing that he had squandered somewhere in the proximity of $500m since the start of his career in 1985. His debtors were everywhere: the IRS, the British Inland Revenue, law firms, financial advisers, music producers, the mothers of his children, former trainers, psychiatrists, wives, attorneys, estate agents, managers, promoters, victims of unwanted and overzealous sexual advances. So submerged in debt was Tyson, *The Ring* magazine was left pondering, 'Even if he wins [his lawsuit against Don King] and collects the full sum, how far can Tyson stretch that paltry $100m?'

Of course, it was all relative. Tyson could probably no longer pop into a car dealer's to purchase a Lamborghini coupé on tick (it had taken some persuasion to prevent him treating himself to a Formula 1 car during a trip to England), but he still had numerous assets: a mansion in Connecticut once valued at $25m went for a bargain $4.1m – despite its twenty-eight bedrooms, indoor racket court, nightclub, theatre and essential everyday waterfall. And then there was his marketability, which was still huge in a lot of places. Not least the Far East, where Japanese promoters were eager to stage a showdown between Tyson and Bob Sapp, a 360-pound colossus and former offensive linesman from the American-football college circuit, under K-1 kickboxing rules.

If money could be made from suing King and kicking the crap out of Sapp, maybe the supposed inevitability of Tyson's ruin and the depressing extension of his boxing career could be avoided. But either way, the forecasts for Tyson weren't great. Here was a man who nearly always failed to keep his emotions in check. It was arguable whether Tyson and the rest of the world were safer when he was slipping through the ropes to fight or stepping out of them to deal with life's little upsets and the small matter of multi-million-dollar debt.

Carl Williams found it hard enough to be an everyday citizen and employee; Tyson's ego had much further to fall. Pinklon Thomas had turned all manner of hell into purposeful enterprise, working with kids and chipping away at their inadequacies; but Tyson was no mentor – he was more like the kids who sat before Mister Pink in their multi-coloured T-shirts, just bigger and angrier and further along the road to no return. Marvis Frazier had grown into a man of God, a preacher whose ministerial trails passed through prisons and churches and community groups and foster homes; religion had provided little shelter for Tyson, who had been betrayed by Christian and Muslim alike. Tony Tucker struggled along in anonymity, working the sordid Toughman circuit along the Florida coast, partially disguised by the grey wisps in his hair and the shades over his eyes; Tyson could shave his head and grow a two-pronged moustache, paint his face with Oceanian battle symbols and bury himself under fur coats and lumberjack hats, but he would always be recognised and hounded.

'I'm a big, strong nigger that knocks out people and rapes people and rips off and bullies people,' he trilled outside a TV awards ceremony in September 2003, before planting a kiss on his latest girlfriend, the actress Luz Whitney. 'I haven't received any dignity from boxing. I received a lot of pain.'

Things just hadn't turned out the way they were meant to. Everything had been so finely orchestrated in the mid-eighties. Whether one believed in the fables about Cus D'Amato or the paternal influence of Jim Jacobs, the meticulousness and ingenuity of Bill Cayton or the robust jockeying of Kevin Rooney, the path originally mapped for Tyson's career had been the envy of all those who came to challenge him. When I asked his old rivals what Tyson most needed in his life today, to a man they named the pivotal figures of the mid-eighties. I asked Carl Williams as we traipsed through the debris of Ground Zero; Pinklon Thomas as we left the gates of the Center for Drug-Free Living; Tony Tucker, as he leaned against a brick wall in Tampa and put on his game face; Marvis Frazier as we waited outside the doors to his church and watched the congregation filter on to the streets of South Philly; Larry Holmes as he gave me a guided tour of his property developments in Easton, Pennsylvania; James Bonecrusher Smith as we sat in the sunshine and watched a regiment of Hell's Angels and war veterans in 'Rolling Thunder' jackets gun past us on their Harleys; Tyrell Biggs as he helped remove sweaty hand wraps from Kirk Johnson's fleshy hands; Tony Tubbs as he careered around the suburbs of Cincinnati without a seatbelt on; and Reggie Gross in letters I posted to him as he languished in a jail cell.

They all mentioned the same names: D'Amato. Jacobs.

Cayton. Rooney. But D'Amato had died before Tyson had become champion, Jacobs had followed three years later. Cayton passed away on 4 October 2003 – a month after Tyson complained that boxing had brought him only pain – and Rooney was just another on the long list of those Tyson had rejected, still listening to ghosts in the Catskills, barely recognisable from the man who used to hug and kiss and slap Tyson in the corner during fights. He had put on the pounds, and he was bald. He was grey stubble and the whiff of Jack Daniel's. And while he would hate to admit it, he was like the men who sat in expectation of Godot, waiting for Tyson to make the call.

May 2004

As I write this now, Mike Tyson's future is as uncertain as his peers', but what he goes through will be no different in kind to what any of the others have faced before him. Even his conquerors have struggled to attain contentment: Buster Douglas survived a diabetic coma and today lives humbly and without fanfare in his hometown of Columbus, Ohio, where he trains his kid brother Billy, himself now an aspiring heavyweight. Evander Holyfield, the anti-Tyson for the majority of Tyson's career, and twice the truth-teller of Tyson's frailties, now shares the same foolhardy dreams as the lesser lights who crumbled where he triumphed. Lennox Lewis at least chose to call it a day while he was still on top of his game, proving – for the time being – that the ending need not necessarily be grim. Even most of the strugglers have yet to crash and burn completely. Though men like Greg

Page and Tony Tubbs and Tyrell Biggs seem prime exhibits of physical, mental and psychological damage, simply getting by for as long as they have done is something of a testament to their will-power and fortitude. And some of that will-power and fortitude is down to boxing.

'Boxing gave a lot of these guys some kind of form and discipline from lives that were otherwise not very goal-oriented,' said Larry Merchant. 'Whatever went on or is going on in their post-boxing lives, the sport did at least give them a few moments in the sun that they otherwise would not have had.'

'Obviously, Mike Tyson's not heading towards a positive ending,' was what Teddy Atlas told me. 'He will just keep on doing what he's always done. He doesn't need to look at any of these other guys to see how he can best go wrong. He'll just do what he's done all his life, which is to never think about anyone or anything else, and how they'll be affected as a consequence of his actions. He's been heading for a cliff face all this time, and now he's just getting nearer and nearer to it.'

'There are two ways of looking at this, and the first is what Larry Holmes predicted a while ago when he said that Tyson would either end up dead as a young man or else in jail for the rest of his life,' said Steve Farhood. 'And there does seem to be that inevitability about him. But I also think Tyson's something of a survivor. After all, if you said back in 1989 that Tyson would still be fighting and making big money in 2003, the response would have been, "No way, how could that possibly happen?"'

It looks like the money and the fighting is reaching its

end. I am certain Tyson will box again, but doubt he will do so more than two or three times. He still has enough to beat a lot of heavyweights out there, and by all accounts he could do with the extra cash. But he fought just the once in 2001, once in 2002 and once again in 2003. He could easily line up a diet of so-called 'tomato cans', and knock one down a month in return for some heavy loose change. But Tyson's financial woes demand big fights, just as Joe Louis's before him. And that means tangling with the kind of opponent who can hurt him, as they did the Brown Bomber.

'What's he gonna do, flip burgers for a living?' asked one of his former trainers, Tommy Brooks. 'No, that's not happening. I hate to say it, but ultimately Mike's either gonna end up hurting someone, or else someone's gonna hurt him.'

'I hope he's looked after,' said Ronnie Shields, another former mentor. 'He's still so vulnerable in certain situations. I just don't know what he'll do when it's all over. Mike and I never talked about that. Never, in all my time with him, did he discuss how he would deal with retirement.'

'Of all the heavyweight champions in history, Tyson has shown the most signs of [being] a sociopath, so I don't really know where that mentality will eventually lead him,' offered Larry Merchant. 'I suspect that ten years from now, some promoter will offer him a fight on TV that will supposedly lead to another title fight. Or else one of those wrestling promoters will make him an offer he can't refuse. And eventually he'll go out with his guns blazing in some incident. Whatever happens, it's unlikely he'll end up destitute. You see, most of Tyson's fans are Tyson fans and not boxing fans. Presumably, they'll follow him to the very end.'

'You know what? I worry when I don't see Mike Tyson on the news,' Bonecrusher Smith had chuckled as we sat in his car in the middle of Raleigh, North Carolina. 'Because when I see him on the news, I know where he is and you don't need to worry. It's when he hasn't been on for some time that you start to think, "Uh-oh, where's he gonna spring up from next?" But even though I may not know where he is right now, I know where he's gonna end up.' Then he had looked at me and smiled, his stout body bulging in its red flannel shirt and grey slacks, one hand patting at the sizeable paunch hanging over his belt, the other wagging an index finger in front of us. Eyes that were peeled back and bulged like a salamander's beneath the dome of his head urged me to get the joke, and when I followed the line of his finger once more I finally got it. Outside, leaning against cement posts and sitting on benches and squirrelling in rubbish bins, wandering men held beer cans wrapped in brown paper bags and argued with their shadows. 'You wanna find Mike Tyson in twenty years' time, you could do worse than check out your local bus terminal.'

The likelihood is that Tyson will borrow pieces from each of his former rivals' destinies. Though the outlook appears bleak and there are many who predict more than just financial ruin for the man before he reaches old age, sporting bad boys can linger – cursing, ranting, drinking and rattling their way along as the years pass by.

Ultimately it is up to each man to decide his own fate. Carl Williams knew that, each night he arrived in Grand Central for the graveyard shift. What was it he had said about looking nowhere else but the mirror to see who was responsible for the faults of his past and the fruits of his future? Whatever the case, I was grateful for the time I'd shared with these men. Grateful for what they had shared with me about Tyson, but more grateful for what they'd shared with me about themselves – about their times in the ring, and the greater fights they'd faced outside.

At the time of writing, Mitch Green is somehow avoiding trouble and keeping out of the headlines. Marvis Frazier is as cheery as ever, still fighting the Lord's corner, preaching to the sceptics in Philly's ghettos, deacon and counsel to many, not least Papa Smoke. In Jamaica, Trevor Berbick escaped charges of breaking and entry when a kindly aunt dropped legal proceedings against him. After asking the former world welterweight champion Lloyd Honeyghan to act as his representative, Berbick is looking to launch a comeback in Britain. He has yet to provide anyone with proof that his loss to Tyson in November 1986 was rigged. Pinklon Thomas continues to work at the Center for Drug-Free Living in Orlando, while not far away Tony Tucker trains fighters on the gruesome, almost no-holds-barred Toughman meatwagon. Tyrell Biggs has bags and will still travel; Tony Tubbs wants to get away from Cincinnati but has no job offer on the line. And the building that Carl Williams patrolled throughout the dark, lonely nights at Ground Zero was eventually condemned and destroyed.

Almost four years ago, I initiated a correspondence with Reggie Gross, one of Tyson's twenty-two first-round knockout victims. Like Tyson, Gross was denied a paternal influence growing up: at three days of age, his father, Russell Alston, was knifed to death during a West Baltimore street fight. Like Tyson, Gross spent several years in homes for juvenile offenders after being arrested for purse-snatching. And like Tyson, in adversity Gross turned to boxing. But as Tyson's fame and reputation exploded, Gross's dreams collapsed. In 1983 he was introduced to cocaine on a car journey to Atlantic City. He never looked back. The following year his five-year-old son died from the terrible burns he received in a fire at his grandmother's rowhouse. Gross soon started running with a friend named Warren Boardley. By 1986 Boardley had become Baltimore's most ambitious and ruthless drug dealer. Gross was employed as hired muscle and more in the Boardley gang's turf war with a pair of brothers named Spencer and Alan Downer.

In September 1986, three months after his Madison Square Garden bout with Tyson, Gross was charged with three gangland slayings: the first on Fayette Street in West Baltimore, when he shot a Downer aide named Andre Coxson once, then a further five times as his victim tried to crawl to safety; eleven days later, two more Downer Gang members had been machine-gunned to death on nearby Gold Street. Gross pleaded guilty to the charges in 1989, explaining at the time that he was 'strung out on heroin' and that on Gold Street 'there wasn't supposed to be no killing'. Gross was handed two life sentences.

Gross's first letters to me concentrated mostly on his time as a fighter. He gave me a short account of his career, mostly detailing the build-up to his contest with Tyson in New York. Attached to this essay was a photocopied picture of him as a smiling and victorious amateur being interviewed in the ring by Sugar Ray Leonard. 'I had a special gift', he wrote to me, 'and I blew it. I know I would have been up there with the best.' In 2001, after Hasim Rahman – a Baltimore neighbour of Gross's – won and then lost the world championship to Lennox Lewis, Gross was the subject of four feature stories in Maryland newspapers. He was grateful for the short burst of recognition. Come the following year, he was receiving the occasional telephone call of encouragement from Tyson and was looking forward to being transferred to a prison nearer to his family in Maryland.

'I've only seen my daughters once in the last twelve years,' he wrote. 'But I have requested a transfer and it could happen any day now. Also, I have been communicating with Mike Tyson again. He sent me some pictures. He a good man and have a good heart. Peace out, Reginald R Gross.'

But come the summer of 2003, Gross had been transferred not to Maryland, but farther west, to Alexandria, Louisiana. His words were now disconsolate. 'I'm still trying to maintain my sanity . . . I'm fucked up.' I had received permission to pay Gross a visit in South Carolina, but his new institution made no such allowances. In the fifteen years he had been incarcerated, Gross had received a single visit from a teenaged daughter, one from a reporter working for the *Baltimore Sun* and a handful from his former trainer, Mack Lewis. But Louisiana was too far away for his daughter to maintain personal contact, the reporter had his scoop and Mister Mack was approaching eighty-five. In November, I heard from Reggie again:

In my fifteen years of being behind the wall, this is the worst prison that I've been in, and it's not the inmates. We're on lockdown now. The whole prison is. This is day eight and I don't know when we're coming off. To tell the truth, this is the most peaceful time. I have to do a year to eighteen months clean before I can transfer again. I been in Lewisburg Penitentiary and Atlanta Penitentiary – which are the worst penitentiary's in the federal system – as far as inmates are concerned; five years a piece in each. Only the strong survive. Then I graduated to FCI [Federal Correctional Institutions] which is suppose to be better, and it is. I got there for staying out of trouble. The bad ass that I was suppose to be, made it. Now I'm just working on my case, trying to make parole if I can't get my case back into court. I was almost five years into my stay at Edgefield but I heard about [Alexandria] through the inmate communications line. It was killings already, fights all the time and it's full of gang-bangers. I never wanted to come back to a place like that again. I made it through Lewisburg and Atlanta, then what happens? They need bodys in Louisiana, my name is called and now here I am, all over again. We're on lockdown now because about forty guys fighting on the yard, twenty Caucasian against twenty black. I was looking through my window in my cell when the fight come off. I knew the lockdown was coming, so I hurried up and filled my containers with ice. Prison is not supposed to be good and happy, I really do understand that. When the judge sentence me to life, he told me to educate and better myself for re-intro into society. I'm doing that. But my release date is 2048. Do you think I'll still be around? But a third of my time is 2009 and

I'm under the old law that says you're supposed to do a third before your first parole hearing. That's why they sent me back into a prison like this. I can handle myself wherever they send me because I'm a man, and I'm respected for not being a snitch. [They're] doing their best to trying to break me, [but there's] only one way to get me started, and that is to put your hands on me to harm me. Tell me, who really wants to be the one to do that and get me started? But that ain't what they're trying to do. It's the mind [they are] trying to get. I do my best to stay from everyone, the guards and the inmates. I stay to myself. I'm a true loner. I don't talk to my cell-mate when we're in the cell – is that being alone or what?! It's hard for me to trust anyone. The things that I really want to say is deep. This is just a little steam I'm letting out here. You can't hold on to too much steam before you burst.

While Reggie Gross battles for his sanity and squeezes every droplet of faith into a parole hearing more than five years away, he knows of only one fact concerning his future other than death: if the parole hearings fail, he will be three years shy of ninety before he gets a second chance at life after boxing.

Statistics and Alphabet Soup

PROVIDING A DETAILED EXPLANATION FOR BOXING'S EVER-expanding proliferation of governing bodies would require many, many pages. Suffice it to say that there is no legal obstacle to prevent your own next-door neighbours from initiating their own sanctioning organisation and rewarding title belts to whomever they please. The four most established governing bodies are: the World Boxing Council (WBC), the World Boxing Association (WBA), the International Boxing Federation (IBF) and the World Boxing Organisation (WBO). That these are the most established is not, however, an endorsement of their legitimacy. Each has been repeatedly guilty of decisions and rulings which stretch the outer limits of the absurd, and all are principally self-serving. If you are looking for a fair-minded idea of who today's real world champions are, buy yourself a copy of *The Ring*, *Boxing News* or *Boxing Monthly*.

It has been commonly accepted for several years that any fighter who won the WBC, WBA and IBF titles in a particular weight class would be described as an 'undisputed' champion – the WBO being the newest of the big four outfits and therefore the easiest to disregard. The term 'linear title' was advocated by *The Ring* during the unification tournament which crowned Mike Tyson undisputed ruler in 1987, when the magazine went to great pains to point out (correctly) that Michael Spinks's claim to the world heavyweight championship could be traced back via linear descent to the retirement of Rocky Marciano in 1955.

The following records contain dates, venues, opponents' names and results of fights. There are several ways in which a fighter's résumé can be recorded and particular differences between American and British presentation. The method below derives mainly from the American version. Here is a key to the symbols used:

KO Knockout: the profiled fighter has won in the specified round, either because his opponent has been counted out by the referee, or because the referee has deemed his opponent unfit to continue.

LKO The profiled fighter has lost this fight by knockout.

W The profiled fighter has won a points decision after the scheduled number of rounds.

L The profiled fighter has lost after a points decision.

WDQ The profiled fighter's opponent was disqualified.

LDQ The profiled fighter was disqualified.

D The contest was a draw.

NC No-contest: an accident, freak injury or post-fight irregularity has prompted the contest to be voided.

Tech. Draw A fight has been declared a draw before it has reached its scheduled conclusion, due to an accident or injury.

Professional Record of Tyrell Biggs

1984

15 November	New York City, NY	Mike Evans	W6

1985

20 April	Corpus Christi, TX	Mike Perkins	KO1
17 May	Stateline, NV	Grady Daniels	KO2
13 July	Atlantic City, NJ	Eddie Richardson	KO3
29 August	Atlanta, GA	Sterling Benjamin	KO7
19 November	Metairie, LA	Danny Sutton	KO7
21 December	Virginia Beach, VA	Tony Anthony	KO1

1986

25 January	Lancaster, PA	James Tillis	W8
22 March	Reno, NV	Jeff Sims	W10
14 August	New York City, NY	Rodney Smith	KO6
14 September	Atlantic City, NJ	Percell Davis	W10
29 October	London, England	Robert Evans	KO5
12 December	New York City, NY	Renaldo Snipes	W10

1987

7 March	Las Vegas, NV	David Bey	KO6
31 July	Corpus Christi, TX	Lorenzo Boyd	KO3
16 October	Atlantic City, NJ	Mike Tyson	LKO7

(Undisputed heavyweight title challenge)

1988

29 October	Milan, Italy	Francesco Damiani	LKO5

1989

4 October	London, England	Gary Mason	LKO7
29 November	Auburn Hills, MI	Bobby Crabtree	KO5

1990

11 January	Atlantic City, NJ	Osvaldo Ocasio	W10
5 April	Auburn Hills, MI	Rick Kellar	KO2
8 December	Atlantic City, NJ	Rodolfo Marin	W10

1991

| 2 March | Atlantic City, NJ | Riddick Bowe | LKO8 |
| 23 November | Atlanta, GA | Lennox Lewis | LKO3 |

1992

18 April	Chandler, OK	Alan Jamison	KO1
7 May	Tulsa, OK	Charles Woolard	KO1
29 May	Amarillo, TX	Mike Faulkner	KO2
18 July	Oklahoma City, OK	Roy Jobe	KO1
19 November	Chandler, AZ	John Jones	KO2
8 December	Tampa, FL	Marion Wilson	W10

1993

17 January	Las Vegas, NV	Mike Hunter	L12
3 December	Bay St Louis, MS	Evgeny Sudakov	W3
3 December	Bay St Louis, MS	Shane Sutcliffe	KO2
3 December	Bay St Louis, MS	Tony Tubbs	L3

1994

| 5 February | Las Vegas, NV | Buster Mathis Jr | L12 |
| 4 April | Tokyo, Japan | Ray Anis | LKO3 |

1995–1996
Inactive

1997

11 January	Mount Washington, KY	Andre Crowder	KO1
19 February	Louisville, KY	Alonzo Hollis	W6
11 September	Ledyard, CT	Larry Donald	LKO2

1998

| 27 August | Atlanta, GA | Carlton Davis | KO2 |

Record: 30 wins (20 by KO), 10 defeats

Professional Record of Marvis Frazier

1980

12 September	New York City, NY	Roger Troupe	KO3
10 October	New York City, NY	Dennis Rivers	KO2

1981

10 April	New York City, NY	Melvin Epps	W6
11 May	New York City, NY	Steve Zouski	KO6
22 August	Las Vegas, NV	Tony Pulu	W6
16 September	Las Vegas, NV	Guy Casale	KO4

1982
Inactive

1983

8 February	Atlantic City, NJ	Amos Haynes	KO5
7 March	Charleston, SC	Mike Cohen	KO2
10 April	Atlantic City, NJ	James Broad	W10
4 June	Atlantic City, NJ	Joe Bugner	W10
25 November	Las Vegas, NV	Larry Holmes	LKO1

(IBF heavyweight title challenge)

1984

25 September	Pennsauken, NJ	David Starkey	KO1
23 October	Atlantic City, NJ	Bernard Benton	W10
5 December	London, England	Funsi Banjo	W10

1985

20 May	Reno, NV	James Tillis	W10
11 September	Atlantic City, NJ	Jose Ribalta	W10

1986

23 February	Richmond, CA	James Smith	W10
26 July	Glens Falls, NY	Mike Tyson	LKO1

1987

1 June	Secaucus, NJ	Tom Fischer	KO2
10 August	Secaucus, NJ	Robert Evans	W10

1988

27 October   Tucson, AZ   Philip Brown   W10

Record: 19 wins (8 by KO), 2 defeats

Professional Record of Mitch Green

1980

8 November	Lake Tahoe, NV	Jerry Foley	KO1
25 November	Hartford, CT	Johnny Pitts	KO3
20 December	New York City, NY	Harold Rice	KO5

1981

22 January	Totowa, NJ	Lindsay Page	KO2
8 February	McAfee, NJ	Robert Evans	D6
21 June	Atlantic City, NJ	Melvin Epps	W6

1982

9 April	Cleveland, OH	Willard Dumas	KO1
2 May	Atlantic City, NJ	Walter Ware	KO1
11 June	Las Vegas, NV	Walter Santemore	W6
14 August	Cleveland, OH	Grady Daniels	W8
2 October	Atlantic City, NJ	Lon Dale Friesen	KO2

1983

| 16 February | East Rutherford, NJ | Jumbo Cummings | W10 |
| 17 July | Las Vegas, NV | James Dixon | W10 |

1984

21 March	Las Vegas, NV	Lynwood Jones	KO1
15 July	Kingston, NY	Young Joe Louis	KO6
31 August	Las Vegas, NV	Sammy Scaff	KO6

1985

| 10 August | Las Vegas, NV | Trevor Berbick | L12 |

1986

| 17 January | Atlanta, GA | Percell Davis | W10 |
| 20 May | New York City, NY | Mike Tyson | L10 |

1987–1992
Inactive

1993

| 26 February | Woodbridge, VA | Bruce Johnson | NC3 |

1994

| 2 June | Melville, NY | Melvin Foster | L10 |

1995

| 18 August | Middleton, NY | Lou Turchiarelli | KO6 |

1996–1997
Inactive

1998

25 July	Lake Worth, FL	Mike Dixon	W8
12 September	Lake Worth, FL	Miguel Otero	L8
2 October	Staten Island, NY	Brian Nix	L10

1999–2001
Inactive

2002

| 9 March | Annandale, VA | Danny Wofford | W12 |

Record: 19 wins (11 by KO), 5 defeats, 1 draw, 1 no-contest

Professional Record of Reggie Gross

1982

7 January	Baltimore, MD	Blufort Spencer	KO1
23 January	Richmond, VA	Charles Roye	W4
24 April	Richmond, VA	John Green	KO1
17 May	Baltimore, MD	Michael Statton	W4
24 June	Atlantic City, NJ	Sonny Crooms	KO2
9 July	Baltimore, MD	Charles Price	W6
23 September	Baltimore, MD	Ric Lainhart	KO6
16 December	Baltimore, MD	Fred Brown	KO2

1983

12 March	Baltimore, MD	'Prince' Charles Williams	KO1
8 April	Baltimore, MD	Blufort Spencer	KO7
5 May	Baltimore, MD	Larry Lane	W8
27 June	Ocean City, MD	Abdul Hakim	KO5
18 August	Baltimore, MD	Franklin Otts	KO1

1984

27 February	Atlantic City, NJ	Marcus Jackson	KO3
11 April	Pikesville, MD	Anthony Witherspoon	LKO7
23 May	Pikesville, MD	Jack Johnson	L10
20 September	Atlantic City, NJ	Jesse Ferguson	LKO3

1985

8 March	Scranton, PA	Jimmy Clark	KO9
28 June	Moosie, PA	Hector Rodriguez	KO3

1986

31 January	Atlantic City, NJ	Bert Cooper	KO8
4 March	Atlantic City, NJ	Henry Tillman	L10
13 June	New York City, NY	Mike Tyson	LKO1

1987

| 30 August | Marbella, Spain | Frank Bruno | LKO8 |
| 11 October | Sao Paolo, Brazil | Adilson Rodriguez | LDQ9 |

1988

| 6 January | Baltimore, MD | Harry Terrell | KO2 |
| 27 June | Atlantic City, NJ | Razor Ruddock | LKO2 |

Record: 18 wins (14 by KO), 8 defeats

Professional Record of Pinklon Thomas

1978

29 August	Seattle, WA	Ken Arlt	W6
31 October	Lacey, WA	Mustafa El-Amin	KO3

1979

8 January	Seattle, WA	Roger Braxton	KO7
20 February	Seattle, WA	Lew Lockwood	KO4
7 April	Billings, MT	Elmo Henderson	KO5
26 April	Seattle, WA	Foma Leota	KO2
23 May	Las Vegas, NV	Lee Holloman	KO2
7 June	Portland, OR	George Jerome	KO2
2 July	Sedro Wooley, WA	Willie Stoglin	KO2
18 July	Las Vegas, NV	Leroy Caldwell	W10
14 December	Atlantic City, NJ	Bobby Jordan	KO5

1980

10 February	Miami Beach, FL	Jerry Williams	KO5
15 June	Clarkston, MI	Frank Brown	KO4
28 August	Las Vegas, NV	Jerry Williams	W10

1981

16 April	Seattle, WA	Lee Mitchell	KO1
25 November	Philadelphia, PA	Curtis Whitner	KO2

1982

23 January	Atlantic City, NJ	Johnny Warr	W8
23 May	Atlantic City, NJ	Luis Acosta	KO2
3 July	Totowa, NJ	Jerry Williams	KO3
14 August	Cleveland, OH	James Tillis	KO8

1983

2 January	Atlantic City, NJ	Gerrie Coetzee	D10
26 March	Atlantic City, NJ	Alfonzo Ratliffe	KO10
24 September	Totowa, NJ	Michael Greer	KO5
27 October	Atlantic City, NJ	Leroy Boone	W10

1984

| 20 June | Hato Rey, Puerto Rico | Bruce Grandham | KO5 |
| 31 August | Las Vegas, NV | Tim Witherspoon | W12 |

(Wins WBC heavyweight title)

1985

| 15 June | Las Vegas, NV | Mike Weaver | KO8 |

(Retains WBC heavyweight title)

1986

| 22 March | Las Vegas, NV | Trevor Berbick | L12 |

(Loses WBC heavyweight title)

| 16 October | Aguadilla, Puerto Rico | Narciso Maldonado | KO5 |
| 22 November | Las Vegas, NV | William Hosea | KO7 |

1987

| 7 March | Las Vegas, NV | Danny Sutton | KO7 |
| 30 May | Las Vegas, NV | Mike Tyson | LKO6 |

(WBC & WBA heavyweight title challenge)

1988

| 9 December | Atlantic City, NJ | Evander Holyfield | LKO7 |

1989

Inactive

1990

23 May	Auburn Hills, MI	Curtis Isaac	W10
12 June	Fort Bragg, NC	Mike Hunter	L10
7 September	Washington, DC	Riddick Bowe	LKO8

1991

| 19 February | Kansas City, MO | Tommy Morrison | LKO1 |

1992

29 May	Greenville, SC	Herman Jackson	KO3
27 June	Greenville, SC	Danny Sutton	W10
31 July	Charlotte, NC	Terry Miller	KO2
1 August	Forest City, NC	Bobby Jones	KO1

8 August	Demopolis, AL	Jim Smith	KO1
14 August	Greenville, SC	Danny Wofford	W10
22 August	Denver, NC	Adolph Davis	KO1
5 September	Daytona Beach, FL	Larry Beilfuss	KO1
19 September	Lumberton, NC	Frankie Hines	KO1
25 September	Charlotte, NC	Kevin Nesbitt	KO1
2 October	Sarasota, FL	Dion Burgess	KO5
22 October	Virginia Beach, FL	Mike Owens	KO3
14 November	Greenville, SC	Craig Payne	W12

1993

29 January	Columbia, SC	Lawrence Carter	LKO7

Record: 43 wins (33 by KO), 7 defeats, 1 draw

Professional Record of Tony Tubbs

1980

14 June	Cincinnati, OH	Bruce Scott	KO1
2 August	Cincinnati, OH	Jerry Hunter	KO4
7 November	San Antonio, TX	Ron Draper	W6
14 November	Miami, FL	John L. Johnson	KO1
22 November	Cincinnati, OH	Larry Sims	KO3
29 November	Los Angeles, CA	Mike Creel	KO3

1981

21 August	Elizabeth, NJ	Dennis Wimbley	KO2
4 October	Newport, VA	Jeff Sims	KO1
21 November	Erlanger, KY	Jesse Brown	KO1
18 December	Pittsburgh, PA	Don Halpin	W8

1982

11 April	Atlantic City, NJ	Baker Tinsley	KO3
12 June	Atlantic City, NJ	Clarence Parker	KO1
7 August	Albuquerque, NM	Clarence Hill	W10
18 September	Atlantic City, NJ	Steve Zouski	KO5

1983

25 February	Cincinnati, OH	Larry Givens	KO7
10 April	Pittsburgh, PA	Jimmy Young	W10
9 September	Las Vegas, NV	Gordon Racette	W10

1984

18 March	Santa Monica, CA	Tom Trimm	KO2
9 November	Las Vegas, NV	Jerry Williams	KO7

1985

16 January	Las Vegas, NV	Tim Miller	KO2
15 March	Las Vegas, NV	James Smith	W10
29 April	Buffalo, NY	Greg Page	W15

(Wins WBA heavyweight title)

1986
17 January   Atlanta, GA   Tim Witherspoon   L15
(Loses WBA heavyweight title)

1987
21 April   Santa Monica, CA   Mike Jameson   W10
30 May   Las Vegas, NV   Wimpy Halstead   W10
29 September   Anaheim, CA   Eddie Gonzalez   KO3

1988
21 March   Tokyo, Japan   Mike Tyson   LKO2
(Undisputed heavyweight title challenge)

1989
20 April   Redondo Beach, CA   Mike Evans   W10
6 May   Pensacola, FL   Eddie Richardson   WDQ8
24 June   Bakersfield, CA   Ladsilao Mijangos   KO3
21 November   Santa Monica, CA   Orlin Norris   NC12

1990
28 July   Atlantic City, NJ   Mike Cohen   KO7
20 October   Atlantic City, NJ   Lawrence Carter   KO7

1991
20 April   Atlantic City, NJ   Riddick Bowe   L10

1992
16 February   Las Vegas, NV   Leon Taylor   KO8
18 August   Pensacola, FL   Lionel Butler   LKO1
14 October   Atlantic City, NJ   Bruce Seldon   W10
24 November   Auburn Hills, MI   Jesse Ferguson   W10

1993
2 February   Auburn Hills, MI   Alexandre Zolkin   W10
27 April   Auburn Hills, MI   Melton Bowen   W10
16 August   Boise, ID   Jimmy Ellis   LKO1
3 December   Bay St Louis, MS   Willie Jackson   KO1
3 December   Bay St Louis, MS   Jose Ribalta   W3
3 December   Bay St Louis, MS   Tyrell Biggs   W3
3 December   Bay St Louis, MS   Daniel Dancuta   W3

1994

22 February	Auburn Hills, MI	Everett Martin	W10
4 October	Auburn Hills, MI	William Morris	NC10
6 December	Auburn Hills, MI	Jimmy Thunder	L12

1995

29 March	Cincinnati, OH	Andre Crowder	KO1
25 August	Atlantic City, NJ	Alexandre Zolkin	L12
20 October	Copenhagen, Denmark	Brian Nielsen	LKO4

1996
Inactive

1997

| 30 August | Mar Del Plata, Argentina | Mario Melo | KO5 |

1998–2001
Inactive

2002

| 29 March | West Lafayette, IN | Michael Shanks | KO2 |

2003

| 17 January | Lemoore, CA | Gilberto Martinez | L10 |
| 25 July | Morgantown, WV | Abraham Okine | LKO8 |

Record: 43 wins (24 by KO), 10 defeats, 2 no-contests

Professional Record of Tony Tucker

1980

1 November	Phoenix, AZ	Chuck Gardner	KO3
24 November	Staten Island, NY	Carol McAllister	KO1
2 December	Toledo, OH	Jesse Clark	KO1
11 December	Chicago, IL	Max Smith	KO5

1981

16 January	San Antonio, TX	Victor Rodriguez	KO2
29 January	Detroit, MI	Willie Kents	KO1
23 February	Atlantic City, NJ	Robert Evans	KO6
9 April	Detroit, MI	Memphis Jones	KO1
30 April	Las Vegas, NV	Chip Tyler	KO7
22 August	Traverse City, MI	Jerry Hunter	KO1
16 September	Las Vegas, NV	Harvey Steichen	KO2
17 October	Traverse City, MI	Frank Farmer	KO1

1982

18 May	Atlantic City, NJ	Grady Daniels	KO5
12 June	Syracuse, NY	Charles Atlas	KO1
15 June	Atlantic City, NJ	James Dixon	W8
30 June	Atlantic City, NJ	Lupe Guerra	KO2
8 July	Atlantic City, NJ	Richard Cade	KO7
12 August	Nashville, TN	Danny Sutton	NC3

1983

7 November	Chicago, IL	James Holly	KO1
1 December	Chicago, IL	Lynwood Jones	KO5
20 December	Chicago, IL	James Dixon	KO6

1984

24 February	Chicago, IL	Larry Givens	KO4
15 March	Chicago, IL	Sam Jeter	KO1
19 April	Detroit, MI	Walter Santemore	KO1
9 May	Chicago, IL	Dave Johnson	KO2
15 June	Las Vegas, NV	Eddie Lopez	KO9
22 September	Grand Rapids, MI	Jimmy Young	W10

24 October	Detroit, MI	O.T. Davis	KO1
2 November	Chicago, IL	Danny Sutton	W10

1985

28 June	Hammond, IN	Bobby Crabtree	KO4
19 October	Monte Carlo, Monaco	David Jaco	KO3

1986

27 February	Detroit, MI	Eddie Richardson	W10
10 July	Houston, TX	Eddie Richardson	KO4
7 August	Houston, TX	Otis Bates	KO2
26 September	Atlantic City, NJ	James Broad	W12

1987

30 May	Las Vegas, NV	Buster Douglas	KO10
(Wins IBF heavyweight title)			
1 August	Las Vegas, NV	Mike Tyson	L12
(Loses IBF heavyweight title)			

1988
Inactive

1989

12 December	Los Angeles, CA	Dino Homsey	KO3

1990

8 January	Inglewood, CA	Calvin Jones	KO5
8 March	Inglewood, CA	Mike Evans	W10
19 July	Seattle, WA	Mike Rouse	KO5

1991

28 January	Inglewood, CA	Lionel Washington	KO1
29 April	Inglewood, CA	Ray Thomas	KO1
3 June	Las Vegas, NV	Orlin Norris	W12

1992

15 February	Las Vegas, NV	Kimmuel Odum	KO2
10 April	Mexico City, Mexico	Mike Faulkner	KO2
22 April	East Rutherford, NJ	Manny Contreras	KO6
26 June	Cleveland, OH	Oliver McCall	W12

12 September	Las Vegas, NV	Everett Martin	W10
7 November	Stateline, NV	Paul Poirier	KO4
13 December	Las Vegas, NV	Frankie Swindell	KO6

1993
8 May	Las Vegas, NV	Lennox Lewis	L12
(WBC heavyweight title challenge)			
December 18	Puebla, Mexico	David Graves	KO2

1994
19 February	Charlotte, NC	George Stephens	KO1
2 July	Las Vegas, NV	Cecil Coffee	KO2
10 December	Monterrey, Mexico	Dan Murphy	KO3

1995
8 April	Las Vegas, NV	Bruce Seldon	LKO7
(Vacant WBA heavyweight title fight)			
16 December	Philadelphia, PA	Henry Akinwande	L10

1996
24 February	Richmond, VA	Orlin Norris	L10
29 June	Indio, CA	David Dixon	KO1
7 December	Indio, CA	Tyrone Campbell	KO3

1997
28 June	Norwich, England	Herbie Hide	LKO2
(WBO heavyweight title challenge)			
18 November	Nashville, TN	Abdul Muhaymin	W10
16 December	Nashville, TN	Jerry Haynes	KO3

1998
| 31 January | Tampa, FL | John Ruiz | LKO11 |
| 8 May | Tunica, MS | Billy Wright | KO1 |

Record: 58 wins (48 by KO), 7 defeats, 1 no-contest

Professional Record of Mike Tyson

1985

6 March	Albany, NY	Hector Mercedes	KO1
10 April	Albany, NY	Trent Singleton	KO1
23 May	Albany, NY	Don Halpin	KO4
20 June	Atlantic City, NJ	Ricardo Spain	KO1
11 July	Atlantic City, NJ	John Alderson	KO2
19 July	Poughkeepsie, NY	Larry Sims	KO3
15 August	Atlantic City, NJ	Lorenzo Canady	KO1
5 September	Atlantic City, NJ	Michael Johnson	KO1
9 October	Atlantic City, NJ	Donnie Long	KO1
25 October	Atlantic City, NJ	Robert Colay	KO1
1 November	Latham, NY	Sterling Benjamin	KO1
13 November	Houston, TX	Eddie Richardson	KO1
22 November	Latham, NY	Conroy Nelson	KO2
6 December	New York City, NY	Sammy Scaff	KO1
27 December	Albany, NY	Mark Young	KO1

1986

11 January	Albany, NY	David Jaco	KO1
24 January	Atlantic City, NJ	Mike Jameson	KO5
16 February	Troy, NY	Jesse Ferguson	KO6
10 March	Uniondale, NY	Steve Zouski	KO3
3 May	Glens Falls, NY	James Tillis	W10
20 May	New York City, NY	Mitch Green	W10
13 June	New York City, NY	Reggie Gross	KO1
28 June	Troy, NY	William Hosea	KO1
11 July	Swan Lake, NY	Lorenzo Boyd	KO2
26 July	Glens Falls, NY	Marvis Frazier	KO1
17 August	Atlantic City, NJ	Jose Ribalta	KO10
6 September	Las Vegas, NV	Alfonzo Ratliffe	KO2
22 November	Las Vegas, NV	Trevor Berbick	KO2
(Wins WBC heavyweight title)			

1987

7 March	Las Vegas, NV	James Smith	W12

(Retains WBC title, wins WBA heavyweight title)

30 May	Las Vegas, NV	Pinklon Thomas	KO6

(Retains WBC & WBA heavyweight titles)

1 August	Las Vegas, NV	Tony Tucker	W12

(Retains WBC & WBA titles, wins IBF & undisputed heavyweight titles)

16 October	Atlantic City, NJ	Tyrell Biggs	KO7

(Retains undisputed heavyweight title)

1988

22 January	Atlantic City, NJ	Larry Holmes	KO4

(Retains undisputed heavyweight title)

21 March	Tokyo, Japan	Tony Tubbs	KO2

(Retains undisputed heavyweight title)

27 June	Atlantic City, NJ	Michael Spinks	KO1

(Retains undisputed heavyweight title and wins linear title)

1989

25 February	Las Vegas, NV	Frank Bruno	KO5

(Retains undisputed & linear heavyweight titles)

21 July	Atlantic City, NJ	Carl Williams	KO1

(Retains undisputed & linear heavyweight titles)

1990

11 February	Tokyo, Japan	Buster Douglas	LKO10

(Loses undisputed & linear heavyweight titles)

16 June	Las Vegas, NV	Henry Tillman	KO1
8 December	Atlantic City, NJ	Alex Stewart	KO1

1991

18 March	Las Vegas, NV	Razor Ruddock	KO7
28 June	Las Vegas, NV	Razor Ruddock	W12

1992–1994
Inactive

1995

19 August	Las Vegas, NV	Peter McNeeley	WDQ1
16 December	Philadelphia, PA	Buster Mathis Jr	KO3

1996

| 16 March | Las Vegas, NV | Frank Bruno | KO3 |

(Regains WBC heavyweight title)

| 7 September | Las Vegas, NV | Bruce Seldon | KO1 |

(Loses WBC title for failing to defend against Lennox Lewis, regains WBA heavyweight title)

| 9 November | Las Vegas, NV | Evander Holyfield | LKO11 |

(Loses WBA heavyweight title)

1997

| 28 June | Las Vegas, NV | Evander Holyfield | LDQ3 |

(WBA heavyweight title challenge)

1998
Inactive

1999

| 16 January | Las Vegas, NV | Francois Botha | KO5 |
| 23 October | Las Vegas, NV | Orlin Norris | NC1 |

2000

29 January	Manchester, England	Julius Francis	KO2
24 June	Glasgow, Scotland	Lou Savarese	KO1
20 October	Auburn Hills, MI	Andrzej Golota	NC3

2001

| 13 October | Copenhagen, Denmark | Brian Nielsen | KO7 |

2002

| 8 June | Memphis, TN | Lennox Lewis | LKO8 |

(WBC, IBF & linear heavyweight title challenge)

2003

| 22 February | Memphis, TN | Clifford Etienne | KO1 |

Record: 50 wins (44 by KO), 4 defeats, 2 no-contests

Professional Record of Carl Williams

1982

22 January	New York City, NY	Greg Stephany	W4
31 March	New York City, NY	Dwight Triplett	KO1
30 April	New York City, NY	Louis Alexander	KO2
28 May	New York City, NY	Donny Townsend	KO1
11 June	New York City, NY	Barry Funches	KO6
20 August	New York City, NY	David Starkey	KO3
22 October	New York City, NY	Michael Greer	KO3
9 December	New York City, NY	Leroy Boone	W8

1983

18 February	New York City, NY	Richard Cade	KO1
24 April	Atlantic City, NJ	Robert Hill	KO3
30 June	Atlantic City, NJ	David Jaco	KO1
16 August	Atlantic City, NJ	Woody Clarke	W10
9 September	Las Vegas, NV	Percell Davis	KO4

1984

7 March	White Plains, NY	Lou Benson	KO2
9 August	New York City, NY	Terry Mims	KO3
23 October	Atlantic City, NJ	James Tillis	W10

1985

20 May	Reno, NV	Larry Holmes	L15
(IBF & linear heavyweight title challenge)			
30 August	Atlantic City, NJ	Jesse Ferguson	KO10

1986

16 February	Troy, NY	Mike Weaver	LKO2

1987

21 June	Atlantic City, NJ	Bert Cooper	KO8
17 October	Atlantic City, NJ	Mike Gans	KO7

1988

27 January	San Diego, CA	Rodney Frazier	KO1

| 27 June | Atlantic City, NJ | Trevor Berbick | W12 |
| 10 November | Stateline, NV | Mike Rouse | KO3 |

1989

| 21 July | Atlantic City, NJ | Mike Tyson | LKO1 |

(Undisputed & linear heavyweight title challenge)

1990

| 24 July | Atlantic City, NJ | Melton Bowen | KO5 |

1991

| 8 March | Atlantic City, NJ | Tim Witherspoon | L12 |
| 15 October | Atlantic City, NJ | Kimmuel Odum | NC10 |

1992

12 January	Atlantic City, NJ	Marshall Tillman	KO2
22 March	Atlantic City, NJ	Jerry Jones	L10
20 August	Atlantic City, NJ	Osvaldo Ocasio	W10
3 November	Ledyard, CT	Jimmy Lee Smith	KO3

1993

| 16 January | Reno, NV | Tommy Morrison | LKO8 |
| 24 April | Birmingham, England | Frank Bruno | LKO10 |

1994

| 22 July | Robinsonville, MS | Alexandre Zolkin | LDQ7 |

1995

| 17 March | Bushkill, PA | Melvin Foster | L10 |

1996

31 May	New York City, NY	Sean Hart	WDQ3
2 August	Melville, NY	Lou Turchiarelli	KO3
27 November	Whiteman, MA	Domingo Monroe	W10

1997

| 13 June | Port Chester, NY | Marion Wilson | W10 |
| 30 October | Port Chester, NY | Anthony Green | LKO7 |

Record: 30 wins (21 by KO), 10 defeats, 1 no-contest